Writing Beat

Writing Beat
AND OTHER OCCASIONS
OF LITERARY MAYHEM

JOHN TYTELL

VANDERBILT UNIVERSITY PRESS

Nashville

© 2014 by John Tytell
All rights reserved
Published 2014 by Vanderbilt University Press
Nashville, Tennessee 37235

This book is printed on acid-free paper.

Text and cover design by Rich Hendel

Library of Congress Cataloging-in-Publication Data on file
LC control number   2014008056
LC classification number   PS228.B6T97 2014
Dewey class number   810.9'0054—dc23

ISBN 978-0-8265-2014-2 (cloth)
ISBN 978-0-8265-2015-9 (paperback)
ISBN 978-0-8265-2016-6 (ebook)

For my love, MELLON,

who opened all the doors!

CONTENTS

Acknowledgments *ix*
A Prefatory Note *1*

PART I ENGAGEMENT

1. How to Write an Essay *7*
2. The Writer as Peeping John:
   On the Nature of Biographical Inquiry *15*
3. Hemlock or Ambrosia: Writing and Editorial Process *34*
4. Notes of a Peripatetic Lecturer *45*
5. Senator Tripletalk and the American Dream *54*
6. Passing Through: Fifty Years @ the Mind Factory *67*

PART II RECONSIDERING THE BEATS

7. Two Notes on Beat Origins *81*
8. The Traveling Writer: Beat Mexico *88*
9. Kerouac's Music *112*
10. Ginsberg Today *130*
11. The Oppositional Writer *149*
12. The Editor as Midwife: Writers and Little Magazines *179*

PART III THE METAPHYSICS OF WRITING

13. Bombing with Words *195*
14. A Writer's Retreat *204*
15. Poetic Faith: Religion and the Writer *213*
16. A Writer's Passage *222*
17. The Donkey and the Written Word *231*

ACKNOWLEDGMENTS

My greatest appreciation is for my wife, Mellon, who inspired so many of the experiences I describe here and always had her camera ready. Mellon has been my most imaginative, loyal, devoted friend, my most reliable source of warmth and love.

This book began when Jean Tamarin, an editor at the *Chronicle of Higher Education*, asked me to write a piece about Allen Ginsberg, which now forms part of Chapter 10 in this book. Another point of departure occurred when Jeffrey Di Leo, dean of the humanities at the University of Houston-Victoria, asked me to speak about the editing process—a talk that ended up on YouTube and is presented here in Chapter 3. Another talk, at the invitation of Daniel Shapiro at the Americas Society, on the Beats in Mexico, stimulated "The Traveling Writer," part of which appeared in *Studies in Latin American Popular Culture*. The essay on William Burroughs's *Last Words* originated in *Bookforum*. Yet another segment of this book was initiated by Ivan Dee, who had reprinted a few of my books and who asked me to write about Jack Kerouac's last years for an online venture called the Now and Then Reader.

I was also led to reconsider the Beats by talks I was invited to deliver by Keith Bollum of the David Turner Warner Foundation in Melrose and Orlando, Florida, and a series of lectures I offered to a graduate seminar at New York University in the fall of 2011. "The Donkey and the Written Word" began as a talk I prepared for the Sigma Chapter of Phi Beta Kappa.

Thanks, as well, to David Chapman of the *South Carolina Review*, to my fellow editors on *American Book Review*, and to Beat enthusiasts Joyce Johnson, David Amram, Regina Weinreich, Bill Morgan, Peter Hale, Ken Stuart, and Hassan Melehy for good cheer and advice along the way. Jaime Wolf offered valuable contractual advice for which I am grateful. Eli Bortz at Vanderbilt University Press was enthusiastic from the beginning and full of constructive suggestions, as was Jeremy Rehwaldt.

Urge and urge and urge,
Always the procreant urge of the world
— Walt Whitman, "Song of Myself"

These novels will give way, by and by, to diaries or autobiographies—captivating books if only a man knew how to choose among what he calls his experiences, that which is really his experience, and how to record truth truly.
— Ralph Waldo Emerson, Journals, January 1841

A PREFATORY NOTE

> It's béat, it's the beat to keep, it's the beat of the heart, it's being beat and down in the world and like oldtime lowdowns and like in ancient civilizations the slave boatmen rowing galleys to a beat and servants spinning pottery to a beat.
> —Jack Kerouac, Desolation Angels

The beat may have begun by striking a hollow log whose sound would resonate and echo the need to gather in either an emergency or for some ritual purpose—or, perhaps, to hear the shaman or storyteller chant once again a shared history. That repeated story was the oral history that gave the tribe a central part of its identity. If the storyteller accompanied himself with a lyre, he was our first musician, but in any event this preliminary historian was often also our first poet, and from him we receive the legends of the Norse or Greek gods, sometimes fashioned with the enormous skill of blind Homer, who may, after all, only be an apocryphal figure himself.

I mean "beat" in a more vernacular sense as well. In the way that a foot patrol officer has a particular sector to police in a defined and regulated manner, with the expectations of the community, knowing that behavior is measured by a code. One can see the ramifications of policing in a dozen television programs, and the evolution of its procedurals and demands from Sherlock Holmes to *CSI* seem manifest. The writer's beat—both the nature of the work and its procedurals—may be less apparent and certainly less visible as matter for mass media.

I'm also interested here in a more mysterious arena than the police officer's precinct or the detective's sleuthing. I've written and edited nonfiction for half a century and so I regard that as my "beat," the territory whose protocol I best understand, whose potential problems and possible dangers I've encountered many times, whose changing opportunities I've always tried to gauge. The priority of nonfiction has always been to tell the truth as well as the writer can. Although surely this is as much a concern for the writer of fiction, the novelist has been known to be more inventive, to distort deliberately, to magnify or minimize for dramatic effect. The job of the nonfiction writer is different, to discern the truth of what actually occurred through the fog of the past, a past subject to defamation, often reconfigured by polemicists, confused by propaganda, obfuscated by faulty memory, or imagined with the license we afford novelists.

This book focuses on the challenges and perils facing any writer today, but particularly the writer of nonfiction. My subject is the process any writer of nonfiction must consider: the way the spoken word can become the launching pad for an essay, for example, the nature of historical inquiry and biography, the craft and consequences of the interview, or the resistance to revision and the implicit opportunity it affords. Some of the essays in this book focus on perennial issues for the writer: the exotic portal of travel and the more mundane presence of a subject as close as the next barstool, the value of seclusion as opposed to a more journalistic exploration of the culture, and the future of the written word as we know it. These essays depend mostly on the perspective of memoir and as such may be anecdotal and instructive, as well I hope as entertaining. I'm not approaching my subject in any programmatic manner, but as an organic expression of what I have experienced myself in the field of action.

Although I have been able to accept journalistic assignments throughout my career and have experienced a taste of the worlds of film and advertising, I am essentially a literary historian focusing on the lives and creative output of modern American writers, particularly those like Ezra Pound or Henry Miller who have challenged and helped change social and literary conventions. In one sense, to the extent that my subjects—and my own much more modest ambitions—reflect our larger needs and aspirations, I am a social critic as well.

I am also using "beat" in its more narrow literary sense, as it applies to a group of American writers emerging after the Second World War, whose members were called a Beat Generation. Some of these writers, Jack Kerouac, Allen Ginsberg, or William Burroughs, for example, have been part of my chosen "beat," and reevaluations of their accomplishments and new discoveries about them may be expected to figure in my narrative.

Finally, this book is what I call a hybrid memoir. It begins with the heartbeat of my own experiences and focuses on what I have learned about the nature of writing. Part of the narcissism of memoir, however, is that the writer gets so caught up in the immediate particularities of recovered experience that the larger context of history and culture is often sacrificed. The vital center of this book, its blood flow, is the social history of the recent past and the legacy of the writers whose lives and literary efforts are reflected here. The crucial element in history—what affords it a future—is how capably its *story* has been shaped and narrated, but that is surely a judgment best left to the reader.

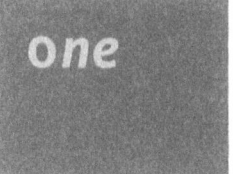# Engagement

CHAPTER 1

HOW TO WRITE AN ESSAY

Reading could lead to a trance of utter lucidity in which, unknown to oneself, one could make the deepest resolutions.
— Henry Miller, Tropic of Capricorn

I don't wish to sound arch, dogmatic, presumptuous, or sententious, but the chemistry is fundamental: I've been relying on it for the past half century.

One begins with a subject. It is preferable to discover a subject that hasn't been entirely sucked dry by St. Augustine and a thousand predecessors, but if you must approach such a subject with the kind of universal appeal validated by all that past interest, the least one can provide is a new perspective. My procedure is to jot down notes as they first flicker in the brain in a rough sort of outline. Sometimes, these reflections can occur at inconvenient moments, such as in the middle of the night when you are dreaming of lost love, or while you are driving a car too fast, late for work, relying on a manual shift with your notebook, your trusty depository, in the cold seat next to you.

Your opening sentence is a signal, as intriguing, elegant, and striking as you can make it. The writer David Shields begins a recent essay with the declaration that "all criticism is a form of autobiography." His terse line is a ring of surprise, coming with the taut certainty of fiat. Fabricating a sentence involves a mental dance of the imagination, a pirouetting and balancing act that is essentially musical. Many writers have honed this craft by reading. As the critic Susan Sontag once observed, "Reading usually precedes writing. And the impulse to write is almost always fired by reading. Reading, the love of reading, is what makes you dream of becoming a writer."

We can learn a lot about how to write by reading, in the same way we all imitate our mother's lip movements in infancy, and learn how to speak by hearing our parents enunciate, watching them manipulate their mouths to form vowels and consonants. That may be why the children of immigrants are left with an accent that is just barely discernable. An immigrant child myself, I read Poe and Jack London, then in adolescence Melville and Joseph Conrad, though I cannot now measure with any accuracy whatever influences any of these writers had on my evolving sense of how to form a sentence. I am certain, however, as Sontag urges, that they motivated me.

In terms of the sentence, I can be prescriptive. The explosive heart of any sentence can reside in a memorable, pungent, or provocative phrase, one that may seem baffling or mysterious at first, but that ultimately makes sense. William James's observation in his *Varieties of Religious Experience* that the affinity between religion and fiction depends on a shared "willing suspension of disbelief"—which he discerns by reading Samuel Taylor Coleridge—exists as an apt illustration.

Such phrases can leap so quickly from the mind that they are best apprehended by a hand notation in a pocket notebook, that venerable practice we neglect in the speeded blur of our computer age. While the phrase may provide the punch in a particularly important sentence, the construction of a deft sentence, like any architecture, requires a conceived plan. As a model for the qualities of poise and delicacy this sometimes requires, I would recommend William James's younger brother Henry, who once explained the secret ingredient of memoir, how the writer uses history: "I draw courage from the remembrance that history is never, in any rich sense, the immediate crudity of what 'happens,' but the much finer complexity of what we read into it and think of in connection with it." The polar tension in James's line depends on the juxtaposed antithesis of rich and crude; it is like a beam that supports the words and makes them hang together so effectively. But James's sometimes ramified and reflexive sentence structure may suggest too carefully calculated and corseted a Victorian model for younger writers today who will seek more gaiety, more swirling, more rhythmic exuberance, as in the opposite model provided by Jack Kerouac in a famous line describing his characters in the beginning of *On the Road*:

> But then they danced down the streets like dingledodies, and I shambled after as I've been doing all my life after people who interest me, because the only people for me are the mad ones, the ones who are mad to live, mad to talk, mad to be saved, desirous of everything at the same time, the ones who never yawn or say a commonplace thing but burn, burn, burn like fabulous

yellow roman candles exploding like spiders across the stars and in the middle you see the blue centerlight pop and everybody goes "Awww!"

Beauty requires no explanations, but the antic pell-mell of this extended line depends on the repeated drumbeats of "mad" and "burn," with each clause building a little longer than the one preceding. Part of its vitality comes from invented words like "dingledodies," a word that connotes something dizzy or jerky, like slaphappy, Harpo Marx in a tub of whipped cream. The power of the line, however, depends on that defining image of the Roman candle bursting among the stars in the firmament. What we are left with is the gasping, breathless excitement of American vernacular with an explosive momentum that just sings. It is an energy that James's more measured propriety perhaps excludes, and James might have shuddered at Kerouac's "Awww!" There may be room for both approaches; one's choice of the formal or more idiomatic usually depends on what is being described.

Sometimes the intricacy of James's constructions, or the headlong rhapsody of Kerouac's, needs the counterpunch of compactness and brevity, a quality one can find in Catullus or Sappho, or more recently in Emily Dickinson or Emerson in his cardinal precept that "Life is our dictionary!" or his more sweepingly romantic observation that "Society everywhere is in conspiracy against the manhood of every one of its members." Emerson's short sentences, like a surprise uppercut in boxing, often express a ringing, profound truth that can lead to epiphany, the knockout of recognition in any essay.

The writer's resources are the tools of analysis, fact, history, or memory, but the two latter categories are subjective and often manipulative, subject to misinterpretation or fabrication, and need to be used with considerable integrity. Personality, as Virginia Woolf once observed, is the "most dangerous and delicate tool" the essayist can employ. While personal experience is often dramatic and compelling, it is not always available or appropriate, and it can appear to be as narcissistic or self-serving as it may be informative or central.

What is crucial is that one sentence should lead to another if you have a story to tell, and narrative is a key element no matter whether the genre you have chosen is fiction or nonfiction. Continuity is the cohesive glue that keeps the reader's fickle eye—and the restless, impatient, and often importunate brain behind it—concentrated on the page. An imperfect analogy, perhaps, would be the jeweler scrutinizing a diamond, his face screwed into his loupe to assess the infinitesimal fractures they call flaws. Reading is a more difficult act of detection because we must consider a series of quite abstract signs that signify best when we can picture the action being described. In general, the writer learns to shun the general, to fear abstraction, to avoid cliché and empty words like "nice," to sacrifice the extraneous word ruthlessly, to pitch the idea in a visible image so graphic that we can see the diamond sparkle or smell, taste, or feel the portrayed object.

Poetry often provides excellent models for such tactile responses, such as the red wheelbarrow in William Carlos Williams's famous little poem, the one he situates in a glaze of rainwater beside the white chickens. Williams provides another clue for the writer. His ears were tuned perfectly to an uninflated diction that is related to actual speech, so natural it never seems self-consciously literary but authentically felt. You can hear it in a poem like "This Is Just to Say," a "found" poem that originated as a simple note that Williams placed on his refrigerator door apologizing to his wife, Flossie, for having eaten the delicious plums she was saving for her breakfast. This tradition of what I would call natural speech is particularly present in American writing: in Whitman the flaneur listening to the slang of apprentice butcher boys on the Bowery in 1854, or Mark Twain, working on the Mississippi and never forgetting the intonations of midwesterners, in Sherwood Anderson's *Winesburg, Ohio*, in Hemingway's "Indian Camp" stories, or in Henry Miller's *Tropics* novels. The writer's work is listening as much as imagining, and what is heard becomes as much an attribute of style as vision does.

Any gathering of sentences into the unit of a paragraph requires connection, a sober or sometimes more riskily poetic logic of association, the knee connected to the thigh, the thigh to the hip and up the spinal cord to the brain that evaluates all. The principle of the paragraph is unity, a relationship of parts acting congruously, helping to advance an argument. While unity or continuity may seem like hopelessly old-fashioned Aristotelian constructs in a postmodernist universe, the comforting harmony it provides helps any writer persuade a reader. The devil of distraction is digression, valid enough in an exfoliating confabulation by Gabriel García Márquez or Roberto Bolaño, but less convincing in an essay.

The essayist—and Orwell is a model—needs to remember the reader's delight and indeed dependence on sheer narrative, as well as clarity in intention and expression. A collection of cohering paragraphs, with the vital transitions provided between them to continue the essential flow, becomes the stream of thought that constitutes the essay. Transitions—at least since Stravinsky's "Rites of Spring" in 1913—have tended to become less logically connected, more associative and imaginative, but they are still necessary for coherence. Then what is important, whether conceived before or after the formation of the essay, is a name to help identify it. The essay title is a trumpet call, a key factor in attracting the reader's attention, a sort of banner or flag preceding the argument and announcing it to an indifferent public.

In the world of journalism or commercial publishing, the writer may not have ultimate control of a title, which is a sort of headline, and may find it replaced by a dry, lifeless substitution. I consider myself lucky to have convinced publishers to use titles like *Naked Angels* or *Paradise Outlaws*, but to record my losses in this regard would only sound like feeble complaining. The editing process commences with one's first sentence and ends as a negotiation in compromise that only occurs if and when the writer has had the good fortune to find an editor to sponsor the work in the first place. Publication is a dark horse, always a long shot, and for every acceptance the writer—at least this writer!—has had to weather a dozen rejections. These can take the form of notes addressed to "Dear Writer" in an e-mail explaining that the publication wants to "pass on this one" (doesn't it sound as painful as passing a kidney stone?) or the submission "does not fit our list"—a euphemism for "we will not go there." The most dismissive and patronizing curt cut omnisciently advises that "this is not your best work."

Even the brutal formulaic rejection, however, may have its benefits, allowing another opportunity for gestation—that potentially most creative space when you reconsider your work and permit it to grow. The best time for me is early in the morning when all is silent except for the first tentative birdcalls. Just changing a word can open a door or lead to a new perspective. Writing is an incremental process, and rereading one's writing, sentence by sentence, preferably aloud to voice the music in a phrase, is critical to any writing process and should recur at every step along the way. Some writers insist they need a critical reading by another reader before any formal submission. This can be quite dangerous if the chosen reader is either too zealous or jealous. What you need is someone who knows how to be constructive rather than quarrelsome, a person who won't deny your style and individuality. I am still looking for such a person though my wife, Mellon, has helped me more than anyone else over the years.

I admit I may have approached the subject of writing an essay too mechanistically for some of my readers and neglected a vital spiritual component. The writer's strength is mostly in a donkey stubbornness, a refusal to accept the negative verdicts of the magazine editors or publishers who feel the work will not profit them. The will to persevere, the power to believe in oneself, even in the face of anonymity, as Walt Whitman or Emily Dickinson did in the nineteenth century, and Franz Kafka in the twentieth, is often what separates a writer from less Nietzschean peers.

Undoubtedly, this is easier for me to write than for any of us to live. Even Polonius might agree that persistence has its limits as a moral principle. The writer may use self-doubt constructively and revise, or it can become a crippling intellectual paralysis diagnosed as the dreaded writer's block. Perhaps the greatest victim of this psychic affliction was the novelist Joseph Conrad, who gave us a glimpse into the extent of his suffering in a letter to his literary agent, Edward Garnett:

> I sit down religiously. I sit down for eight hours every day—and the sitting down is all. In the course of that working day of eight hours I write three sentences which I erase before leaving the table in despair. . . . It takes all my resolution and power of self-control to refrain from butting my head against the wall. I want to howl and foam at the mouth but I daren't do it for fear of waking that baby and alarming my wife.

Conrad was writing in English, which happened to be his fourth language. Born in Poland, his second language was an uneducated Russian heard in one of the czar's prisons where both his parents developed tuberculosis and died young. He learned French as a seaman in the French merchant marine. Retired from a career as a British seaman where he advanced from cabin boy to captain, he struggled to write. However, with his East European accent, he was forever insecure about his command of the English language, which was not the result of schooling but acquired pragmatically by work at sea. He had adventures to relate—stories of enigmatic spies, anarchists, and smugglers—the result of voyages around the world, and despite encouragement from writers like Ford Madox Ford and Henry James, finding the right words and the proper diction was a protracted torture for him. But he persevered, wrote *Heart of Darkness* and many other novels, and received the recognition that he deserved. Nevertheless, Conrad's efforts assume mythic proportion.

As George Orwell admitted in his essay "Why I Write": "Writing a book is a horrible, exhausting struggle, like a long bout of some painful illness." Over the years, as I conducted workshops in nonfiction or creative writing, many students have approached me, explaining that they could not fulfill the assignment, complaining that they were "blocked." The fear they felt develops from a failure of confidence. The offer of more time might merely prolong the block and turn it into a Sisyphean boulder. I would hesitate to tell such a student writer that travel to a remote and very different culture might release the block and lead to the discovery of a subject because then they might never complete the course or might hazard a journey that may be too dangerous today. I certainly would not share the story of William Seward Burroughs, who ended a protracted block by shooting his wife at close range in Mexico City in 1951 and then wrote *Junky* and *Queer* during the year of his trial. Homicide is clearly too insufficiently therapeutic, too drastic a strategy for me to propose.

Instead, seeking to encourage, I used to tell them a story that may be partly apocryphal, but like most good stories it serves an instructive purpose. The writer Jack London lived with his mother in Oakland, California, early in the twentieth century. They were quite impoverished and London earned his keep working in a cannery and then shoveling coal for ten cents an hour. He had been writing, writing, writing since his teens, but all he had received were condescending notices of rejection. He gathered all the rejected material and placed it in a pile, stating that when it reached his height, he would accept that as a karmic sign to stop trying. The material accumulated to over five feet. London was a good-looking young man, but only five foot four. When his stepsister's sixty-year-old husband approached him and said he needed help to go north to the Klondike because gold had been discovered, London decided to accompany him. He felt he had nothing to lose and digging in the coal was backbreaking labor. The sketches he wrote about life in the mining camps were immediately accepted—a new subject matter often creates a platform for any writer, which may be why so many writers like Orwell or Hemingway began as journalists.

London ended up as the most successful writer in the history of California with a forty-thousand-acre estate and a yacht he would use to sail around the world. I just loved *White Fang* and *The Call of the Wild* when I was a boy, and I would have had less occasion to rejoice in my youth had I been deprived of the ability to read those books. That quality of spiritual stamina and the sheer monumental will to continue the work had sustained Jack London when he was an inch away from failure, which is why I have suggested that persistence may be even more useful to the writer than talent itself. It is an inspiring story: I believe it may have helped some of my former students, and I hope it encourages you.

Note to the reader: I must admit that the chapter you have just read was rejected by some thirty editors of magazines like the *Hudson Review* and the *Kenyon Review*, cooler publications like *McSweeney's* and *Tin House*, and more desperate possibilities like the *New Yorker* or the *Paris Review*, where one's work can linger in the slush pile for months before being scanned by an apprentice. After more than a year of lonely circulation, an angelic editor in South Carolina heard its message and offered to publish it, and for that I am grateful.

CHAPTER 2

THE WRITER AS PEEPING JOHN
ON THE NATURE OF BIOGRAPHICAL INQUIRY

The artist is present in every page of every book from which he sought so assiduously to eliminate himself.
— Henry James

In fact, biography cannot imitate life; it has to get rid of the chaos and clutter; it rejects the habitual and extraneous detail of our days; it rearranges its material; it tells a flowing story—something our lives never were.
— Leon Edel, "The Age of the Archive"

I. A Tripartite Hybrid

Begin with a thumbnail of history: "his story" as an ancient figure like Plutarch might have put it, or "her story" as Sappho might have seen it even earlier. Both the novel and biography have similar traditional roots in letters and journals. The novel is much younger than either the poem or the drama, less connected than these earlier genres were to an oral tradition that preceded the written word. As elaborate and voluminous a product as the novel depends entirely on the fifteenth-century technological innovation of the printing press. It took until the middle of the eighteenth century for the use and availability of Gutenberg's invention, originally used for Bible production, to become so widespread that longer fictions would be made available for an educated, leisured, mostly genteel female public.

Another source for the evolution of the novel, and a signifier of its social potential, is more disreputable: rumor or gossip. Robert Darnton, in his account of early French fiction, *The Forbidden Best-sellers of Revolutionary France*, describes the process where the habitués of Madame Doublet's Parisian salon entered in a ledger the news—in French *les nouvelles*, from which we derive the term novel—of outrageous aristocratic marital improprieties. In a time of strict monarchic censorship, such ledgers were passed secretly from region to region and became an early prototype for the newspaper and the novel. Rumor and gossip may motivate the contemporary biographer more than the novelist though they are necessarily approached with the perspicacity of a Sherlock Holmes and the systematic peering of a psychoanalytical lens.

The novelist's stepchild is biography, a genre that could not be applied to the lives of writers before the Renaissance when they were still mostly anonymous scribes. Shakespeare, after all, near the end of his life only has the idea of publishing his plays under his own name after he hears that Ben Johnson already has done it. Shakespeare dies early in the seventeenth century, and we have barely enough documentary evidence to verify his existence as a writer.

The biographer is a curious tripartite hybrid: part inquisitive reporter, part historian who tries to interpret a past era, part storyteller with a dramatic sense of timing the possible. To some extent, from a psychological perspective, perhaps the biographer is more of a voyeur than we expect, like a transfixed, gazing infant, dependent yet nourished by the subject's activities, accomplishments, and defeats, the ingredients of a life that may seem more vital and engaged than our own.

There is a parasitic quality to the biographer's curiosity that may leave some readers queasy. Edmund de Waal notices near the end of his remarkably evocative memoir, *The Hare with the Amber Eyes*, the "slightly clammy feeling of biography, the sense of living on the edge of other people's lives without their permission."

With an almost Faustian eagerness to use any means to discover a truth, particularly if it has the salacious or scandalous edge that results in sales, the biographer has sometimes been accused, as Jean Cocteau put it describing Ezra Pound, of not knowing how far to go too far. This can result in what the novelist Joyce Carol Oates has termed "pathography"—the sensational exaggeration of an artist's emotional excesses and vulnerabilities so as to present a distorted picture of a life.

No one understood better than Henry James, who made a bonfire of the letters he had received, how a snooping curiosity could become an obsessively gross violation of privacy and propriety. Such tension underlines his novelette, *The Aspern Papers*, where James's narrator avidly pursues the papers of an American romantic poet James names Jeffrey Aspern, papers that are in the possession of old Juliana Bordereau in her Venetian palace. Presenting himself as a prospective lodger and ingratiating himself, the narrator courts Juliana's middle-aged, unmarried grandniece Tita, flattering her and taking her out in a gondola along Venice's romantic lagoons. No blunt summary can do justice to the delicate shadows and shades of sentiment that James manages. When Juliana dies, Tita implies that the narrator can have the papers he desperately desires provided that he marries her—which he cannot bring himself to do. The narrator's overtures and flirtation, however, the seductive charms of persuasion, suggest one of the biographer's perennial temptations and a dangerous border of propriety is intimated by Ms. Bordereau's very name.

Generically, though some feast on the form, readers tend to have less sympathy for the biographer's craft and the perils it presents than with the poet's or fiction writer's creative anguish. While the poet may struggle with alcohol or angst, the biographer always needs to consider the vulnerability of the spine, the aching back resulting from long hours and sometimes years of archival research, reading diaries, journals, and correspondence.

The poet can compose quite independently in a garret or park; the biographer begins in an institutional archive usually controlled by fastidiously decorous reincarnated Victorians who would shudder if you sneezed or accidentally touched the wrong page. I spent a few years working on the huge Pound cache at the Beinecke collection at Yale. Enclosed in its gleaming white, marble sarcophagus, I always felt its custodians regarded me as if my fingernails were dirty, my trousers insufficiently pressed, my soul smudged and presumably larcenous.

Such scrutiny only serves to compound the difficulties faced by any biographer: the awareness that what you are perusing may be full of unreported gaps, that as you search for illuminating clues beyond the mundane you are blinking in a darkened area, seeking glimmers of light, unaware at first that the concerns and proprieties of an earlier moment may be quite different from what you are used to seeing. At the same time, the biographer may so easily become the victim of a subject's projected view—the way the artist may wish to be seen.

Think, for example, of Jack Kerouac's *On the Road* where his protagonists with masculine bravado hitchhike or drive recklessly back and forth across America. Kerouac, in fact, hated driving and mostly took the Greyhound bus, which compromises his public image as a virile adventurer. Myth, as David Shields argues in *How Literature Saved My Life*, "is the attempt to reconcile intolerable contradictions." The very business of art often depends now on the fabrication of an accompanying myth of the artist's struggle and the gestation of the work, a myth that needs to be powerful and persuasive enough to attract an audience. Is it any wonder that many biographers can be sucked into its vortex and duped?

The most personal and defining aspects of a life are often unmentioned, repressed or disguised, and artists using reams of paper, their descendants and executors, still tend to be zealously protective of a future reputation. At one point, Ezra Pound lived with his wife and mistress—rivals each with a child by him—in the same squeezed quarters in Rapallo, Italy, during the Second World War. Even the most diligent detective will not learn of any conflict, nor will any details of Pound's other paramours be retrieved, except by innuendo, insinuation, or implication. So is Pound, the iconoclast of modernism, who proclaimed "Make It New," still a grand Victorian, as concerned with a fashioned persona in life as well as his art? On the other hand, a more contemporary figure such as Anaïs Nin may be too willing to tell us, as she did when her diaries were published in the 1960s, more than we need or wish to know.

The great challenge for the biographer is presented by the imagination. For biography to succeed, the skill of the novelist is required to select a pattern of events as part of a continuous narrative. Unlike the novelist, the biographer tries to reinvent an actual existence, a person whose feelings and thought process may be unrecorded or irrecoverable. The novelist has invented a protagonist, but the biographer needs to consider the risk of hidden circumstance, of violating the factual, the inconsistencies of contradictory accounts. Both the novelist and the biographer share the knowledge that what they are proposing is merely a plausible illusion, a story convincing enough to attract and retain a reader's fickle attentions. The biographer is always less secure, aware that the life presented depends on the need for dramatic peaks that may distort the truest picture as much as that picture is ultimately shaded by a subject who may have left much out.

If the subject is still alive, the biographical portrait can seem damaging, unbalanced, with insufficient awareness of the gray nuance that so often colors a life. If the subject is recently deceased, a zealous literary executor can block access or prevent quotation from unpublished material, sometimes even after a manuscript has been completed. For the biographer, writing about the dead is usually safer than trying to describe the activities of the living. The dead have become historical;

the living may become hysterical, hypersensitive, querulous, obsessed with reputation, eager to perpetuate self-fabricated myths.

II. *Mensonges Vital*

The late 1960s was a turbulent period and the possibility of profound change seemed imminent. That expectation was as contagiously uplifting as it was a cause for pervasive anxiety. We were living in a historical era punctuated by moments of mass hysteria: riots, political assassinations, thousands of marchers surrounding the Pentagon demanding an end to the Vietnam War. At Queens College in New York, where I was a very junior assistant professor, with a singular beard and hair that was long enough to guarantee the early termination of academic employment, a hundred students and faculty had placed their bodies on the Long Island Expressway, blocking traffic eight miles to the midtown tunnel. We did not see this sort of activity every day or every century.

I taught in the evenings then, in the School of General Studies. I had been hired by the dean of that division, who happened to subscribe to *Partisan Review*, and the magazine had printed a moody poem I had written about a rape. The poem had been admired, also, by Marianne Hauser, a colleague in the English Department who taught creative writing. Marianne was a brusque, commanding, but tiny woman who spoke in a guttural voice with a Swiss German inflection. A highly opinionated, feisty novelist of some underground repute, she amused me. I called her the matador because she was so sinewy, rail slim, and she wore very tight black leather trousers. Though she was elderly, old enough to have been my grandmother really, she was so spirited she seemed decades younger, almost my contemporary. Sometimes I gave her a ride to the Village after classes and occasionally I met her for coffee before classes.

It was on one of those serendipitous meetings—actually in the first week of classes at the end of August 1969—that Marianne invited me to join a group of friends who were coming to her apartment in Washington Square Village for drinks the following night. She told me Anaïs Nin was also invited and might appear. I lived only a few blocks away, and liked to drink.

That first night in September the air was particularly moist and warm, and there were over a dozen people in Marianne's living room.

I was thirty years old, by far the youngest person there and, I noticed, one of the only males. Most of the guests were crowded around Nin, whose dark hair was crowned high on her head, giving her an extra few inches of height and a poised but posed appearance. I may only have imagined it, but she seemed to be almost searching for prey in the room, and there was something of the vampire or only the coquette in her inquiring glances. She was wearing white heels and a light, white gossamer gown just inches off the floor. The delicacy of the fabric suggested fluency and she glided alluringly in the room.

Half an hour later I was able to reveal myself as an admirer. I told her I had been a student of Henry James's biographer Leon Edel at NYU and had read her story "Under a Glass Bell" in a seminar on the psychological novel. Actually, I had proposed writing my doctoral dissertation on Henry Miller to Edel; Miller, of course, had famously been Nin's secret lover in Paris in the early 1930s. Edel advised me that I would never get a university position if I wrote on Miller and that instead I should focus on Henry James. Edel did tell me he had met Miller in Paris several times during the 1930s, when Edel was working for a Canadian newspaper as a foreign correspondent. Miller never seemed like the rambunctious buccaneer of *Tropic of Cancer*, but instead was always turned out in suits his tailor father had made for him. I did not know that Edel had reviewed the first published volume of the *Diary* in the *Saturday Review of Literature* in 1966, placing Nin accurately among the surrealists "in the last backwater of Romanticism," and suggesting that the diaries should be "quarried with caution."

Nin mentioned that she was often out of town, giving lectures or working on a screenplay in L.A. There was a calculated deliberation, a stilted quality to her speech that was intriguing. She was in New York, caring for her husband Hugo, who was recovering from surgery to correct a detached retina. Somewhere in the conversation, I can't any longer recall the segue, I told her I thought that her story "Under a Glass Bell" was a deliberate inversion of Edgar Allan Poe's classic tale, "The Fall of the House of Usher." Smiling coyly, she denied having ever having read Poe. Her assurance made me feel a bit foolish.

I was familiar with the legend of the journalist who had asked William Faulkner whether he had read *Ulysses*, Faulkner's flat denial, and the journalist's assertion that after the death of the great novelist he found a copy of Joyce's novel annotated in Faulkner's hand. Too dense to realize that an artist is usually reluctant to divulge a source to a young unknown, I persisted.

In a little example of spontaneous pedantry, I pointed to the snapped guitar string at the conclusion of Nin's story, and remarked that Roderick Usher's guitar improvisation was the only sound he could tolerate. Roderick was a hypersensitive *ennuyé*, as was Jeanne in "Under a Glass Bell." Both inhabited a dream world that alienated and isolated them from most human concerns.

I began to list some of the parallels between the houses in each story, the description of windows, curtains, and servants; the "dark and intricate passages" of the Usher mansion and the "labyrinthine stairway" of Jeanne's. Usher, I added, is described as being the last stem of his genealogical line, and Jeanne's face seemed "stemless as she monologued endlessly." Usher's sister Madeleine is cataleptic, like Jeanne and her two brothers, and in both stories the illness of the siblings is reciprocal and possibly compounded by incestuous longings: "If I am sick they get sick. If they are sick I get sick," Jeanne confides. Sometimes, as if to confound any connection between the stories, "Under a Glass Bell" inverts what Poe supposes. Roderick, for example, fears shadows, while Jeanne is at ease with them.

With a look that seemed quite satisfied, yet slightly petulant or even pouting at the same time, Nin let me filibuster without interruption. Shadowed by mascara, her eyes seemed veiled, her lips painted with a white lipstick, and her unlined face smooth and heavily made-up. She seemed much younger than she actually was, able to move in the room with a sort of feline liquidity of arms and legs, but she said nothing. Finally, I proposed that both Roderick and Jeanne clearly express their fears of going mad. At the end of Poe's tale, Madeleine rips her way out of the tomb in which she has been prematurely interred, and in a mirror in "Under a Glass Bell" Jeanne sees an image of herself in a tomb wearing a crinoline with its silk covering eaten away.

All these parallels, no matter how ingeniously perceived, were merely coincidental, Nin announced with a Cheshire smile, since she had not read the Poe story. The calm steadiness of her position was deflating to say the least. I felt exposed in all the preposterousness of the presumptuous academic professing to explain the origin of a text to its creator. Subsequently, perhaps in another sort of academic denial, I would develop my theory in an essay that Richard Centing was kind enough to print in an early issue of a little magazine devoted to Nin studies called *Under the Sign of Pisces* in the winter of 1971.

A decade later I got an assignment from a slick New York magazine to describe Nin's love affair, one of her calculated launches into what Breton called *amour fou*, with Henry Miller in Paris of 1932. Reading Nin's letters and published diaries, I stumbled on her declaration in the middle of the first volume that Les Ruines, the castle where Nin's father had abandoned his family, looked like the sort of setting invented by Poe. To understand the crumbling gloom of such a setting, she probably had read Poe's stories. So as Henry Miller might have put it, I had been "played"!

Miller owed a lot to Nin because the frankness he perceived when he first read parts of Nin's diaries in 1931 confirmed the unliterary and erotic direction he wanted to take in *Tropic of Cancer*. His romantic delusion was the hope that Nin would leave her banker husband for him. After her failed pregnancy, when he followed her to New York City in the spring of 1935, he realized she could never actually break her emotional bond with her husband and the security he represented.

I must admit to feeling more bemused than betrayed when I discovered the acknowledgment of Poe in the first diary. While I may have been subject to one of Nin's *mensonges vital*, or "the lies that give life" as she rationalized it in an unpublished diary, I had not been duped. I knew fiction's twin is often fabrication and art is related to artifice. My article received a lot of attention, enough to trigger a contract for a book.

One response, however, was at least disquieting, a threatening letter sent by an attorney in Los Angeles on behalf of a man named Rupert Pole, who apparently had been scandalized by my assertions. In the age before cell phones Pole had innocently been bigamously married to Nin, had been her West Coast spouse. The lawyer warned me not to write another word about Anaïs Nin so, of course, I did. *Passionate Lives* had been intended as a biography of Miller, but because his son Tony proved too difficult for me to negotiate with, it turned into a study of modern romantic marriage with a chapter on Miller that included Nin. Rupert Pole never sued me; perhaps his attorney was clever enough to realize I could prove each one of my allegations, no matter how outrageous some of them might have seemed to Pole.

There was a coda to the time when I met Nin and perplexed her with Poe that still haunts me though. At the end of the evening, after I had valiantly or fatuously failed to persuade Nin of the correspondences in the stories, and after I had enjoyed a few more glasses of wine, I was seated on a couch—was it leather or vinyl?—waiting for my head to clear before leaving. The excitement of mingling guests and animated conversation had entirely abated as there were only a few stragglers left. I felt a bit like an uninvited guest at a failed séance where the ghost had refused to appear. Anaïs was to my left on the couch, listening intently to another woman who abruptly left the room.

What happened next surprised me: suddenly, Anais was curved into my lap, her head just below mine and her whitened lips slightly parted. Did her look seem appealing, expectant, or confused? Was this was an overture, a test, a calculated strategy to detour me from the track of my comparison, or the sort of accidental misstep that can occur to the inebriated? It was such a transient moment, such a brief flicker in the cosmos, evident I suspect to no one else still in the room. I smelled jasmine, but instead of arousal, I remember my body constricting, tightening, my lips and fingers turning slightly colder as I slipped her gently to the side and then quickly escorted myself out the door.

III. In Search of the Grail

Unlike fiction, biography can be hazardous and access to any subject can depend on tests establishing trust and credibility. I don't suppose that such tests are as consequential or as picaresque as the quests that form the earliest part of English literature—the Arthurian legends with the king of an ailing realm dispatching his knights to recover the holy grail, a symbol of salvation—but they can be full of surprising twists.

Most always, when writing about modern or contemporary figures, the biographer will attempt to validate the recalled truth of past experience through personal interviews with the subject, if possible, or with those who knew the subject. The emotional dynamics are often delicate and can certainly affect the extent and accuracy of access.

I can never forget, for instance, interviewing the novelist William Seward Burroughs in 1974 in a loft space on the Bowery in Manhattan, and asking him about the circumstances of shooting his wife Joan Vollmer Adams in Mexico City in 1951. Burroughs had seemed distant before my question, his replies blunt, mechanical or in the flat, uninflected mode he called "factualist." With this question though, he stiffly rose from a long metal table and retreated to a far corner of the room, mumbling a reply I could not hear and my tape recorder could never capture. That question ended my interview like a door closing.

So clearly tact and timing can affect the process of any interview. Sometimes, an interview can finish before it begins or at least before anything useful is said. In 1982, for example, I tried to interview a minor Beat poet named Ray Bremser in Boulder, Colorado, as part of a documentary film I had written on Jack Kerouac. Bremser, a former drinking buddy of Kerouac's, had been incarcerated several times and did not quite understand why I wanted to interview him. He was both nervous and surly, full of a coiled tension that made me apprehensive. When he sat down, I noticed a bulge in his knee-high boot, so I asked him about it. With a grin and a flourish, he pulled out a stick of dynamite. Pointing it directly at me, he explained that in the West miners used dynamite to excavate claims, and also to ward off potential claim jumpers. The aggressiveness of his response and a feeling of unpredictable irresponsibility were intimidating enough for me to abort the interview.

In ways I could not really understand at the time, I was being tested by Burroughs and Bremser, and those were tests I fumbled. I would like to recount two occasions when I inadvertently passed tests, enabling me to gain the assistance of figures who could become crucial informants for the story I wanted to tell.

IV. Afternoon with a Faun

My first book, *Naked Angels*, was a very early attempt to write the history of a group of writers who had met in the precincts of Columbia University near the end of the Second World War and were known as the Beat Generation. The three leading figures in what would emerge as a literary movement, William Burroughs, Jack Kerouac, and Allen Ginsberg, had been introduced to each other by one of Ginsberg's Columbia classmates, Lucien Carr.

Kerouac's latest biographer, Joyce Johnson in *The Voice Is All*, describes Carr—nineteen years old, a blonde, elfin young man—as having the appeal of a faun. Wiry and wily, Carr also had a more arrogant, impetuous side. He had been expelled from several good prep schools and was clearly rebelling against any conventional expectations with an extroverted wildness demonstrated by his sloppiness and an utter disregard for his appearance. In a time when students were expected to wear ties and jackets to class, he could appear in a torn white shirt and no socks. Both Kerouac and Ginsberg were drawn to him as a catalyst.

Carr's family was from St. Louis and part of affluent set that included Burroughs. What was unusual about Carr was that he was being relentlessly pursued by his former scoutmaster, David Kammarer, a large redheaded man with a flowing beard and a high-pitched often hectoring voice who had been one of Burroughs's few childhood friends and was part of the same elite circle in St. Louis. A jealous, obsessive stalker, Kammarer had followed Lucien on August 13, 1944, to the West End, a workingman's bar on upper Broadway near Columbia and an early Beat drinking hole. After a night of drinking, Kammarer led Carr through Riverside Park to a secluded area near the Hudson River where he attempted to force himself sexually on his younger companion. Defending himself, Carr fatally stabbed his antagonist with his scout knife, weighted the body with rocks, and rolled it into the river.

This sad and shocking murder was reported in the tabloids and formed a strange bonding ritual for the Beats, who by then were sharing a large apartment at 419 West 115th Street, near Columbia University and a few blocks from where the event had occurred. There was a trial, and Carr was sent to Elmira Penitentiary for two years after pleading to a charge of manslaughter. What was interesting, however, from any literary perspective was that Burroughs and Kerouac decided to collaborate on a novel about Carr and Kammarer, contributing alternating chapters in a style that imitated Dashiell Hammett and Raymond Chandler. Although the novel, *And the Hippos Were Boiled in Their Tanks*, would only appear in print seventy years later, it demarcates the beginning of the Beat Generation.

Twenty-five years after the murder, in the early 1970s, I had been progressing through the Ginsberg Archive at Columbia University and had read "A Journal of a Fall," a notebook account Allen had kept about Carr. I was eager to interview Carr. I knew that he had a career as an editor at United Press International, a news agency located in the Daily News building on East 42nd Street. Carr was brusque and evasive when I called, clearly reluctant to talk about the past. After several subsequent calls, he finally agreed to meet me after work.

Carr was knotted and gnarled by middle age, his blonde hair was mixed with white strands, his fingers stained by tobacco, his voice rasping from too much smoke. He was still thin with the same swagger of brash confidence that once had so much appeal for his Columbia contemporaries. He brought me to an unpretentiously proletarian bar, a long narrow standing-room-only place where one might come for a quick shot during lunch hour or after work. What I remember most about the room were its dingy yellow walls, the sour stench of beer as if the floors had been cured in it, the stale cigarette smell in the air, and the blare of a hundred people trumpeting the news of their day and, perhaps, their prospects for the night to come.

Carr immediately ordered a double martini, and I asked for the same on the rocks. When I took out my small tape recorder, he grimaced and told me he preferred that I not use it, that the din in the room would make the tape inaudible anyway. It soon was clear that a conversation more than an interview might ensue, with Carr directing questions about my background and interests as if he were hiring me at UPI. I knew from having interviewed men who had served time in prison—such as Herbert Huncke, another catalyst figure for the Beats—that they could be suspicious, that they could easily size me up as an FBI informant.

I was still naive, and Carr quickly ordered another round of drinks. He had managed to decoy, avoid, or disparage every question I tried to ask about his time at Columbia, his association with Kerouac, Ginsberg, and Burroughs, or his relationship with Kammarer. Laughing frequently, boisterously, he seemed to be sneering and sharply cynical. Smirking maliciously, I thought he was taunting me. When he spoke at all, he would turn his head away from me, his voice deliberately lowered in a harsh slurring growl.

We were on our fourth round—a single for me instead of doubles—when I dimly began to understand that this was a sinister test in Hemingway machismo, a game for which I had little aptitude, a diabolic drinking contest for which I was entirely unprepared. My knees were buckling and I was gripping the railing on the top of the bar with one hand, already "three sheets to the wind" as the sailors used to say, incapable of now even asking another question, wondering whether I had enough balance and money to pitch into a taxi for home.

Carr began talking to an acquaintance in the news trade when a minor miracle occurred. Standing erect in the noisy crowd at the bar was a tall, burly fireman in full regalia, holding his drink in one hand and a long javelin-like steel rod in the other still-gloved hand. In New

York City, unlike Paris, it is against the law for a police officer or firefighter in uniform to order a libation in a bar. This firefighter, a striking presence, looked something like a red-cheeked Roman warrior about to depart for battle. He wedged himself at the bar beside me and, absurd as it may seem, engaged me in a discussion about Franz Kafka's bewildering story "A Country Doctor."

He was perplexed, he claimed, by Kafka's impotent protagonist. "Perplexed" is the exact word Kafka used in the beginning of his bizarre tale in which a physician is stripped naked by his patient's family when he is unable to provide a cure, so this encounter seemed part of a design I could not quite yet decipher.

Loudly, the fireman demanded to know whether the fumbling physician represented some disguised fantasy. Was he a ritualized scapegoat figure unable to even detect the wound of his ailing patient just as earlier he had been unable to save Rose, the servant he had never previously noticed, from the marauding ravishments of a mysterious groom? And wasn't there a connection, my fireman leered, between the patient's infected wound with its rose-red worms and the assault on the servant? Was the wound—now my fireman seemed to be almost lewdly whispering—a displaced or repressed memory of the unnoticed Rose, and was she not the sign that the doctor's life had been unlived, wasted in routine?

These questions were catapulted, a barrage I was too inebriated to contain. Slowly, I realized that this firefighter had been my student in an accelerated program for adults at Queens College several years earlier when I had asked the class to compare Kafka's story to "The District Doctor," an earlier, more realistic tale by Turgenev. Carr, of course, could not know this. He was utterly fascinated by the fact that a man of the people, a lifesaver, would engage me on the esoteric subject of Franz Kafka.

At this point, I had earned my credibility with Carr but I needed my own doctor. An absurdly weird version of the grail maiden had miraculously appeared, validated the purity of my intentions, and declared me suitable to receive the grail no matter how drunk I had become. But I was too bleary and weakened by the gin to continue. My fireman former student bought us a fifth round that I could not finish, and I was helped into a taxi, hoping that on a future occasion I might learn something more tangible from Lucien Carr.

v. A Venetian Romance

When the fiery young poet Ezra Pound met Henry James in London in the spring of 1912, the older, more Victorian man of letters advised him that his ideas were too heretical. With his acutely refined sensibility, James, called "The Master" by some of his contemporaries, had hit the mark precisely, and later Pound would be regarded as the most controversial of American writers.

During the fourteen years he lived in London, Pound profoundly affected the art of poetry with his theories of imagism and the formation of literary modernism. To support himself, he had written both the art and music criticism for the *New Age*, an upstart newspaper with a Nietzschean slant. Just prior to his departure in 1920 he reviewed a recital by a young American violinist named Olga Rudge.

Pound encountered the violinist again at Natalie Barney's salon in Paris. A slight, demure, graceful presence, Olga was drawn to the flamboyant poet whose words so often sounded like brilliant explosions: "Beauty must never be explained," he would declare, or "Beauty is merely a brief gasp between clichés." Pound was married to Dorothy Shakespear, a fact that failed to prevent the infatuated Olga from following Pound to Italy when he left France in 1924, or from becoming pregnant and giving birth to Pound's daughter, Mary. Pound found occasion to travel with Rudge when she performed in various parts of Europe, and he even wrote music for her to play. Together, they discovered a cache of lost Vivaldi manuscripts, and Olga organized a series of concerts in Rapallo, the town on the Italian Riviera where Pound lived. During World War Two, Dorothy and Olga shared residence with Pound despite the fact that they were rivals "who coldly hated each other," according to Mary.

At the end of the Second World War, Pound was arrested and tried for treason by the American government because of a series of reckless, mostly incoherent radio broadcasts he had made in Rome during the war. It was difficult for a democratic system that values free speech to execute one of its leading writers, so instead Pound was incarcerated for thirteen years in St. Elizabeth's, a mental institution in Washington, D.C. Pound became a pariah—the Benedict Arnold of literature—but a procession of American artists came to visit him at St. Elizabeth's, venerating him as an icon of outspoken candor. After his release in 1958, due to pressure by Ernest Hemingway, T. S. Eliot, and most strategically Robert Frost, Pound lived mostly with Olga until his death on his eighty-seventh birthday in her home in Dorsoduro, Venice, in 1972. Most of his final decade had been spent in a deliberate silence, an act of either monastic contrition or dramatic strategy to avoid explanations.

Thirteen years later, I moved to Venice. I had spent several previous years researching Pound's life at the Beinecke collection at Yale, at the Lilly Library in Bloomington, Indiana, and at the Humanities Research Center in Austin, Texas, where large collections of letters and papers were archived. Contracted by Doubleday to write a biography of Pound, I thought that, at the least, I should avail myself of the pleasures of living in one of the most exquisite places in Europe. With only faintly reverberating echoes of *The Aspern Papers*, I very much wanted to meet Olga Rudge.

Pound's publisher, James Laughlin, liked my first book *Naked Angels* and had given me her address. I wrote from New York and when I received no reply, thinking of the "publishing scoundrel," the unnamed narrator of *The Aspern Papers*, I wrote again. As Henry James himself might have put it, I did not receive the favor of a reply.

I arrived in Venice in the spring of 1985 with seventeen bags and suitcases and my wife, Mellon, who was then doing a lot of fashion photography. We had flown to Milan and then taken a train across Italy with our clothing, a small archive of research material, and photography equipment. We had so much baggage with us that Mellon forgot to take her portfolio off the train; fortunately, it was retrievable because Venice was the last stop.

We took a motorboat—the only way to navigate Venice's circuitous canals with a load of luggage. Our temporary destination was the modest Pensione Wildener conveniently located near the Piazza San Marco and the center of Venice. Our room featured a spectacular view of the Grand Canal, but since I planned to stay for a year, we needed to rent lodging.

Our first week was spent in fruitless searching, getting lost in the twisting ancient geography of Venice and being astonished by its beauty, unchanged since the height of the Renaissance. The cobblestoned alleys were a kind of destabilizing unbalancing act, a tilting of perspective. Venice was a fantasy of Renaissance architecture, Byzantine grace, and baroque intricacy: the labyrinth of canals, the lapping presence of the sea and its salty tang in the air, the glittering reflections of the changing light off the water at sunset, the mysteriously curving and angled houses with elongated windows and their blistered facades of yellow, orange, and red were all like invitations to consider. While there were places to purchase, little or nothing was available to rent.

Finally, Mellon, a beautiful young woman with much more courage and savoir-faire than I could ever muster, said she was going to ask an officer in the American Express office for assistance. I declared that would not work: American Express was there to sell traveler's checks, not to secure accommodations unless in a fancy hotel like the Danieli. An Italian man who spoke English and worked at American Express must have fallen in love with Mellon immediately because he asked her to return at five o'clock. When he saw that I was with her, he appeared crestfallen but gallantly escorted us on a twenty-minute walk, over the Accademia Bridge to Dorsoduro and the huge palazzo of a restorer of Titians and Canalettos. He owned a small duplex villa in the Campo Santa Marguerita, near the grand palazzo where Robert and Elizabeth Barrett Browning had lived a century earlier. He would rent to us, provided we could pay him immediately in cash for the entire period. Taxes, most Venetian businessmen felt, were an inconvenience that could be circumvented.

I wired my American bank for money, converted it to casino stacks of liras, signed some official papers declaring my legal rent to be a fraction of the sum I gave to my new landlord, and, as the saying goes, hoped for the best. The next day we discovered that our room in the *pensione* had been part of the lodging where Henry James had composed one of his late masterpieces, *The Wings of the Dove*. Since I had written a doctoral thesis on James's late fiction, this seemed like an annunciation, a charmed augury of exceptional tidings.

Soon, I was installed in my new workspace and Mellon departed to continue her fashion work for Sipa Press and *W* magazine in Paris. I wrote a third time to Olga Rudge, this time including my new telephone number, heard no response, and went to work at my writing.

Unless it was Mellon calling from Paris, the phone hardly rang. Cramped at a very small and uncomfortable writing table, I spent the days bent into my evolving manuscript, writing a longhand page in the morning and then typing a second draft after lunch on a portable Olivetti typewriter. A book page a day, I hoped, would allow me to complete my project in a year and meet my deadline. In the evening, I would unwind with a grappa or an *averna* and a two-hour perambulation through the streets and alleys of Venice, often ending up in a little trattoria for dinner. I stopped in most of Venice's four hundred churches along my way, marveling at the Raphaels and Tintorettos I would find adorning the ceilings and altars.

One morning, still unshaven, unwashed, and only partly dressed, steeped in my work and perhaps even a little dazed by the force of my own concentration on my material, the telephone rang. And I heard a whispering, vaguely British, but certainly correct accent. The woman speaking—it was Olga Rudge—requested that I meet her immediately, and gave me the address of an art gallery ten minutes away.

Rushing my morning ablutions, I hurried to the gallery only to see a tiny, white-haired woman barely five feet high with an overflowing shopping cart that she asked me to convey. Unlike Juliana Bordereau of *The Aspern Papers*, who shielded her eyes with green eyeshades, Olga Rudge looked directly into my eyes with a furious intensity, her little body tense with rage. There had been a terrible misunderstanding, she explained. She had brought a collection of Pound memorabilia to the gallery for a visiting delegation of Pound scholars who had come from America to begin the celebration of the centenary of Pound's birth in Hailey, Idaho, in 1885. The gallery, however, was only prepared to offer her one wall, which she found too insulting to bear.

"But what will I do now?" she plaintively inquired, completely at a loss. I volunteered to hang the memorabilia in her home. We walked around a few curving streets to 252 Calle Querini, a former gondolier's cottage down a dark, narrow alleyway, a few steps from where Igor Stravinsky had lived, near the Customs House and the Salute Church, and minutes away from Peggy Guggenheim's museum on the Grand Canal. The "hidden nest," as Pound called it, was on three floors, with about 250 square feet of space on each landing, a large room and a smaller one on each. The third-floor room, originally where Olga practiced the violin, had been Pound's study and his final resting place. This was where I was expected to display the collection of posters, books, photographs, broadside poems, and letters.

Olga told me there was little time remaining and I got right to work. What was framed I could hang with a hammer and nail; what wasn't could be taped from the back or displayed on a few small tables I found on the lower floors. I had no experience arranging art and associated gallery openings with the opportunity to consume as much wine as possible. Far from adept, I could never manage to hang a picture without a tilt; I had built my own bookshelves with warped wood and was known, to my wife at least, as "Mr. No-can-do" when it came to matters like using a hammer. The Muse of the Arts, however, must have been in the room with me, and at the end of two hours, Olga came in beaming.

There was still a little time left and she offered to take me to lunch, a simple pasta and a glass of red wine on a small canal on the Rio Fornace. When we completed our repast, she said we had to return to receive the American scholars whose arrival was imminent. I demurred that now I really needed to shower and shave, and that I was exhausted. I was not actually tired but knew that if I met the American Pound scholars from the University of Pennsylvania, Wisconsin, Indiana, Michigan, Maine, and who-knew-where, I would be cannibalized, devoured by their jealousy, metaphysically torn apart by maenads who despised biographical inquiry but were profoundly envious of the opportunity. These scholars had spent their lives annotating *The Cantos*, unconcerned with the dynamic of creation and the life behind them. So I escorted Olga back to the Calle Querini and left.

I returned many times during the following months. Once she met my wife, Olga loved her and allowed Mellon to photograph me seated in Ezra Pound's high-backed, elaborately woven wicker armchair, looking like a pleased potentate. She claimed she had not allowed anyone to sit in that chair since Pound's death. Betrayal of trust is, of course, a key issue in Henry James and is the deciding factor in *The Aspern Papers*. Olga seemed to trust me—after all, I had helped her when she was in need—although I knew I could not fully trust her. She was fiercely loyal to Pound's memory, minimized his anti-Semitism, arguing that it was normative for Europe and America prior to World War Two, and rationalized his sympathies for Mussolini by arguing that there was considerable support for him, as there had been for Adolph Hitler, in America in the early 1930s.

Olga was ninety years old when I met her and she became a limited confidante; she was lithe and nimble and, though she could be forgetful and sometimes confused about dates, her mind seemed relatively clear and able to recall details from the past. Generally, she seemed to breathe an indomitable inner strength. Once she scampered up a ladder to where her books were shelved to retrieve a heavy coffee-table art book with a picture she wanted me to see. Mellon asked her the source of her energy, and she replied that she drank lots of milk. I encountered her one morning on a vaporetto, steady and grasping its railing with the poise, good cheer, and willful resolution she usually displayed.

When I was preparing to leave Venice that winter, Olga's friend Pablo Casals was giving a recital in Venice. She expressed interest in attending so I offered to escort her. She refused, saying that we would need to reach the concert hall by taking the vaporetto, a lurching ferry moving in what could be very choppy waters. She could not see that well at night, she explained, and could no longer trust her balance, even with my arm supporting her. So she understood the vulnerabilities of aging.

Mellon and I attended the concert. Casals, very old himself then, played the cello surrounded by an intimate audience seated around him in gold-and-burgundy velvet chairs in a palatial space with high frescoed ceilings and stone walls. The sound of the cello was bittersweet and enthralling.

There is a sad Jamesian coda to the story, however. I returned to New York where in 1987 *The Solitary Volcano*, my biography of Pound, was published. Seven years later, I was invited with my wife to return to Venice to speak at its film festival about the legacy of the Beat Generation because of a featured group of Beat-related films they were showing. The Venetian officials in charge needed an authority on the subject to address them. During the festival they accommodated us for four days at the Hotel Des Bains, on Lido, which Thomas Mann had used as the setting for his great story "Death in Venice."

When I tried to reach Olga Rudge I was unsuccessful and heard that at ninety-nine she had become frail and was now living with her daughter, Mary, in a castle in the Tyrol, three hours to the north. Previously, they had been estranged with Olga as independently as always trying to live alone in the "hidden nest."

However, Olga had been victimized by a scoundrel of another sort than the one depicted in *The Aspern Papers*. Philip Rylands was the director of the Peggy Guggenheim Foundation and managed her museum in Venice—Peggy Guggenheim had died in 1979. Rylands and his wife Jane convinced Olga to set up an Ezra Pound Foundation that the Rylands would administer to disseminate Pound's writing. For seven thousand dollars they acquired more than two hundred boxes of Pound's papers from Olga, which they later sold to the Beinecke. The art world is redolent with deception and appropriation, and Olga had not been able to fend for herself at the end. She died a few years later at the age of 101.

CHAPTER 3

HEMLOCK OR AMBROSIA
WRITING AND EDITORIAL PROCESS

Life is our dictionary!
— Ralph Waldo Emerson

When I think of the relations writers have had with editors, I almost inevitably recall Jack Kerouac's enthusiastic delight in the spring of 1951 when he burst into Robert Giroux's office and unrolled the manuscript of *On the Road*, a novel he had typed on a homemade scroll in three weeks, working with little sleep, drinking cup after cup of coffee, some laced with Benzedrine.

Giroux—who ran Farrar, Strauss and Giroux until his death in 2008—was then a talented young editor at Harcourt Brace who had accepted Kerouac's first novel, an imitative, apprentice effort called *The Town and the City*, and forced the recalcitrant Kerouac to cut a third of it away.

The excision was wrenching for Kerouac even though he knew he was still in the process of discovering his own voice. According to William Burroughs (who may well have exaggerated the claim), Kerouac had already written over a million words, beginning at the age of eleven. Conventionally organized, *The Town and the City* was especially influenced by the sweeping prolixity of Thomas Wolfe. Wolfe had been edited by Maxwell Perkins at Scribner's, who also edited Hemingway and Fitzgerald, and who not only cut away huge sections of Wolfe's work, but reassembled and reconfigured other sections to the extent that later critics could question the nature of authorial responsibility—call it the "authority"—particularly with Wolfe's later fiction. In the 1920s, Perkins was probably the most powerful and discriminating fiction editor in America, and, several decades later, Giroux was a prescient editor with antennae sensitive enough to detect the new.

When Giroux began to examine the unraveled manuscript of *On the Road*, he could see that it was virtually one endless stream of exuberance, an exfoliation punctuated primarily by dashes, so he naturally spoke about the necessity of editing. Kerouac's astonishing response was to roll up his manuscript and walk out. This stand was dangerous from any editorial perspective: it negated the role of the midwife of book production; it diminished the potential control of any publisher's representative. Kerouac may have been agitated by the hot flush of his own breakthrough, but his response to an editor's quite normal request was probably one of the more drastic and reckless in the history of American literature.

The state of impasse this presents seems universal for so many writers. I know, for example, from my own little history, that with each of the books that I've been fortunate enough to conceive, write, and see published, there was only one person in this huge country besides myself who cared enough about my idea to encourage me to see it through—and that was my editor. So it is difficult to imagine the courage—or is it a place located somewhere between impetuosity and folly?—to tell that person, "Well, I don't really need your help, your questions, suggestions, corrections, emendations, and qualifications. Since some spiritual power—call it 'god' or Dionysus if you like—dictated this to me, a reed bending in the wind, would it not be blasphemous to revise?" Would Moses have argued with the god whom he could not even name as he inscribed the Ten Commandments, asking for a word to be substituted or recommending a semicolon?

I suspect most writers are subject to the conflict between the heated demands of the heart's inspiration and more conventional approaches to making writing accessible and perhaps acceptable. *On the Road* finally appeared in 1957—six very long years after its composition. The published version was conventionalized by two editors at Viking Press—Helen Taylor and Keith Jennison—the rollicking, cascading rhythms of Kerouac's scroll, its surging momentum and endless variability punctuated and organized into predicate and verb propriety. Some might say that Viking's version of what Kerouac had written represented a literary castration, especially after reading *Visions of Cody*, a novel written with the freedom of *On the Road*, in the same year of 1951, but considered unpublishable and only published posthumously. To its credit, or perhaps as testament to how many copies have been sold, Viking Penguin did publish the scroll version of *On the Road* in 2007.

When I was writing my first book, an early history of the Beats called *Naked Angels*, my editor was Joyce Johnson, who had been Kerouac's lover in 1957. As an editor at McGraw-Hill when it still had a trade division, she was more responsible than anyone in America for the revival of interest in Kerouac in the 1970s as she began posthumously publishing and reprinting many of Kerouac's novels. My book, which was published by McGraw-Hill in 1976, was an early attempt to chart the history of the Beats and to determine the value of what they wrote. The title itself—*Naked Angels*—might indicate a subversive advocacy. Even Allen Ginsberg advised using the more anthropologically accurate title of *Naked Humans*.

Young, intemperate perhaps, I would not listen to him or to Joyce Johnson. She complained that sometimes my language sounded too passionate, too rambunctious, too infatuated with my own linguistic overreaching to induce the credibility the Beats needed after two decades of systematic condescension and outright dismissal by establishment media. My response to Joyce Johnson's objections—and it does seem jejune to me today—was to accept other advice from Allen Ginsberg and spend most of 1974 in Mexico on a fellowship from the National Endowment for the Humanities, trying to revise and reimagine my material.

Ideally, any writer acts as a primary editor, often, at first, trying to overcome a latent, intoxicating narcissism. My practice is to read the work aloud, slowly and deliberately, listening to the rhythm of sentences and attending to the connections, logical or psychological, between them. Oaxaca was distant enough from New York to help me, especially since I had no easy telephone communication. I was able to create valuable transitional sections for my manuscript on the sunny terrace of the Pensión Suiza in Oaxaca, which, hotheaded still, I insisted should appear in italics! I omitted chapters on poets like Gregory Corso, Gary Snyder, and Lawrence Ferlinghetti to focus on what had begun in New York City at the end of World War Two. I think I learned from Joyce—and her own calm, controlled prose was a model—that charged language is not always convincing, that an avalanche of anger does not itself persuade, that words broiled in oil do not often result in clarity or cohesion, that rhetoric, as Yeats once put it, is often the will straining to do the work of the imagination.

Actually, I had learned other lessons about the editing process even earlier. When I was preparing for doctoral orals at NYU in the 1960s, my study partner Harold Jaffe and I compiled material for two anthologies.

We called one of them *The American Experience: A Radical Reader*, and it was intended to be the first exploration of the political and cultural turbulence of that era. As editors, we chose writing we found to be powerful, provocative, and representative of the new: Malcolm X, Lenny Bruce, Timothy Leary, Ginsberg, and others.

At that time there was virtually nothing in print to help explain the conflicts of 1960s America. Jaffe and I had no agent, but we were familiar with the telephone. Of course, in those ancient times one could actually reach an editor that way. We wrote a proposal and shopped it around to those who expressed interest, managing to create a small bidding war because we believed in simultaneous submission. We had been advised that sending a proposal to more than one publisher at a time was an impropriety, a protocol violation of the genteel code supposedly operative in the publishing industry. Nevertheless, we ignobly adopted this strategy as a means of survival in a world where we realized the odds were against us, where we did not have years to wait patiently and politely to evaluate rejections, or to sit on Samuel Beckett's desolate heath expecting an answer that might never even come.

We received a very generous contract from Harper and Row—I bought two handmade suits—but when we turned our project in, our signing editor informed us that his bosses had found some of the material we included too raw or offensive. This was an aspect of the editorial process that Kerouac knew implicitly, and I suppose so many novelists prior to William Burroughs's *Naked Lunch* knew it, as Edgar Allan Poe once put it, as the shadow of their shadows.

The publisher, who was committing to a capital investment in your words, had the potential to lose, especially considering the vast educational market, and so your great Victorian aunt Mammon, who served watery tea without sugar and had always despised your long hair and crossed-leg manners, became an informal cultural arbiter. The publisher's role was to censor whatever seemed to violate her sense of the socially accepted as was the case in modern American literature from Theodore Dreiser's *Sister Carrie* to Henry Miller's *Tropic of Cancer*.

Obliquely, in a hushed, undertaker's undertone, it was suggested that we could be successfully blacklisted by commercial publishers. We didn't believe we were being quite confronted by gangsters and, ultimately, we negotiated a compromise: we would remove selections that the Harper overlords found sexually transgressive, but not writing that we saw as developing new political consciousness such as Malcolm X's "The Ballot or the Bullet." We could not make Harper happy and our sighing signing editor—an effusive giant in cowboy boots from Texas—spent the rest of his career in contracts. However, the book sold very well both as a trade item and as a university text. Hopefully, it may have even helped foster some change.

Over the years, the taboo nature of my subjects—writers who quarreled violently with established values—has subjected me to the pressures of editor's qualms and anxious signals that cultural nerves meant to be hidden are being exposed. Allow me to consider two examples.

In the winter of 1987, Nona Balakian, an editor with the *New York Times Book Review*, asked me to review *The Last Museum*, a novel written by a visual artist named Brion Gysin. In Paris in the late 1950s, Gysin had introduced William Burroughs to what they called the "cut-up," a technique allowing Burroughs to insert a selection from a news clipping or a writer he admired into the fabric of his own text without attribution—what painters called "collage" and contemporary musicians "sampling."

Set in a bordello, *The Last Museum* was deeply influenced by Burroughs, who had provided an introduction. As a reviewer, I thought it my job to describe some of the bizarre dream sequences and burlesqued scenes of twisted sexuality.

I submitted the review only to hear from Balakian that the *New York Times* could not print it. When I asked why, the editor's icy retort was that she worked for a "family newspaper."

Since I knew Gysin deserved attention and quite possibly the novel would not receive any other notice, I agreed to let her tone down the review by omitting the more salaciously insalubrious details of its plot, at least those that seemed, that late in the history of Christian civilization, too threatening to the families gathered around the fireside.

On another occasion in the following year, I was less accommodating. Working on a book on Henry Miller, I wrote an account of Anaïs Nin's serial polyandry in the early 1930s in Paris, the period when Miller was writing *Tropic of Cancer*. She supported Miller with an allowance, paid for his room in the Hotel Princesse and later for an apartment in Clichy, shared his bed before afternoon tea, and ultimately subsidized the printing costs of Miller's bombshell book when it was completed in 1934.

My subject, however, was Nin's remarkable sexual voracity. Besides her stolid husband, the banker Hugo Guiler, Nin would also sleep with a progression of other men during the course of the day, including two of her psychiatrists, Dr. René Allendy and Dr. Otto Rank, and her cousin Edouardo Sánchez. So my piece was titillating if not voyeuristic. And my primary sources were Nin's copious diaries and the large correspondence she shared with Miller.

Fame, the very glossy magazine that had commissioned the piece—which I called "Two Spies in the House of Love"—promptly assigned their cooking expert to edit it into "house style," which almost always is a euphemism for dull prose. The editor wanted to poach my chickens in cream sauce when I had already deep-fried them. She also seemed intent on omitting most of the details I had provided for the sake of authenticity, from the furniture in Nin's rooms in her estate at Louveciennes, just outside Paris, to the salty insinuations of her tongue.

Confident that I could sell my story to *Vanity Fair* or *Playboy*, I flatly refused all her recommended alterations, causing an editorial impasse. When Gael Love, the magazine's editor in chief called me, desperate to meet her deadlines, my unsympathetic and perhaps brutally crude response was "Fuck *Fame!*" I should not have responded so violently, though it was a true register of my absolute contempt for the magazine then; I suppose it would have been more cute or clever to have quoted Jack Kerouac's wish that "I'd rather be thin than famous." I must admit that when the piece appeared *exactly as I had written it*, I was extremely gratified.

The piece caused enough interest to lead to a contract for a book called *Passionate Lives*. The title was the publisher's cliché, not mine, and its lesson is that writers aren't always allowed to use the titles they have invented.

Any title is a headline, a telegram to a sleeping public. When I edited Carl Solomon's last book (he was the dedicatee of Allen Ginsberg's "Howl"), he was working as a walking messenger and just could not imagine a title for his little collection of pithy, humorously absurdist essays. I suggested *Emergency Messages* because of the frequent urgency in his voice. That idea worked, at least as far as Carl and his publisher were concerned.

But *Passionate Lives* was about five highly competitive modern marriages, and in each a writer was transfigured by a ravaging love that charged and changed the ways the writer spoke to the world. In each case, what the writer had to say was vitally transformative. One of my subjects was Henry Miller, and my desire had been to call the book *Plenipotentiaries* after a line in *Tropic of Cancer* in which Miller's nihilistic hero declares that he is "here as a plenipotentiary from the realm of free spirits." The head of the division of the conglomerate publishing my book decided that no one in America would know what "plenipotentiary" meant, as if I were trying to confuse his consumers with a book about penitents or penitentiaries.

Clichés, however, do have some value in the world of publishing, which is closely related to its cousins in advertising. Once, when the State of New York ran out of funds to pay the instructional staff at the City University of New York where I still teach, Mellon got me a job with the Don Wise Agency, a small firm located on Forty-Second Street, just off Fifth Avenue in Manhattan. I remember its location only because of its centrality, so close to the place of "absolute madness and fantastic hoorair" Jack Kerouac described at the end of the first part of *On the Road*, "with its millions and millions hustling forever for a buck among themselves."

My assignment was to write a history of wallpaper for the Imperial Wallpaper Company of Chicago, which wanted a brochure for its fiftieth anniversary. I learned how wallpaper originated in Europe during the Renaissance with the delicate rice paper used by the Chinese to line teak tea chests, paper that the French and English used to paste on the walls above their fireplace mantels; the rice paper was followed by the rich textures of the parchment proclamations issued by Henry VIII. After turning in my copy, I met with Don Wise, feeling like a dwarf in a giant office that looked down on the New York Public Library across the street. He congratulated the research that supported my history of wallpaper—he praised its elegance!—but complained that my language was too fastidious because I had failed to employ any clichés! He had the piece entirely rewritten by one of his trained subordinates, probably an expert in baking buttery croissants, to the extent that it was quite unrecognizable by me. My only consolation was the compensation, though the check seemed somehow redolent of grease.

I do not mean to imply that the editor is the writer's perennial antagonist. Many writers, and I include myself, have worked as editors, though university positions, if one is lucky enough to be able to find them, do afford any writer more time to do the work. An editor's differing point of view can have intrinsic value serving to sharpen an argument or clarify its causes. An editor can sometimes see the logical flaw of which you were unaware, or may suggest a path you just could not discern. Ideally, an editor cultivates your collaboration, responding with tactful sensitivity and some linguistic discretion, as well as the honesty to remark, "I don't think this works and here might be another way. . . ."

However, we understand that today's labor market employs fewer editors to do more work for less pay. Pressured by a dozen clamoring projects, each more weighty than Michelangelo's marbles, the editor may not be fully attentive when necessary. We've all heard of the editors who merely acquire but then never inquire, those more concerned with commerce than quality, or those so harried by their own crowded schedules they can only offer vague injunctions to "remedy this or redo that!"

When the World Trade Center catastrophe occurred, I was working on a hybrid memoir called *Reading New York* contracted by Knopf. Since the Random House building was being frequently evacuated due to emergency drills and false alarm threats, it became quite difficult to contact my editor, a most capable person who had probably stashed her cash under a mattress and was ready to flee.

Much of the now-invisible editorial responsibility to verify thought and language seems relegated to the deft curiosity of the copy editor, a shadowy presence as the manuscript is prepared for the galleys stage who points to the misused word, the incorrect fact or chronology, the dangling infelicities, the awkward construction, or the flaccidity of the extraneous. Even the most diligent copy editor, however, can detour a preposition as the esteemed Harvard don Harry Levin pointed out in a consequentially caustic dismissal of my Pound biography in the *New York Review of Books*, the most austere and circumspect of review organs.

I had four different editors during the decade I devoted to *The Solitary Volcano*. My project had begun inauspiciously when I announced it to my mother—the primal editor and the reason I became a writer—during our last dinner before she would be taken away to die in an awful hospital battle with leukemia. "But how could you?" she remarked, outraged by Pound's notorious anti-Semitism, the very poison that had driven her to seek refuge in this country.

Another editor bluntly told me to bury my evolving manuscript in a drawer for at least a decade. Her successor, fascinated by Jean Stein and George Plimpton's *Edie*, a popular biography of Edie Sedgwick, one of the glamorous members of Andy Warhol's entourage, advised me to turn seven years of research based on several thousand letters into a pop collage. My book would be more imaginative, she assured me, if I added juicy conversations even if no records existed.

A third editor was such an evanescent disappearance I never spoke to her. Then, an editor from *Vanity Fair*, a magazine I had already written for, asked me for a piece exploring Pound's first meeting with T. S. Eliot, only to offer me a kill fee after I wrote it because all available space had to be reserved for Dominick Dunne's stories on the murder trial of Claus von Bülow. The intrigues of socialites, I understood, usually trump the predicaments of poets!

My fourth editor was Fran McCullough, a noted cookbook editor with the girth to prove it, and when we met in 1985 in Venice, Italy, where I was actually writing my book, a page a day, I took her near my lodging in Dorsoduro to the Antica Locanda Montin, Pound's favorite eatery, and the next night by vaporetto to Harry Cipriani's on the island of Giudecca, a restaurant patronized primarily by Italians who knew that most Venetian cuisine was inferior, fit only for tourists who would not know better. I realize that unconsciously I must have been trying to bribe or at least butter favor with my editor through her palette but, alas, she too was discharged by monolithic Doubleday before ever reading a page of my book.

Pound himself, of course, was the most adept and brilliant editor of his time. Modernism's sharpened focus begins with his linguistic prescriptions, his warning against the sentimentality caused by painted adjectives, the kind of excess leading to what he once called "emotional slither." In an essay ("A Retrospect") he proposed a poetic line as durable as bone or granite, and, as he advised in a letter to his friend Iris Barry in July of 1916: "I think there must be more, predominantly more, objects than statements and conclusions, which latter are purely optional, not essential, often superfluous and therefore bad."

As an editor in London, Pound helped T. S. Eliot, Frost, and Joyce get their initial recognition, and he profoundly affected Yeats with an informal tutorial on imagism at Stone Cottage during parts of three winters before World War One. I suspect he was the person most responsible for building Eliot's confidence, making him believe that he could have a voice that would be heard, getting "The Love Song of J. Alfred Prufrock" published in *Poetry*, albeit on its last page because Harriet Monroe felt her subscribers would not be able to understand the poem, and entirely reorganizing "The Wasteland," which Eliot then dedicated to him as *Il miglior fabro*, the greater craftsman. Hemingway may have given Pound boxing lessons in Paris in the early 1920s, but I believe that when Pound read his first stories, he helped hone Hemingway's style according to the imagist precepts Pound had been propagating. The chiseled minimalism that became so well-known as Hemingway's style was more due to Pound than to Gertrude Stein's more Jamesian indirection and circumlocution.

By the time I submitted my Pound manuscript to Marshall De Bruhl, Doubleday's editor in chief, I had no active editor. I felt flattened to insignificance, to say the least, by his imperturbable acknowledgment that he had never even heard of my project. Much to my relief, a month later in the unbelievable and almost unbearable cacophony of the Oyster Bar in Grand Central Station, he announced that he so admired the book he would not change a word. It sounded like a muffled annunciation, divine but one made ambiguous because of the clatter of dishes and the oceanic volume of noisy conversation Though I could barely hear him in the din, his revelation caught me off guard and left me choking on a shrimp.

I realize how rarely this sort of editorial sanction occurs in the production of any book. I do wonder what would have happened had Robert Giroux responded similarly to Kerouac's sprawling scroll in 1951. What is most astonishing to me about the six subsequent years during which Kerouac could not find a new publisher for *On the Road* is his persistence despite all the difficulties any writer encounters, the isolation, the psychic consequences of concentration, and more mundane reports of work-for-hire contracts, the end of midlist publishing, the disappearing market for serious fiction. Most of all, faced with rejection and unsympathetic editors, a writer needs a strong dose of practically indomitable belief in one's creative capacities, the measure of which in Kerouac's case is the six novels he wrote in those six years from 1951 to 1957, despite his anonymity, often desperate circumstances, and considerable depression. It makes me marvel that anything except celebrity confessionals and cookbooks get written and certainly published at all.

I do not offer this memory as a final reflection on the editing process, its perils and promise. I learned much more about what an editor can accomplish and what I would call the donkey burden of that role when my friend, the novelist Ronald Sukenick, persuaded me to help edit *The American Book Review*, a magazine he was starting to allow more prominence for the writer's voice. It would become an opportunity for me, he said, to give back to the literary community. And he was right, as over the years I was able to help then unknown but genuine writers like Luc Sante, who would receive his first publication in *American Book Review*.

One of my key responsibilities for *American Book Review* in its early days was finding the most interesting books to assign. I would assort several large canvas U.S. mail sacks a week right on the street outside the Cooper Square Station in lower Manhattan, where *American Book Review* had its postal box, and then load the sacks into my old Toyota. Then I would drive the poetry books a mile downtown to Rochelle Ratner on Spring Street. Rochelle had a fiat on poetry; she was the scrupulous Robespierre of our small editorial crew who scrutinized excessive praise searching for a "sweetheart" review. Most of the rest of the books were destined for resale at the Strand Bookstore and I would slide the sacks down the basement stairs of that venerable emporium of used books. This was a primary source of support for *American Book Review* along with a few modest grants from arts councils.

Imagine my shock when once, loading the books still in their official postal mail sacks, I was apprehended by two excited postal inspectors who claimed I was stealing the United States mail! Even on the Lower East Side of Manhattan, theft can hardly be considered an editorial prerogative. Editing, like writing, has its hazards.

CHAPTER 4

NOTES OF A PERIPATETIC LECTURER

*I should not talk so much about myself
if there were anybody else whom I knew as well.*
—Henry David Thoreau, Walden

Early in June 1998, I was invited to speak about the legacy of the Beat Generation at a conference sponsored by the Roosevelt Study Center in Middleburg, Holland. Rather than being central as the name of the small city of Middleburg would suggest, Middleburg is located near the southern border with Belgium. Two centuries ago, the European "lowlands" were arbitrarily divided by Spain, and Belgium was created as a means of weakening Holland.

I was born in Antwerp, Belgium, very close to Middleburg and the Dutch border, in 1939 and had been forced to flee with my parents when the Luftwaffe began bombing in 1940. My father, who had been raised in Amsterdam, called me his "little Dutch boy" when I was growing up in Manhattan—which, of course, had been originally settled at the start of the seventeenth century by the Dutch and the French-speaking Belgian Walloons who worked for the Dutch West India Company.

I had been in Middleburg for a few days, impressed by the civility and tranquility of the Dutch. My impression was that Middleburg was a bustling community inhabited by over a hundred thousand citizens on bicycles, few of which seemed chained or locked. Even the police were on bicycles, which made them seem less effectual, less serious in a way, without the flashing lights and sirens that trumpeted their arrival in New York City. When I visited a local tavern one evening—the place, incidentally, officially designated to sell marijuana—I was surprised to overhear agitated Dutchmen still concerned about the single murder that had occurred in their province within the past year.

The following afternoon, with a few hours to spare and a learned presentation or two I could well afford to miss, I took the train to Antwerp. I had been to the city previously, admired the gargoyles and Gothic arabesques perched deliriously on buildings, smelled the salt tang of the port, marveled in the Rubens Museum. I even still had family that lived in Antwerp, but I only had time to visit the great fourteenth-century Cathedral of Our Lady, the largest church in the lowlands with its four-hundred-foot spires and the capacity to contain thousands of worshippers. It was a particularly bright afternoon and the refracted glimmering from the stained-glass windows—there are fifty-five of them in the cathedral—was mysteriously warming through the incense and the foglike dimness of the vast church interior.

The centerpiece on the high altar, a painting by Rubens of the Virgin, enraptured, being lifted to heaven by a choir of angels in a swirl of concentric energy and sheer, spectacular radiance, particularly compelled me.

Travel can be disorienting, but imagine my shock when, exiting the church and crossing a small side street, I saw two bare-breasted women in high heels and G-strings vigorously bending and beckoning to me from a storefront window! I was still in a somewhat transported state, blinking in the sunlight after seeing Ruben's romantic vision of Mary's ascension, but now suddenly plunged into a Breughel painting dominated by a tall, leering, madly gesticulating, masturbatory female with very long, tangled black hair and pallid, spectrally white skin, seemingly inviting me to dance. Her brazen red-headed companion had the reddest, most lascivious lips, which she had manipulated into a provocative oval shape. She was caressing herself, one hand on her breasts while the other seemed to be pumping under the G-string. The redhead seemed heated with tiny drops of moisture above her upper lip.

I just stopped short in the middle of the street, caught in a frozen gape, an endless nightmare moment of bizarre stasis. Were these twisting figures the mythical sirens who had tempted Ulysses and his sailors returning from Troy? Was I to be snared in a dance with the devil from which there could be no escape? Despite the fecund promiscuity of the illicit language he was able to use so freely, I suspect even Henry Miller might have been flabbergasted. I admit I was not exactly the ingenue from Winesburg, Ohio; I had certainly seen some of the old seedy Times Square, but I had never been presented with anything so flagrantly, so salaciously enticing. I know it would be unfair to characterize the redhead fondling her pendulous breasts as diabolical—perhaps the more politically correct allusion is to the sort of animal voluptuousness one senses in Fellini or Pasolini.

I think I was stunned by the violence of the juxtaposition of Ruben's vision of Mary miraculously looking like a robust woman in her prime being elevated at the end of her life by angels, a beautiful though fleshly painting in a sacred place, and the profane suggestion of the gesturing women in the storefront window just outside the church. While I had read Breton and Artaud and studied surrealism, I guess I had never experienced an illustration so brutally visible. After a few more moments, feeling like some embarrassed rube, I managed to stumble off and found the next train back to the safety of my conferees. At the Roosevelt Study Center I knew I could expect nothing more surprising than some slight condescension or intellectual disagreement. University professors and writers, even when gathering to discuss the rambunctious figures of the Beat Generation, tend to be unalluring, decorous, and restrained.

Over the course of a half-century academic career, I've been to many such meetings, mostly occasions for windy discourse where the best one can hope for is a couple of brandies for a jolt of reality. I have been fortunate enough to have received invitations to present my ideas in Europe and Asia, and in various parts of the United States. There are several times that stand out from the rest, though the impact of whatever I had to say depended less on my ideas than the indigenous circumstances.

In 1975, for example, I decided to spend my sabbatical year in Southeast Asia. Sabbaticals are supposed to be devoted to pursuing research, but I was tired of airless libraries and the scrupulous diligence of footnotes. I had spent the previous five years researching and then writing the first history of the Beat Generation, and my book *Naked Angels* was in production in New York.

My wife, Mellon, had received a travel fellowship from *National Geographic*, and, perhaps because I had been a National Endowment for the Humanities Fellow, I was offered the opportunity to speak at Asian universities in a tour organized by the United States Information Agency (USIA). I could speak about American literature and culture; about Ralph Waldo Emerson, Henry James, Pound, and Eliot; or about more contemporary figures, depending on what the host institution determined would be of interest.

I lectured in Jakarta, in Jogjakarta where it seemed as if every man rode a bicycle in his sarong, elsewhere in Indonesia, and in Bangkok to small but respectful audiences. I often had the queasy feeling—familiar to me from my own students in New York—that no one really comprehended or had enough command of English to respond to my remarks, that these talks I was offering were only a form of diplomatic politesse, a subtle form of American cultural propaganda.

In general, at airports and railroad stations, I was received as an official representative by American embassy officials or local government attachés who often wanted to control every move I made when I was not in the lecture hall. Once, in India, the rector of Benares Hindu University complained on greeting me that I "was scantily clad"—it was so hot I appeared in sandals and just could not wear a jacket or a tie. In Lucknow, my two escorts—I wondered whether they were police agents—were furious when I slipped off to the heart of the market, a congested mile from my fancy hotel, to purchase a sari for my wife. This was 1975 when kidnapping Americans was not as fashionable or lucrative as it has become, but I now think my angered handlers knew much more than I did.

In Bangkok, the unbound galleys of *Naked Angels* were delivered to me via diplomatic pouch. After I corrected them, Mellon and I took an elegant but ancient train, wood paneled in its interior like the Orient Express, overnight to Chiang-mai where I was scheduled to talk about American transcendentalism. At dawn, from the slowly chugging train, only a few inches above flooded rice paddies, we saw the farmers rowing to their fields. At the station in Chiang-mai, we were greeted by a young Thai displaying a large placard, my name displayed on it in big letters as if I were running for political office, and he drove us silently to a small teak inn located on the Mekong River. The river overflowed our first night there and the dirty water was waist high for blocks around, but the staff at the Chiang-mai Guesthouse acted as if this were normal and promised the water would soon subside.

In Chiang-mai, Mellon was often away, photographing the opium substitution program for the United Nations Development Fund, taking helicopters with Lieselotte Waldheim-Natural (the daughter of the then UN secretary-general) to the Burmese border, so she did not attend my lecture. I spoke about Emerson's radical assertion that "society everywhere is in conspiracy against the manhood of every one of its members" and his acolyte Thoreau's even more provocative arguments in "On the Duty of Civil Disobedience," blaming Northern merchants as much for the slavery system as plantation owners. I suggested that all progressive American thought emanated from the circle of followers around Emerson in the 1840s. I must have seemed strident to my Thai audience that afternoon, trying to illustrate how a small band of abolitionists and suffragettes could counter the inertia of a nation with the persuasive power of their ideas, but no matter what I said or how vehemently I expressed it, I felt suffused by a benign atmosphere of placidity.

I spoke for nearly an hour, and then I think a minor miracle occurred. The university was only twelve years old in 1975, and its motto seemed quaintly Emersonian: "Where nature nurtures beautiful intelligence!" It was an especially warm afternoon, and the windows in the room I was lecturing in were wide open. At the exact conclusion of my talk a tiny, intensely glowing yellow finch or canary flew into the room, did a stately 360-degree circuit, paused on the windowsill as if to survey those in the room, and then darted away. I cannot claim to be an ornithologist, but it seemed to me at least (though I wonder whether anyone else either noticed it or even found it unusual) like an annunciation of sorts or an omen.

One consequence of my remarks—perhaps it was due to the yellow transit of the bird—was that the dean of the humanities came up to me after the lecture and offered me a position with a stipend of one hundred dollars a month. It does sound like very little—it was the sum I received for each of my talks—but it would have gone quite far in Chiang-mai then: a modest dwelling, possibly even a servant, and the most delicious foods I had ever eaten. I thought of the great critic William Empson in Japan and I was more flattered than tempted.

I also had the obligation to USIA to complete the lectures they had arranged, particularly a tour of universities in Northern India, which I began in November. After a series of lectures at six different universities, the high point of the tour had been set for the University of New Delhi, then considered the finest academy in the north. India was a fascinating country, with cows wandering its sometimes very dusty thoroughfares, even an occasional elephant, and files of elderly women bearing loads of firewood. But New Delhi represented progress and change and I was excited to be there.

My subject was Anglo-American modernism, and I chose to focus my talk on Ezra Pound's incendiary attacks on a corseted Victorianism, on what Pound called Tennyson's "petty embroideries" and the general linguistic inflation and abstraction of Victorian poetry. For Pound, the Victorians were only perpetuating a romanticism that could no longer speak honestly to the breakdown of culture he observed in the years prior to the First World War. Instead of the preaching in poems of some of the Victorians—for instance, Tennyson's "Locksley Hall"—he admonished his followers that "poetry can never be the packmule of philosophy" and "beauty can never be explained." Beauty, he proposed, was as fugitive as "a mere gasp between clichés," and instead of the long expansive poems of the nineteenth century, he offered very compact, brief poems influenced by Catullus and haiku. He rejected what he saw as the conventional ornateness of the Victorian period and the architectural clutter of its literature; instead, Pound concentrated on the dynamic image, placed a radical focus on the visible and the tactile that disregarded the old metrical regularities and rhymes, and was seen as revolutionary by a group of American and British poets eager to reshape the medium.

I spoke in a large hall that lacked ventilation and smelled slightly of mustard. I thought I heard some murmuring as I spoke. Some of my auditors seemed to be squirming uncomfortably in their seats. I did not understand that the intellectuals of India loved the language that had served to unite their vast country, and consequently the literature of their former Victorian masters. These British writers were so revered that no one could safely criticize them. It did not matter to my audience that these ideas were expressed by Pound in London from 1911 to 1913 and that they were potent enough to change the ways in which English would be written in the twentieth century by followers such as T. S. Eliot and Ernest Hemingway. Somehow, I was informed, I had insulted my hosts, and the second part of my tour, to Hyderabad and points south, was summarily canceled. Perhaps I should have safely reconsidered Emerson or the later fiction of Henry James? Suddenly, I had become the persona non grata of the universities of India.

Naturally, I felt rebuffed and rejected. Mellon was waiting for me in Kathmandu where no one wanted to hear a lecture unless it was on improved techniques for growing beans or potatoes. We took a public bus three hundred miles to Pokhara, a bus that hastened around the sheer, harebrained, terrifying curves and precipices of the Himalayas. The road had been completed only five years earlier, and formerly one had to walk there from Kathmandu. From Pokhara we walked for weeks on an ancient dirt trail—up five thousand feet every morning and then down four thousand feet in the afternoon—to approach the base of Annapurna, the second-highest mountain in the world. Every step seemed to take us further and further away from civilization. There were no machines or mechanical devices anywhere, no electricity or indoor plumbing and very little protein. What would I have given for an egg or a can of sardines? All I could purchase was a bracelet made of five metals from a Tibetan guide who sold it to me for five rupees—a dollar! I still wear it on my wrist as a reminder of how high I could ascend.

Every evening after trudging all day on the dusty trail, buoyed by the most dazzling views of the unspoiled Himalayas at every step, we would inevitably arrive at a straggling collection of mud-baked huts and small wooden houses, one of which was for travelers. In the *losmen*, for a quarter, we could lay our sleeping bags down in a common room and share a meal of rice and lentils. In the morning, after a greasy *charpati* and tea, we would continue on our way. We bathed in the coldest streams and defecated at the side of the path, but felt more cleansed and exhilarated than ever before.

We had been walking back into the Middle Ages with every step and never reached Annapurna because I succumbed to a very bad case of dysentery. I think I learned more on that trek to Annapurna about beauty and eternal verities than in any of the universities I had so blithely passed through. I have not returned, however, afraid that by now there are vendors with carts selling Nathan's hot dogs and Coca-Cola along the trail.

I don't wish to mislead you, though. I had not transcended. I resumed my New York life of university teaching and writing. I had been affected by my year away—one mundane sign, perhaps, was that I found it impossible to enter a supermarket for a year. I would lecture when invited at places like the National Arts Club on Gramercy Park, the Americas Society on Park Avenue, or the Tang Museum at Skidmore College in Saratoga Springs, but the golden fire of the fugitive canary never reappeared.

In the United States, my lectures often came with strange discolorations, the weirdness of poetry in a world of affluence. In Victoria, Texas, a town near Houston with the stately old residences of oil barons only a few miles from tarpaper shacks, I was asked to speak about the editing process. The talk was posted on YouTube, but that evening I was also expected to read from one of my books at a cocktail fundraiser for the magazine that had invited me. I was being asked to sing for my supper in a sumptuous oil tycoon's mansion that made Gatsby's garish ostentation seem in good taste. The walls were festooned with huge, realistic paintings of hunting scenes and the grim stuffed heads of bison, bears, and tigers. Someone wearing too many diamonds and looking as regal as Lauren Bacall was descending a grand, circular, black marble staircase with a gold rail. All I could think of as I read my passage about growing up in Manhattan was Daisy Buchanan crying in Gatsby's silk shirts. The distraction made me falter slightly in my delivery, but maybe the bourbon was partly to blame.

There is something different about the wealthy, as Scott Fitzgerald informed us so eloquently, and we live in a country with enormous abundance. I can offer one final illustration. A few years ago I was asked by a foundation to come to Melrose, Florida, to talk about the evolving reputation of the Beat writers. The foundation acquired several large-scale photographs and asked Mellon to present a slide show and talk about her mentor and friend, the photographer Robert Frank. A sleepy, sprawling town of mostly modest cottages, Melrose is northeast of Gainesville and about an hour east of the Gulf. I balked at accepting at first because I was told we would fly into Jacksonville and then be driven three hours or so across the state, west to Melrose.

We were greeted at the airport by a white stretch limousine that could have accommodated a rock group with all their instruments, sound equipment, and a few leggy groupies. The chauffeur opened the glass partition explaining that the intercom did not work properly. When he heard we were from Greenwich Village, he assumed we were faded rock stars or famous for something. No matter how we tried to dissuade him, he kept turning his head around intermittently through the long drive to question us. We were seated thirty feet behind him, on a huge circular seat next to a bar. I felt like Elvis without the boots, but the driver's lack of attention to the road before us was quite disconcerting.

When we arrived in Melrose, our driver deposited us at Chiappini's, a gas station–cum–grocery store where a delegation of thirty or forty very casually dressed Floridians, in shorts and sandals, paraded around with bottles of beer and a surfeit of cheer. They might have been expecting Elvis, but they seemed like a gaggle of yodelers, rejuvenated hippies at a college reunion. This was their regular evening gathering place, but the enthusiasm of their reception was genuine, and it was another sort of cocktail party in the humid heat of gas fumes.

An hour or so later we were driven to a seafood restaurant by David Turner Warner—a Hemingway type with huge literary ambitions and the same capacity for alcohol—whose foundation had invited us. Our hosts were generous and hospitable, but after dinner we were accommodated in a cobwebbed room with decrepit furniture in a rambling old house where we were the sole occupants. We were told the house was being renovated, but it seemed as if Tennessee Williams or Stephen King had designed it. The next evening our talks were preceded by an hour or more of fortifying lubricants, beer and wine, Jack Daniel's and one-hundred-proof vodka—"the better to assimilate the ideas of the visiting lecturers" as the grinning wolf told Goldilocks. But I will spare you the details.

CHAPTER 5

SENATOR TRIPLETALK AND THE AMERICAN DREAM

*A politician is an arse
upon which everyone
has sat except a man.*
—E. E. Cummings

1. The Way We Are

As an infant, I was never kissed by a presidential contender, much less a congressman or councilman, although once as an undergraduate I had the good fortune to be seated next to Eleanor Roosevelt. I met my presidential aspirant when I was an adult because of a profile in the *New York Times*. I had written a hybrid memoir about a twenty-year friendship with a few members of the Beat Generation, which HarperCollins was publishing in the fall of 1999. It was my last book in the twentieth century and was particularly special for me because its core was a series of photographs my wife, Mellon, had taken of writers like Allen Ginsberg and William Burroughs years earlier.

Dee Dee DeBartlo, the publicist at HarperCollins, a bright, energetic young woman, fell in love with Mellon as almost everyone does and had arranged that the *Times* do this profile. They wanted their reporter to write the piece in the middle of August and insisted that the interview occur in our apartment in the city. We were spending our summer in Vermont, my old Honda was ailing, and I was reluctant to drive back anyway, but when Dee Dee offered a roundtrip limousine and driver, we knew we had to do it.

Usually, the subjects of *New York Times* profiles are politicians or major power players, not authors. Joyce Wadler, the *Times* reporter, kept her piece light and lively, and it was the most effective publicity I had ever received.

The article was read when it appeared by Lorraine Miller, a New York State Supreme Court judge. She was adjudicating the inheritance that Peter Orlovsky had received from his life companion, the Beat poet Allen Ginsberg, one of the best-known poets in America who had died in 1997, leaving his academic pension benefits and other funds to

Orlovsky. Orlovsky, also a poet and with a reputation for wildness, had used drugs and alcohol promiscuously. He was living in a recovery facility on Broadway and 101st Street, a block from where I had spent my childhood. Judge Miller was afraid he might be exploited. She wanted to know whether I would consent to being appointed his guardian, a prospect that did not appeal to me because I knew how much trouble Peter had caused for Allen.

When I refused to act as guardian, Judge Miller—a feisty woman who radiated authority—asked whether I would visit Peter to report on his well-being. Peter was especially fond of Mellon, so we went together and met him in a grim little waiting room where we had been seated for twenty minutes. Peter had a taciturn side as well as an explosive surrealist capacity to act out, and I remembered him as the vibrant dynamo running the tractor on Ginsberg's Cherry Valley farm with cowboy bravado, but now he was quite sobered, depleted.

We took him for a short walk to the Soldiers and Sailors Monument in Riverside Park so Peter could sneak a smoke; there he told us he wanted to move to a Tibetan ashram in Vermont where he would spend the rest of his life. I never saw Peter again, although Mellon always wanted to drive up to the ashram in Barnet, Vermont, to bring the photographer Robert Frank, who had once made a touching film about him.

Mellon invited Judge Miller to our apartment to discuss Peter's prospects, and we saw her subsequently as friends. When she told me she wanted to write a book about her experiences on the bench, I offered to help and suggested the title *Disrobed*. As far as I know, she never wrote the book, but through her we also became friends with a prominent New York attorney. This attorney invited us in the middle of December 2006 to meet John Edwards.

The former senator from North Carolina had been the Democratic Party's vice-presidential nominee in 2004 after receiving almost 20 percent of the primary votes, and he wanted to launch another presidential run. The invitation-only event was scheduled to occur in Bunny Mellon's Central Park South penthouse.

My wife, by six degrees of separation, had always been interested in the Mellon family because her father, Maurice Quint, had worked for Andrew Mellon in the Treasury Department. Bunny had been married to Andrew Mellon's son Paul for over a half century. Paul Mellon was a billionaire heir of the Mellon banking fortune, and Bunny had inherited her own pharmaceutical fortune because of a grandfather who invented Listerine. Known as an art collector and a horticulturalist, she had been a close friend of Jacqueline Kennedy's and at her request had redesigned the Rose Garden in the White House when the Kennedy family lived there. The Mellons were the sort who could endow museums like the National Gallery in Washington, D.C., and buy or sell an American presidency if they contributed enough financial support.

I was not inclined to attend the event, but Mellon was very eager to go, so off we went. We were ushered into a ballroom. It was late enough in the afternoon to see the sun setting in the west through the floor-to-ceiling plate-glass windows; the whole expanse of Central Park lay below us in dappled light, a regal estate of 843 acres just for the pleasure of the citizens of New York. A squadron of servers brought wine and succulent hors d'oeuvres, baked oysters and shrimp, various melting concoctions and cheeses, enough to feed a lowland community in New Orleans, devastated by Katrina, for a month. The event was a fundraiser, and almost everyone I met was a well-connected New York attorney. Edwards was running late and the wine and delicacies continued to circulate.

I admit to being slightly looped when Edwards began his pitch. Edwards had standard liberal credentials—for universal health care, abortion rights, a citizenship process for illegals—and considerable populist appeal. Bunny Mellon and others believed he had a Kennedy charisma with his own New Frontier to explore. As a family man who had four children with his wife, Elizabeth, an attorney, he stood for family values. He seemed even more sympathetic because his son, Adam, had died in an automobile crash in 1996 after winning an essay contest sponsored by the National Endowment for the Humanities. Another clue for me was a photograph I had seen of Edwards and Peter Coyote in Manchester, New Hampshire. An actor whom I admire and one of the original West Coast Diggers of the late 1960s, Coyote looks uneasy and guarded. Singer Jackson Browne is between him and Edwards, and Browne has his arm embracing Edwards's shoulders affectionately. Coyote, far to Browne's side, doesn't look sure he is in the right place. Edwards has the flamboyant, beguiling smile—the heartland look—that always wins elections in America. It does make one wonder whether, in the end, dentists and cosmeticians have as much to say about who rules America as Nancy Reagan's astrologer.

In his four-hundred-dollar haircut, Edwards looked fabulous, glowing vitally with an inner fire that seemed to pour out of his eyes and suffuse his presence like a golden aura. Was it rock conviction, an infusion of inner light, a Viagra flush, or the red-hot Mercedes convertible Janet Joplin promised could make us all happy? He seemed so sincere, so soulfully concerned about the poverty of others. His voice, with its downhome southern inflection, was soothing, friendly, sweet as maple syrup on a summer sundae. Was I the only person in the room who noticed the disquieting way his words seemed to slide sideways out of his mouth? When I looked around the room, everyone else was standing intently in two-thousand-dollar suits, many of them pinstriped, three-piece uniforms of corporate wear. Was he like Jimmy Carter asking *them* to join his construction crew, to volunteer to build new housing for the poor?

Maybe I'm suspicious, but the words, though mellifluously persuasive, sounded sanctimoniously like the oily piety of the well born and privileged. Edward's talk did not seem to be a case of the doublespeak that Orwell decries in his famous essay, "Politics and the English Language," where he warns of "unscrupulous politicians, advertisers, religionists" who deliberately abuse language to confound or mislead us. He genuinely seemed to want to help the impoverished in America, and at the very least he was calling attention to the problem. I knew Edwards had working-class origins though he had made a fortune as an attorney, mostly representing families in medical malpractice insurance claims, enough money to have personally contributed over three million dollars to his own senatorial campaign in 1998.

What no one in that spacious room knew was that Edwards was in the process of building a thirty-five-thousand-square-foot home for himself and a fifteen-thousand-square-foot home for one of his daughters. It does sound unfair to suggest—a man has to live somewhere—but his home could probably have accommodated that entire swamped lowlands neighborhood of New Orleans I mentioned earlier.

Two facts are relevant here: Edwards was running on a family-values decency platform and his wife, Elizabeth, was later diagnosed with breast cancer. I should also mention that no one in that room with so spectacular a view knew that a few months earlier John Edwards had succumbed to a woman who flattered him in a New York hotel with the apparently irresistible cliché "you are so hot!"

Rielle Hunter may have stalked and snared him—her name has an allegorical quality that makes this seem possible. As a party-loving teen from Fort Lauderdale, she arrived in New York as Lisa Jo Druck—the name, with its connotations of drunken intercourse, is as suggestive as the more notorious one she kept after her first marriage. In her early twenties, she met the quintessentially New York novelist Jay McInerney. Her affair with him inspired his 1988 novel *The Story of My Life*, told in the voice of a cocaine-addled plaything. After moving to Los Angeles, she married an attorney, Alexander M. Hunter III. In Los Angeles, she tried to write movie scripts—apparently the most enticing opportunity available—and had a video production company.

Almost a year after the fundraiser where I watched John Edwards warmly hug my wife, where I heard his penthouse supplication for contributions to the church of his ascension, a scurrilous tabloid called the *National Enquirer* published an article alleging an affair and Rielle's pregnancy, which Edwards denied with enough sangfroid to air-condition all of New Orleans in perpetuity. There were rumors of a scandalous sex tape like Paris Hilton's, and a lying cover-up provided by Andrew Young, one of Edwards's assistants, who claimed he was the daddy. It seemed as if the writers of *Entertainment Tonight* were scripting American politics.

This reflection began with Allen Ginsberg who, in one of his last poems, "The Ballad of the Skeletons," exclaimed, as part of the bitter parody of his disappointment with our system, "my family values mace!" Edwards, the family-values Democrat, seemed quaint and now quite irrelevant in an age when even children can access the pornography industry, second only in influence in America to guns and war. Manufacturing anything else, from shoes to cars, seems to occur with more efficiency and at less cost in Asia. As meaningful work, even work like Jack Kerouac's mother had in a shoe factory, becomes harder and harder to find, family values themselves seem more like political slogans than matters of ethical concern.

As his own former campaign chairman David Bonior claimed, "John Edwards betrayed us all."

Rielle Hunter had been the videographer for Edwards's presidential campaign, and the suspicion was that she had been supported during her pregnancy by funds siphoned from that campaign. In 2011, after Elizabeth had died from cancer, Edwards was charged with using over a million dollars of the money he had raised for his political purposes to provide for Rielle's care and comfort. The FBI questioned Bunny Mellon at Oak Spring Farm, her four-thousand-acre estate—four times the size of Central Park—in Upperville, Virginia. Three-quarters of a million dollars of her money were alleged to have been fraudulently used to support Rielle. No one knows how the heiress, a centenarian, answered the investigators. Did she politely or curtly inform them that the way she spent her money was only her concern, or did she lament the millions she lost in two Ponzi schemes?

The court process ended in a mistrial—is that the way we exonerate politicians?—and Rielle would write the seamy tell-all *What Really Happened*. We'll probably see the Hollywood soaped-up version soon, a love story with some whining recrimination but without violence. Although McInerney had told an earlier part of her story, it was probably at least as strangely paradigmatic as Edwards's. This *is* the way we are now. It would take a novelist with the pessimism of Herman Melville when he completed *The Confidence Man* at the end of a spoiled career, or one with the barbed wit of Mark Twain, a specialist in American tall tales and cons, or one as stubbornly perspicacious as Theodore Dreiser to show how fully it reflects the American experience in an age of entropy and decline. Dreiser could propose a fitting title—*Another American Tragedy*.

II. A Monumental Howl

> Q. What is the chief end of man?
> A. To get rich.
> Q. In what way?
> A. Dishonestly, if we can, honestly if we must.
> Q. Who is God, the only one and true?
> A. Money is God. Gold and greenbacks and stocks—father, son, and the ghost of the same—three persons: these are the true and only God.
> —Mark Twain, "Revised Catechism"

I live in Greenwich Village, about a mile north of the former World Trade Center, a neighborhood that was locked down after the catastrophe in 2001 with air that still smelled like plastic a month after the disaster, even though Christine Whitman, the former governor of New Jersey and George Bush's environmental protection commissioner, counseled that the air was fit to breathe. The World Trade Center was the symbol of the financial heart of the American Imperium just as Washington, D.C., is its political center.

Many Americans deny the consequences of what I have termed an imperium, although I live in the Empire State and know better. The United States has small armies permanently stationed in places such as Okinawa, Japan, and Wiesbaden, Germany, and the forty-seventh parallel in Korea a half century after the end of World War II—and a network of military bases all over the globe—so our nation has either considerable fear or interests to protect. This military system girdles the globe. Though we have no emperor calling the shots, it signifies the enforcement of authority and costs a fortune to maintain.

The military complex also denies the ideals of the Founding Fathers from George Washington to Thomas Jefferson who warned of the dangers of foreign military entanglements. They had studied history and understood that as any empire—whether the Greek, Roman, or more recently the Napoleonic—expands through conquest, it loses strength at the center. When systems in nature expand too rapidly, they often reach a point where they begin to contract, when entropy leads to collapse. At first the empire, or its managerial elite, benefits economically from military procurement and conquest; ultimately, greed leads to financial peril, miscalculation, wheelbarrow inflation, and bankruptcy.

Such notions are considered unpatriotic, I should point out, and are rarely observed except by bitter outsiders such as the late Gore Vidal or poets including Lawrence Ferlinghetti, who once observed that our political symbol is the eagle, a large and fierce hunter-bird, which in our case flies with two right wings.

On Monday, September 17, 2012, my wife had an appointment with the National Gallery. The day before, I drove our weather-beaten Subaru, which has already taken us over a hundred thousand miles, to Washington, D.C. We made an incorrect judgment on the Beltway and ooops!—we were right across from the Pentagon, confused about our route. Suddenly, a white SUV swooped around us and motioned us over. The driver, a tall, ruddy redhead, saw that we were lost, decided that with our dog madly barking we did not resemble terrorists, and politely redirected us to downtown Washington.

The first story I noticed on the front page of the *Washington Post* on Monday morning was on the resumption of wolf hunting in five states. The headline above the wolf story read "Afghan Insider Attack Kills 4," referring to the recent wave of assassinations of American soldiers by supposedly allied Afghan military and police. The second paragraph of the article bears particular notice: "The insider attack came on the same day that NATO warplanes killed nine women gathering firewood in the mountains outside their village in an eastern province, according to local officials, adding to long-festering outrage over civilian casualties." The planes that dropped their bombs on the women from Laghman, a province east of Kabul, are identified as NATO rather than American, a more likely probability. I can report having seen lines of such women, many of them old and white haired, bent under bundles of kindling or containers of water, during the time I spent in Southeast Asia. These were the same women George Orwell observed when he was a policeman in Burma and whom he felt were invisible to the British. Although I could sympathize with their burdens, the visible emblems of a third world existence, I never expected to see them bombed. In the era of locked cockpits after 9/11, we now have the more sinister terror of drone warfare, where a man or a woman pushing a button in the American heartland of Ohio or Texas can determine the annihilation of innocents anywhere gathering wood or water in the mountains.

If anything, downtown Washington, D.C., is a place of Napoleonic pomp and grand majesty. Some of its buildings, such as the two framing the Naval Memorial near Pennsylvania Avenue, could have been plucked from Paris, the broad sweep of Pennsylvania Avenue inspiring wonder. But there were, as well, pockets of homeless and the mentally disturbed—an elderly white lady screaming on a corner of how she had been sexually harassed by African Americans, a sharp contrast to hundreds of government workers heading for work with the sober determination of bees returning to the hive. People seemed busy, even the traffic cop I saw littering a candy wrapper while operating an upright electric Segway.

After breakfast, I accompanied my wife, Mellon, to the National Gallery, where she was showing a curator photographs she had taken over the years of Robert Frank. I headed with our dog Frank out to the National Mall. Frank, a rescued Canaan, is named after the photographer Robert Frank. Mellon, our dog, and I had all been to Washington last when Robert Frank's work was exhibited at the National Gallery in 2008, a few days before President Obama's inauguration.

We had paraded up and down on the National Mall then, frigid in the wind and over frozen ground, but warmed somehow by the pride any citizen must feel in the nation's capital. Now it was summer's end, a perfect seventy-five degrees, but the mall from Third Street to Seventh was all torn up and clogged with machines working to improve drainage and contain rainwater for irrigation. Walking north to the Washington Monument, I was able to escape the noise of the work—pump priming or ecological?—which, apparently, has been continuing during the Obama presidency.

The grass on the nation's mall was green and cut—the grass that Walt Whitman, our national poet of democracy, had accepted as a central metaphor for the creative regeneration of nature. When, during the Civil War, Whitman had worked as a clerk for the Department of the Interior, he had been discharged when an official in his department had opened his desk to find a copy of "Song of Myself," Whitman's epic announcement of the American Dream. Long before the computer age, Whitman could cross Pennsylvania Avenue and find clerical employment in the Department of Indian Affairs. This was the period when he spent years visiting the wounded in hospitals after his day of work.

The Civil War was the great turning point in our national history, and one key measurement of the change was the growing influence of corporate structures during the postwar period. When the victorious Union general Ulysses S. Grant was elected president, he was known for leaving the White House at lunch to repair to the lobby of the Hay-Adams hotel just across the street. Grant was happiest on horseback—he had been a cavalry officer—and hated the confines of the White House. He was also alcoholic and could satisfy his tastes in the lobby of the hotel, which had a bar. Often, he would spend entire afternoons there, and the corporate emissaries who needed his support began to see him at a cocktail table in the hotel lobby.

Though it has even earlier antecedents, this is one of the popular origins of the term "lobbyist," and it has particularly vernacular flavor. Today, the lobbyist is often a former congress member or senator who had been denied reelection; that person still knows many members of the House or Senate, and so has considerable access and becomes a useful resource for corporate influence in the decision-making process. If de Tocqueville were to revisit the United States now, 150 years after writing *Democracy in America*, he might decide that we are less of a democracy and more of an oligarchy with lobbyists as oil for the system. With an Orwellian touch of "newspeak," they are called "government affairs consultants."

Frank and I walked toward the soaring Egyptian obelisk of the Washington Monument surrounded by fifty flags fluttering in a circle, its primal purity like an elongated finger into the sky. I sat on a bench to note the sheer thrust and power of the white marble tower, like the frozen image of a rocket going to outer space. Frank began to howl, a monumental, mournful, resonant wail, something he might express when left alone, but hardly appropriate so close to the White House.

Frank is the descendant of a biblical breed, a canine creature whose forebears evolved when they retreated back to the desert when the Jews were forced out of Israel by the Romans two thousand years ago. Lately, American fundamentalist sects, on pilgrimages to the holy land, have been getting Canaan dogs, then bringing them back and breeding them in the South. Looking at Frank's paws for signs of a possible abrasion, I saw the dandelion mixed in with the grass and thought Whitman would have approved. Now, Americans tend to pour weed killers on their bluegrass lawns, unconcerned by the fact that the poison inevitably seeps below, affecting the water we drink with our morning coffee.

Whitman had little stake in the American Imperium though. As a journalist in the 1830s and 1840s before becoming a poet, he had visited the holds of the slave ships in New York harbor and knew that slaves had been recruited to construct many of the federal buildings in Washington. He had written about our eighteenth president, Franklin Pierce, who "ate dirt and excrement for his daily meals, liked it, and tried to force it on these states." Whitman was referring to Pierce's notorious compromising with Southern slave owners, but his words showed that the great reconciler who thought the grass was a "uniform hieroglyphic" or the "beautiful uncut hair of graves" could be intemperate if aroused.

III. The Empire City

> *To walk in money through the night crowd, protected by money, lulled by money, dulled by money, the crowd itself a money, the breath money, no least single object anywhere that is not money, money, money everywhere and still not enough, and then no money or a little money or less money or more money, but money, always money, and if you have money or you don't have money it is the money that counts and money makes money, but what makes money make money?*
> —Henry Miller, Tropic of Capricorn

I want to tell you about my West Village neighbors. First, there is the homeless man I call Captain Willy who has lived on my corner for twenty-five years. He used to have an apartment on my street, but ran into hard times, was evicted, so he began sleeping in an alcove across the street from his former residence. Arrested and incarcerated for vagrancy, he always returned to what was familiar. Finally the police stopped arresting him because he provided "eyes on the street" for them and tried to prevent incidental street crime when he could.

Willy has a history even Charles Dickens could not invent. Son of an Air Force man who died when Willy was twelve, Willy left his home at age thirteen in Riverhead, Long Island, in 1967 because his mother had never stopped beating him. In North Carolina, he picked cotton in the fields with an African American family who sheltered him until he joined the Marines. Fourteen, with fabricated papers, he was sent to Vietnam after training to be a field radio operator. In 1969, he was captured in battle by Vietcong. Though he was tortured for information and crucified, he managed to escape in the jungle, and received a Silver Star for his trouble. Had he been captured by the Chinese, he confided, he would have been immediately executed since they took no prisoners in Vietnam. Now, "they own us," he added bitterly, referring to the billions of dollars of our national debt the Chinese have been financing through the purchase of Treasury Bills.

The war left him a designated hero with an alcohol problem, and he spent the next decade driving a taxi in Miami until his drinking began to interfere with his driving and his pugnacious nature got in his way. In danger of losing his hack license, he was tempted by one thousand dollar fares—meet a boat at dawn and receive a package—and then was induced to drive for a few mob hit men. There was an FBI shootout, the windshield and all the glass in the car shattered, and the two men in pinstripes for whom he was driving were DOA in the bloody back seat. A cooperative witness, Willy spent a year in jail, mostly in solitary to prevent mob retaliation.

When he was released in 1980, Willy came to Manhattan. The only work he could find was as a bouncer at Badlands, a notorious gay bar on the corner of Christopher and West Street, facing the highway and across from the river. I used to feel a slight chill in my spine walking past it. Badlands attracted an edgy clientele; it was a raw and sleazy dive where men used their fists for sex as well as intimidation. Willy broke up the fights and made enough money to pay the rent for his apartment on my street. He lived in a tenement near Seventh Avenue that had a crack den, the street in front of his building littered with vials every morning. When the AIDS crisis shut down all the dives like Badlands, he was out of work. With a past record and depleted savings, he decided to become the Bartleby on my street corner.

It must have been a hard life, and for years he got by selling discarded furniture to the antique stores that used to line Bleecker Street and less valuable finds in front of the St. Mark's Church on Second Avenue. Now and then, I would give him a twenty. I know others gave him money, food and fine clothing too. He is in a wheelchair now, and although he is only fifty-eight, he looks eighty-five. He has a room across town in subsidized housing on Houston and Avenue C, a battery-powered wheelchair, and receives his VA disability. It is never quite enough, so he returns to his corner occasionally and begs for assistance, mostly to raise money for prescribed medication he says he can't afford. In the past, affirming he was "a loyal and honorable man" he promised to repay me though I knew enough not to count on that prospect. He may be a con man—he always shows me the prescriptions—but I would prefer to help him when I can rather than write checks to institutional charities where some funds may or may not eddy down to the unfortunates of our world.

Willy is a vestige of the old neighborhood. When Mellon and I moved into a rent-controlled railroad flat in the West Village, it was still working class. The docks were still active, though dying, and longshoremen lived there so they could walk to the piers for the early morning shake-up. The woman who lived on the floor below me was the bookkeeper for the St. Luke's Church on Hudson Street, and the one above me was a secretary. The top floor was inhabited by Gerry Donovan, who dragged up the marble stairs, heaving with his club foot in a heavy boot after working until midnight as a doorman at the New York Athletic Club. One of Gerry's five brothers, all of whom were born in that apartment, was a longshoreman though he had moved to New Jersey.

In the two decades that Willy lived on the corner, through summer humidity and winter ice, the neighborhood became gentrified. All the Bleecker Street antique places had to relocate for cheaper rents, the artists fled to Hoboken and Brooklyn, and the secretaries and clerks to Queens and other areas. We may have lost our local hospital, but my building is now inhabited exclusively by Wall Street financial people and professionals—architects, doctors, and lawyers. The brownstone just opposite was a regular location for the television show *Sex and the City* because Sarah Jessica Parker, who played Carrie Bradshaw, supposedly lived there. They kept me up all night for years with bright lights and blaring directorial bullhorns. Now legions of tourists come to pay their respects, gazing as reverently as if they were visiting Jesus's manger in Bethlehem.

Actually, the gawking tourists may be closer than they imagine. The director Andre Gregory, who played John the Baptist in Martin Scorsese's *The Last Temptation of Christ*, lives in my building, as does Willem Dafoe, who was cast as Jesus. One year younger than Willy, he's appeared in over eighty films. A serious actor, with an apprenticeship in off-Broadway theater, he usually plays villains, outlaws, or deeply flawed figures. Lean, wiry, with at times an almost mean look, he has an engaging if devilish smile that can turn into the malicious leer displayed by his character Bobby Peru in *Wild at Heart*, my favorite of his films. Dafoe is perhaps best known for three Spider-Man films in which he played the Green Goblin.

He rarely attends our small coop meetings, and when he does, he has nothing to say. I have seen him carrying groceries and depositing his trash in our common receptacle, but all I get is a furtive, almost guilty smile of faint recognition. He is only here a few months of the year, and I often see him being picked up by a black limo. Captain Willy, on the corner in his wheelchair, is smoking the cigarette stubs he has scavenged from the gutter.

CHAPTER 6

PASSING THROUGH
FIFTY YEARS @ THE MIND FACTORY

He most honors my style who learns under it
to destroy the teacher!
—*Walt Whitman, "Song of Myself"*

1. Those Who Can

For the past fifty years, I've taught writing at Queens College, one of the senior branches of the City University of New York, in the vast system of learning serving over a quarter of a million students. When I announce the length of my service, some people look puzzled, some dazed, others shocked. A generous few will politely aver that I look too young to have been treading water in a bureaucratic maze for half a century. I know that around the country there are other academicians who continue to teach into their seventies and eighties, in spite of infirmities, the subtle, almost inevitable bias of ageism, and the desires of administrators anxious over budgets to replace older faculty with less expensive talent.

I also realize how anomalous my continuing to teach might seem to many of my students. Some of them surely regard me as a hoary fossil who received a "D" in a course called penmanship in the third grade, who admits he wrote his first two books by hand. Probably I sound like the fire-spitting dinosaur of legend who still advises his students that they are expected to know the meaning of the words they are asked to read, that the best readers are the most deliberate, that the perennial underlying purpose of the university has been to master language. Without such effort (whether the "language" in a course informs the world of physics, chemistry, Beowulf, or Dante) the student will be less equipped to navigate the world.

In a culture that emphasizes speed and efficiency, reading can become skimming. Indeed, college teaching, like many other fields, seems threatened as a future career option as the need for trained instructors becomes diminished by technological innovations that tend to replace people with computers, books with animated films, and as classrooms disappear to blink online from Phoenix in perpetuity. In the twenty-first century, any notion of permanent employment, of loyalty to a firm or a system that sustains a work career for the long run does seem like some arcane medieval heresy in a historical moment that almost universally now presents a dire, Darwinian employment prospect.

Professionally, all teachers have suffered from George Bernard Shaw's flip adage that competent people actually do things in a real world, repair plumbing fixtures or body parts, while teachers preach or pontificate in the classroom, ideally removed from the exigencies of sweat and blood. In this jaundiced view, teachers become theoreticians of life rather than practitioners. Actually, Shaw should not be blamed for his oversimplifying observation that "those who can, do; those who can't, teach." The remark, which has the acerbic cut of genuine humor, is made by a character in a play, *Man and Superman*, whose attempt at writing a novel has been dismissed as hopeless by his creative writing teacher. It expresses the character's disappointment rather than forming the foundation of a philosophy or a general truth about a profession.

I had some experience as a child actor, and read Shaw's play as an undergraduate student because I was interested in writing for theater. Coming from a bourgeois background, I understood that writing was a risky professional path, that every writer needed a fallback strategy, a way to pay for pizza while the rejections mounted. Unlike my contemporary students, I attended a university without the burden of tuition and debt, but since I no longer wished to live at home, I had to find a way to support myself. Working as a waiter, I learned to scrutinize every detail on the table from a smudged wineglass to the fine black hair perched on a soup spoon, to move as expediently as a sparrow darting for a crumb, as swiftly and gracefully as possible, to act courteously with a smile, and, most importantly, to remember exactly whatever the diner had ordered. The work was almost athletic—a race from dining room to the scowling chef's station and back—but also good for the mind and its powers of observation.

My point, though, is that despite Shaw's quip, and like most teachers, I have always been a worker, from the time in the third grade when I began going behind bars in musty taverns on upper Broadway at midday on weekends, collecting the caps of beer bottles for recycling, to the time I delivered groceries in my neighborhood when kidnapping young boys was not a metropolitan hazard.

Always the tallest kid in the class, shaving by thirteen, I found my first full-time work at fifteen—a summer job in Long Beach, Long Island. I persuaded an employment agency that was not interested in my age or the child labor laws to send me to a hotel where I was hired as an emergency replacement to operate an elevator manually from 4 p.m. to 2 a.m. On the boardwalk, the Breakers offered studios for the season and its clients would ascend with sandy feet and glistening faces from the beach in the late afternoon, then descend for dinner, tanned, perfumed, and relaxed, and then reascend usually after some perambulation on the boardwalk, a few of them with a tipsy leer and lurching steps.

Still imbued with youthful innocence, even I could ascertain, given the abbreviated transit of a six-flight elevator ride, that a suave, gray-haired gentleman with oiled hair who lived on the top floor, an acting teacher he claimed, was courting a very gracious, demure, fine-featured slightly younger woman who was sharing her room on the fourth floor with her elderly mother. What impressed me particularly was that he reappeared one hot night just before my shift ended, after his midnight cigar stroll for air on the boardwalk, wearing a jauntily angled yellow Fedora. Surprisingly, now he was arm in arm with a much younger female companion in a breathlessly tight blouse and pink shorts whose perfume had mixed with sweat and smelled slightly rank in the close confines of my creaking, wooden Otis elevator. I suppose I was merely a voyeur in training, though each time another scantily clad hooker ascended for her assignation with the dapper lothario, I felt a bit disappointed as well as soiled. I was certainly not entitled to such feelings, and maybe I can now see that on some impossibly romantic level, I was in love myself with the betrayed party from the fourth floor.

The work I found while in graduate school fulfilled me less than what I could discern on the endlessly up and down elevator rides with the aggravating ring of the impatient passengers waiting to be transported. I became the registrar in the emergency room of New York Hospital, a fancy enough title for the admitting clerk working a compressed weekend double shift from 4 p.m. to 8 a.m., a hard Friday and Saturday night's work in the world, which allowed me the leisure of taking classes during the week. Even when faced with occasions of enormous distress,

I was still obligated to obtain medical histories and to arrange for billing or insurance prior to the patient's treatment.

Despite my objections, entering patients, confused by the extent of their own apprehensions, often mistook me for the doctor on call because I had to wear a white hospital jacket. I wanted to become a doctor of words: to prescribe happiness with poems, I wonder? Very early one morning, I admitted Norbert Weiner, the great cyberneticist whose calculations led to the computer. Looking strained and grave, I didn't know whether he would ever emerge from the hospital alive. The registrar's job taught me how grimly absurd life could appear, even to as miniscule a cog as myself in the giant organization of a fifteen-story hospital, and how arbitrarily chance could cause catastrophic consequence.

The most difficult part of my life occurred after my Saturday morning shift ended, trying to stay awake in the student union building at New York University, waiting for an 11 a.m. seminar on American transcendentalism. I felt like the famous caricature of Emerson as a transparent eyeball except that mine desperately wanted to close. Maybe it did not help matters that my instructor, a distinguished scholar but a Methuselah in his eighties, spoke in whispers and raised eyebrows.

II. An Academic Refuge

I was always good at school, able to express myself forcefully and persuasively in class and in my essays. I used whatever money I had saved from my days as a waiter to finance the year's tuition for my M.A. I confess I enjoyed the work of being a graduate student, analyzing the changes in the eight versions of Walt Whitman's 1855 poem "Song of Myself," for example, and I received excellent grades though my intentions were not completely honorable.

The Vietnam draft was beginning in the early 1960s, and that was a war in which I had little inclination to serve. I needed to stay in school to get deferred, but my savings were quickly depleted. I was too proud to ask for assistance from my father, a small-time diamond merchant on Forty-Seventh Street who took the subway to work every morning and who would have advised me that money was what banks provided.

Life can be serendipitous. When I applied for an assistantship, teaching first-year students at New York University the fundamentals of writing, I was turned down, despite my outstanding record, on a particularly hot spring day by a pudgy, sweating professor directing the composition program. I later learned he was a rabid woman chaser and that my chances would have been greatly improved had I been able to display some shapely ankle, dimpled knee, or prominent cleavage. Crushed, I retreated to the Grace Church on Broadway, a silent downtown architectural beauty, fell to my knees, and mourned my dismal prospects.

A week later, a man wearing what looked like dazzlingly white pajamas and a white turban walked up the four flights of my tenement building bearing a telegram. He was not the Sikh prince of one's dreams but a Western Union messenger who had appeared because I did not have a telephone. His news was so astonishing I gave him a five-dollar bill, all the money I had left and a generous tip in that time of relatively deflated currencies. One of the classes I had taken was a Ph.D. seminar on Henry James, taught by Leon Edel, whose five-volume biography on James had won the National Book Award. Professor Edel had so liked my essay on James's short story "A Bundle of Letters" that he had recommended that I be appointed as his graduate reader.

This position came with a stipend as well as free tuition, and meant I would be grading my peers—in the early 1960s enrollments in the humanities were considerably larger than they are today. Soon I was reading for Edel's graduate class in the psychological novel and another one in modern American literature taught by the English Department chairman, an esteemed senior Americanist named Oscar Cargill who had been teaching at NYU since the novelist Thomas Wolfe taught there and called it "the School of Utility Cultures."

Soberly serious and gruffly ministerial, Cargill sent me on what was then called the "Old Boys' Network" to Queens College. With a commanding voice, Cargill declared to someone on the receiving end of his telephone that he was sending this boy—me?—over "but he was only passing through." The proper translation of this coded message was "give this graduate student a temporary part-time position if you value our relationship." Hopeful naïveté, I suppose, prevented me from understanding how a position teaching remedial English would contribute to the developing exploitation of American higher education as institutions began to raise tuitions while staffing classes with inexperienced adjuncts who were learning how teach. That was 1963; today, according to the U.S. Department of Education, 1.3 million of the 1.8 million faculty teaching in two- and four-year institutions are part-time adjuncts, and even a floating adjunct could be assigned a graduate class.

A ten-mile train and bus ride from my apartment, Queens College was situated in a place inauspiciously named Flushing that seemed like an Ohio suburb with plenty of trees on wide avenues, manicured lawns, and private houses. With a campus that is large for any metropolitan university, Queens College has its entrance on a street called Kissena Boulevard, which meant "running brook" in the language of the indigenous people who had inhabited the area before the Dutch drove them out. The running brook is no longer part of the landscape.

I was interviewed perfunctorily at registration in a gymnasium by an assistant chairman who knew Cargill and may have wished to curry favor or just stay in contact. While he tried to speak to me, he was answering the anxious queries of a swarm of registering students. I was self-consciously insecure: my hair was too long, and I had begun a goatee. The college at that time still maintained a dress code and guards at the gate would turn away women wearing pants or shorts and men in jeans. The din of the milling students and the blare of the PA system announcements all added to my confusion.

I felt out of place, a singular sock swirling in a noisy washing machine. The borough of Queens was much more conservative than vertical, aspiring Manhattan. Queens was the burial ground of the city, dominated by the endless cemeteries that help determine its character. Then it was primarily inhabited by the families of police, firefighters, postal workers, and civil servants; now it is one of the most ethnically diverse places on planet earth, and this change has been reflected in the student population at the college.

For the next two years, like some flickering gnat in the twilight, I completed my graduate classes at NYU and taught two sections a semester at Queens College. I liked the intermediate-level course in nonfictional prose because I could construct my own syllabus and use models such as George Orwell and Henry Miller. I cannot confess to liking the drudgery of more remedial classes in the fundamentals of composition for which anyone deserves double pay. Economy was the primary lesson I could communicate to my writing students: how to find the fat in the sentence and trim it like a butcher for the health and vitality of the expression, how to avoid abstraction or at least objectify it if possible with some visible image or tactile sensory response. That small step would usually take a semester, though most of my students never mastered it.

III. An Ear to the Ground

American public universities were expanding in the 1960s. I was still merely "passing through," as Cargill had insisted, when the dean of the School of General Studies at Queens College in 1965 offered me a full-time position as a lecturer.

While this more than doubled my income, it aroused some territorial suspicion in the English department. Its chairman, a formidable Renaissance scholar—an expert on Sir Edmund Spenser's manipulation of the chivalric code—was not happy about my appointment since he had not initiated it. "I know nothing about you," he told me, snickering slightly, when he summoned me to his office, "but I'm keeping my ear to the ground!" His ear did not look dirty, but the remark had an ominous edge, an old pre–Civil War frontier expression referring to the troubling sound of mounted Indians on the warpath.

Even though I was writing a dissertation directed by Edel on narrative changes in the fiction of Henry James in the 1890s—a paleface and clearly not a redskin according to the well-known distinction provided by the critic Philip Rahv—I believe I was always seen as a raiding warrior by the older professors who ran the department. In 1968, when I completed my Ph.D., I was promoted to a probationary assistant professor's position, one that might get me tenure after five years of evaluation of my publications and classroom effectiveness.

I knew I had a lot to say and a lot to write, so I adopted the strategy of teaching in the late afternoons and evenings. Since these were the least desirable hours, I could teach electives, offer a poetry course on Yeats, Eliot, and Pound, or spend an entire semester on James Joyce's *Ulysses*. The students were much livelier than the usual undergraduates. In the evening sections, most of them worked in the world. They were the elevator operators and waiters of my earlier training. They tended to be older, independent, eager, and outspoken. I will never forget the construction worker in a creative writing class, a sturdy young man intoxicated by Joyce and haiku, who would arrive every week bearing a case of warm Guinness stout on his shoulder. That class soared.

A change in status was immediately reflected in office arrangements. Originally, I shared a desk in a large room with twenty others located in the airless bowels of the library. When the dean anointed me with a full-time line, I was moved to Whitman Hall, a funky, old three-story structure, originally part of the reformatory that had preceded the college. The building had been used to house delinquent boys only a few decades earlier, but now was dedicated to the English Department.

My third-floor garret was occupied by Helena Brewer, a senior scholar, whose husband had been the president of a small school called Olivet College in northern Michigan. Much later, when I was writing the life of Ezra Pound, I learned that Brewer had offered Pound a post in 1937. Had Pound accepted, he would have avoided the treason trial that made him so controversial and ended with a dozen years of incarceration. Instead, with typical intemperance and imagistic power, he refused Brewer's offer, writing that "all you college presidents should be boiled in oil."

The Brewers were quietly genteel, quite undeserving of any such fate. Helena had a bad back, so she was allowed to have a small couch situated under a dormer in her office for rests between classes. I used the office only when she was not on campus and thought that, like some Sigmund Freud of the academy, the frayed and faded yellow couch signaled that I had distinctively arrived.

My couch privileges were very temporary, and I was assigned (or sentenced for the next two decades) to a little box in a new building without windows. Whitman Hall was razed, replaced by a new academic tower, mostly for administration, which still dominates the campus and provides a decent view of Manhattan from its upper floors. In what I saw as a snub to American poetry, the new building was not named after Walt Whitman, who like Ben Franklin was one of our greatest autodidacts. Before the Civil War, Whitman had actually taught at the Jamaica Academy, a primary school located less than five hundred yards away that discharged him after a semester for what was termed "indolence" and because as the son of a Quaker he refused to strike his wards when they were disobedient or did not learn properly. Pound, incidentally, who had declared, "I don't teach, I awake!" was fired summarily from his only teaching job at Wabash College in Crawfordsville, Indiana, in 1905. These writers were inspiring, though they clearly might not provide reliable pedagogic models.

IV. My First Last Lecture

As a young assistant professor in the 1970s and 1980s, I was expected to specialize in Henry James, but found I was becoming more interested in Henry Miller. My anthology, *The American Experience: A Radical Reader*, had been published by Harper and Row and managed to create some national controversy. In the early 1970s students all over the country were protesting against American involvement in Vietnam, and even at Queens College students were blockading buildings. The college organized a series called "The Last Lecture" where theoretically one could offer a final professorial assessment. Deans and department chairs dominated the series. As a token voice of junior faculty, and because my anthology had presented many of the angriest voices of the 1960s, I was asked to offer one. I knew I couldn't hold the interest of agitated students with a talk on the refined sensibilities and the mannerist world of Henry James, so I chose to speak about the Beat Generation, a group of writers who had emerged while I was an undergraduate but had been mostly denigrated ever since. A large group of faculty and students heard me out, and I knew I was reconsidering something vital and new.

I managed to revise a number of my graduate school essays to satisfy professional journals, to mine my dissertation for others, to appear in *Partisan Review*, and I was fortunate enough to place my last lecture talk as an essay in the *American Scholar*. Although I had already published more than some of the senior members of my department, I was told I needed a book if I hoped to remain at Queens College. While this qualification did not seem to be a universal requisite in those days, it did echo the sound of the raiding party's reverberating hooves.

I was writing a book, but not to satisfy any stuffy academic expectations. *Naked Angels* was an early history of the writers of the Beat Generation that grew out of my piece in the *American Scholar*. It would be accepted by McGraw-Hill's trade department, a big commercial publisher that would release it in 1976. Subsequently, it was translated into a number of foreign languages. That had to impress the professorial caste whose expectations usually were never much more ambitious than a modest university press edition that might reach a few colleagues.

When I proposed a course on the Beats to the curriculum committee, which controlled new course offerings, several of my more conservative colleagues, perhaps condescendingly, reminded me of my former interest in Henry James as if it were a religious or at least a sacred professional obligation. I did teach a course on the Beats at the New School, a few blocks from where I lived in the Village, and then to an overflow class of over a hundred students at Rutgers University before I could convince my colleagues that this material might attract more students to the department than John Milton or Henry James.

v. My Heart-Shaped, Red Plastic Ticking Clock

Academic life was changing as the mimeograph machines used for duplication were being replaced by photocopiers. When I began teaching at Queens College, there was talk of disbanding accounting; now, the premium seems to be on vocational skills, and accounting and computer sciences are our most popular majors. In a time when foreign language departments shrink, consolidate, and are phased out of existence, can English be far behind?

I used to write by hand, and the college had created an office that would type manuscripts for faculty. When I moved to Venice, Italy, to complete my biography of Ezra Pound, two women in that office kindly typed what I mailed, chapter by chapter. Perhaps that book exhausted the resources of the office, but it was closed forever in the new computer age, and I knew technology would have to become more instrumental in my life.

I had been educated in the old-fashioned lecture system and when I came to the college, every room was equipped with a wooden lectern used by the instructor to support lecture notes. That model, which had persisted in universities for centuries, was slowly replaced in the 1980s by one that resembled group therapy, whose goal was to get as many students as possible to express opinions. The classroom would now be informed, as the very hierarchical novelist Vladimir Nabokov nastily put it, by active student participation, which meant "letting twenty young blockheads and two cocky neurotics discuss something that neither their teacher nor they know."

I was a student in the 1950s, part of what was termed the "Silent Generation"; I've certainly brayed enough in classes to compensate for that reputation. As a student I was vociferous, even once foolishly standing in a class to denounce Henry James's world as too fastidious, too elegant, too removed from the life of the streets. While class participation might be a way to avoid the burden of preparing a formal lecture, dependence on student response has debatable value. When I complained to various deans and college presidents that the lecterns had suddenly disappeared as if abducted, my protests were simply ignored. Pathetically, all during the 1990s, I carted around a portable metal lectern, a clumsy reminder of a forgotten world.

Ironically, now I can use as a substitute lectern the tall equipment box in the corner of my "smart room" containing a DVD player and other electronic equipment. I'm not too fuddy-duddy to avoid the opportunity presented inside this box, and will often find a way to use film or audio as a dramatic vehicle for fifteen minutes or so. My YouTube posts seem to impress my students more than anything I have still in print.

My rough estimate is that I've evaluated some five million words of student writing, much of it adequate to the task, very little of it compelling. I stopped teaching graduate students because too many of them were schoolteachers primarily interested in boosting their pay. I do encourage questions in class, although mine often seem to vanish like slowly lifting fog in a silent void until, rhetorically, I answer myself. Students who have been forced to digest Derrida and arcane theoreticians seem to have less appetite for Kafka, Beckett, and literature in general, but I can provide no statistical argument to buttress such conjecture.

The contagion of the present moment, perhaps a function of reduced attention spans caused by television and facilitated by the computer, is rampant plagiarism. So many students repeat gross oversimplifications found on the Web, citing them without acknowledgment, unaware that five of their classmates will have used the same inane slogans. I tell them, partly facetiously, that while the Web works for the booming American pornography industry, it is not as valuable as a good book, and one of the virtues of university training is learning how to discover the books that speak with authority.

At the same time I understand my students as an informally extended family. Some of them have met in my classes, subsequently married, and invited me to the wedding. I have been to a bris, baptisms, anniversaries, and recently to a seventieth-year birthday celebration where I was seated next to a hedge fund billionaire. Occasionally, I hear excited shouts of "Professor!" and I encounter former students in the streets of Manhattan: once, a uniformed police sergeant named William Malone in my local Rite-Aid confessed to me he had never been able to understand the Kafka story on which his paper had been based, and it still bewildered him. Am I wrong, or did he seem to regret the class was over?

In the last few decades of the twentieth century, I helped administer my local chapter of Phi Beta Kappa and my department's honors program and writing contest; now I get soda for the Special Occasions Committee, though I have brought in more than a few bottles of champagne for retiring colleagues I admire. Many of my colleagues left in relative youth, hoping to finish the novel begun twenty years earlier; some fled as soon as they were eligible for pensions.

Evidently, I've endured. Recently the educational bureaucracy of the City University offered to honor my service with a little gold pin, a tiny token routinely awarded for those who have taught for thirty five years—which I had already received fifteen years ago. This minute fact had been obscured somehow in their computer systems, but what it meant to me was that the past fifteen years did not signify.

As my department's oldest and longest-serving member, I'm asked whether I am contemplating retirement myself. Like some somber Soviet commissar, I quip that "I'm on the five-year plan," that twice a decade I ask myself the same question. I would earn more with my pension than I can by continuing; in effect, I've been working for free. However, I know that I will not stop before physical infirmity or mental disequilibrium. My spiritual purpose remains to remind my usually somnambulistic students (who may inhabit more of a virtual existence than I realize) that there are miracles to wake them. My heart knows that my joy still depends on perceiving the world as it changes and using the word to articulate that change, and that the stimulation provided me by the university pleases both my mind and soul.

I have no grand expectation: near the end, I will probably be rewarded with another pin, an embossed certificate, or maybe the Wizard of Oz from behind a dark curtain will surreptitiously slip me a heart-shaped, red plastic ticking clock as a measurement of my fortitude. At my retirement party, after too much champagne, I probably will imagine the Wizard as my old chairperson behind his desk cluttered with the piles of paper that signify bureaucratic activity, that esteemed Renaissance scholar of yore, asking with a voice that sounds as mechanical as a shrug: "What, are you still loitering here, still passing through?"

TWO Reconsidering the beats

CHAPTER 7
TWO NOTES ON BEAT ORIGINS

"You can't interview a hipster because his main goal is to keep out of a society which, he thinks, is trying to make everyone over into his own image."
—Norman Mailer, "The White Negro"

1. Seismic Sounds

When Herbert Huncke, in the spring of 1944, introduced Burroughs, Kerouac, and Ginsberg to morphine via "the mainline"—that is, injected in the veins above the wrist—he was accomplishing a revolution in the sensibility of American writers. Gertrude Stein may have changed direction and moved to Paris to write after she inhaled the nitrous oxide provided by William James at Harvard at the start of the twentieth century, but Huncke's introduction may have been even more profound and penetrating, a ritual communion of transgression.

Huncke was a haunting figure with a ravaged face and a "doomy charisma," as the novelist Jonathan Lethem once put it in a piece in the Talk of the Town section of the *New Yorker*. The word "beat" was frequently used by Huncke, a Times Square hustler with stories about his circus experiences who became a code figure for the Beats, an emanation of a subterranean underground world and a street sensibility they admired. The term derived from African American slavery, and "beat to his socks" was an expression of the most "total and despairing image of poverty," as the novelist James Baldwin once explained.

For Huncke, "beat" did not signify confused values or loss as Stein had characterized Hemingway's generation; it meant exhaustion, being beaten down, burdened and crushed by the weight of the world, all the blather of being flattened out by the hard knocks of negative experiences leaving him too impoverished to find money for food or housing. In that exposed, defeated, vagrant state, an individual could afford to be extremely open and candid because there was nothing to lose. Humiliation was not a possibility because one could not descend any further, and the emptied-out state might allow one to be more receptive to vision. As Allen Ginsberg later explained in a letter to his aunt

Hannah Litzky in June 1958, Huncke's being "beat down to his naked human core" could result in a kind of religious illumination.

The term was popularized by novelist John Clellon Holmes in an article, "This Is a Beat Generation," that was published in the *New York Times Magazine* in November 1952. Holmes had heard Kerouac use the term to describe a painter named Iris Brody, "a ragged skeletal but illuminated junky girl we knew," as Ginsberg put it.

Kerouac and Holmes had been walking in the East Village and Kerouac casually commented that Brody did not represent any vestige of the lost generation, but something new—a "beat generation." In his article, Holmes argued that the "nakedness of mind and soul" that created the beat state was a result of being "pushed up against the wall of oneself," in other words existing without hope or resources, not disillusioned like the writers of the 1920s, not suffering from any loss of faith but certain of the need for it. Despite being beaten down or perhaps in some strange way because of it, they still had a will to believe in a spiritual path.

Kerouac extended the meaning of beat to beatitude in, of all places, a June 1959 *Playboy* article on the term's origins. Kerouac's Catholic childhood and his explorations of Buddhism as a means of weathering his own disappointments when his novel *On the Road* was not published in the early 1950s certainly helped to further such a perspective, one he later popularized in a novel called *The Dharma Bums*.

Kerouac's emphasis on beatitude was repeated in interviews and on television, most notoriously when he remarked on the John Wingate television show that he was "waiting for God to show me his face." On one level, he may have been attempting to correct some of the condescensions of mass media, particularly the caricatures of the Beats in a 1959 *Life* article by Paul O'Neill that displayed an apartment with a potbelly stove, an unfinished poem in a typewriter, bean cans, and a baby playing with beer bottles on the floor. The negative stereotype of the Beats as unwashed, unmotivated, uneducated delinquents who scribbled whatever came to mind was compounded by the San Francisco gossip columnist Herb Caen after the Soviets successfully launched their Sputnik satellite. Derisively, he called the young people who were reading Kerouac "beatniks," and the name became a sticky label with a subversive connotation.

Kerouac articulated what he meant in a piece called "Aftermath: The

Philosophy of the Beat Generation." The group he envisaged had bonded because of a "special spirituality":

> A vision of crazy illuminated hipsters suddenly rising and roaming America, serious, curious, bumming and hitchhiking everywhere, ragged, beatific, beautiful in a graceful new way—a vision gleaned from the way we had heard the word *beat* spoken on street corners on Times Square and in the Village, in other cities in downtown-city-night of postwar America—*beat*, meaning down and out but full of intense conviction. We'd even heard old 1910 Daddy Hipsters of the streets speak the word that way, with a melancholy sneer. It never meant juvenile delinquents; it meant characters of special spirituality who didn't gang up but were solitary Bartlebies staring out the dead wall window of our civilization.

The "solitary Bartlebies" to whom Kerouac refers would become the descendants of Melville's absurd protagonist. Bartleby is a scrivener, or clerk, who refuses—on the singularly subjective grounds that "I prefer not to"—the quite conventional demands of the indulgent Wall Street attorney who employs him to copy legal documents. Bartleby is the fictional cousin of Henry David Thoreau who was incarcerated in Concord, Massachusetts, when he refused to pay a poll tax to vote and wrote "On the Duty of Civil Disobedience" in his jail cell. The message of antinomian resistance of that essay would travel a century later as far as Mahatma Gandhi in India and Martin Luther King. Bartleby ends up incarcerated, curled in the fetal position in Melville's story, withdrawn from the world of getting and spending, and staring at a wall—the "dead wall window of our civilization" in Kerouac's formulation. Bartleby's despair is one of the beginning points of the Beat recognition.

II. The World of Cool

The Library of America's recent publication of several large volumes of Kerouac's fiction and poetry is another step toward literary canonization, a process that often takes as long as any official declaration of sainthood, though it may be more subject to dispute.

The press release accompanying the Library of America's *The Cool School* begins by assuring me that "from music, to television, to fashion, hipsters are everywhere today." Actually, with the mordant wit he often displayed, the former *New York Times* book reviewer Anatole Broyard once argued that the hipster's state of mind was inevitably *nowhere*. He might have added that the television screen is the last place one should expect to find anything hip.

Glenn O'Brien's anthology—he playfully calls it his "compendium of orphans"—provides enough examples to illustrate the paradoxical metaphysics of nowhere. In a pithy but insightful introduction, he establishes his *terroir* and defines the geography of the place he is exploring: "To be hip is to belong to an underground, a subculture or counterculture, an elective tribe located within a larger community, outsiders inside. It is detached from the main thing and proud of its detachment."

A street person, a spiritual outlaw, an outcast, heretic, or pariah figure, the hipster uses language as part of a disguise, assuming an alternate set of values. As James Baldwin once explained in a letter that the *New York Times* published on July 29, 1979, the hipster's argot was African American in origin, "an alchemy that transformed ancient elements into a new language" formed out of "brutal necessity" whose rules were dictated by whatever messages the language needed to convey. Like Gnostics among the early Christians, that language is often coded, multilayered, swiftly mutating, and often deliberately ambiguous.

The hipsters kept talking, as Jack Kerouac maintained in his *Playboy* piece, about "personal experience and vision, nightlong confessions full of hope that had become illicit and repressed by War, stirrings, rumblings of a new soul . . . [until] Huncke appeared to us and said 'I'm beat' with radiant light shining out of his despairing eyes." So Kerouac got the term that would replace the "lost" of the Hemingway era from a furtive Times Square figure, but Kerouac's ability to *hear* and dramatically manipulate the term into the rubric by which his generation became known is characteristic of his imaginative power.

The hipsters, with their protective veil of detachment, saw themselves immediately after World War Two as "cool," a relative, provisional quality that like grace could not be faked, but became an attitude that spread internationally. O'Brien might have done well to have included a section from Amiri Baraka's *Blues People*, where he defines cool as the ability "to be calm, even unimpressed by whatever horror the world might daily propose." Baraka's context is a century of segregation, and cool was the mask of equanimity assumed by a saxophone player like Lester Young, wearing shades on stage instead of a silly Sammy Davis grin.

In its heyday, hip became a reactive model for the embalming conformities and insecurities that the early Beats felt in the 1950s. Historians tend to emphasize the ways in which Cold War hysteria was manufactured, a construct invented by Washington lobbyists to enable the military-industrial complex and guarantee prosperity. The "Take-Cover" nuclear drills, the pervasive terrors of the Red Scare, the creepy insinuations of McCarthyism, and the poisonous untruths of informers resounding in the ears of the House Un-American Activities Committee all led to the purges in government, in Hollywood, in the universities, and even in the civil service. The 1950s were also the decade in which the Warren Court ended American apartheid with the *Brown v. Board of Education* decision in 1954 and then a few years later sanctioned *Tropic of Cancer*. In New York City, a DJ named Allen Freed with a rhythm-and-blues format started playing Little Richard, Chuck Berry, Bo Diddley, and finally Elvis. Lawrence Ferlinghetti helped create a new vitality for the alternative press scene with City Lights and its publication of *Howl* in 1956. A year earlier, Mailer had published his seminal essay, "The White Negro," in a new magazine called *Dissent*, a name that signified the antinomian discontents that would help redefine national priorities.

Of course, there was very little that could be considered "cool" about any of this, and Kerouac in *Playboy* had coyly suggested that most of his Beat writer pals "belonged to the hot school, naturally since that hard gemlike flame needs a little heat." O'Brien includes Mailer's essay as well as Kerouac's "The Origins of the Beat Generation" (the *Playboy* article). These two selections, along with Anatole Broyard's "Portrait of the Hipster," form the emotional core of his anthology.

Some of O'Brien's selections, such as the ones from jazz musicians Miles Davis and Art Pepper and an interview with Kerouac's hero Lester Young, help us to understand the dark corners, the sometimes elliptical or private concerns of the hip or cool cosmos. O'Brien gives us a short vignette by Huncke describing the openness of a Times Square "pad" right after the end of World War Two, a sort of Beat salon with white furniture and Persian blue walls. He includes Carl Solomon's "A Diabolist," a five-hundred-word composition against ennui that probes the relationship between perversity and a new reality, the surrealist desire to "turn things around to make the ugly beautiful."

O'Brien reprints poems by Gregory Corso and Bob Kaufman, Diane di Prima's recollection of first discovering "Howl" (though her warm memory of sharing a bath with Ginsberg and Kerouac might have provided a better illustration), and Ed Sanders's "Group Grope" description of neo-beats merging fornication with poetry on the Lower East Side, circa 1961. Along with essayist Seymour Krim's "Making It," an inciting description of an age when the "address book replaces the soul," such selections do a lot to capture the desperate and animating energies of the moment. A few of O'Brien's choices in the final third of his book, attempts to find contemporary illustrations of hardboiled hip, such as "Beatnik Executives," his own gentle parody of "Howl," fall flat.

The limitation of O'Brien's collection is that it depends on excerpts, a taste of hip diffidence here or a flash of apocalyptic rage as in the Burroughs selection from *Nova Express*. While such sampling has a place in any critical methodology, it is often not lasting or substantial enough for us to remember the flavor. The difference between a taste and a full meal is more than volume or duration and defines the quality of the experience.

The advantage of any anthology, however, is that it can highlight salient issues that prove central. This requires some discrimination in the selection process, and a good example of O'Brien's success in this sphere is the ten-page selection he takes from Joyce Johnson's *Minor Characters* where Walter Pater's "gemlike flame" glows. Johnson observes that after the publication of *On the Road*, Kerouac noted a "cool that was colder and deader than any hipster's earned fatalism." Kerouac had been the first to exclaim that the Beat mood had died in 1952, probably as soon as his friend John Clellon Holmes announced it to the world in his article in the *New York Times*. I cannot forget that when I met William Burroughs in 1974, he flatly denied belonging to any Beat Generation.

The problem of using hip as a handle, an organizing principle for an anthology, is that the Beats were more polymath, nurtured also by such uncool passions as Buddhism and the political awareness that caused Ginsberg to organize the protests against the Vietnam War that became the soul of the counterculture. Active protest is never hip or cool; the hipster uses subterfuge to avoid authority. As the newspaper man John Leland puts it in his deft *Hip: The History*, "there is something inescapably nerdy about compiling a history of hip." I knew Carl Solomon pretty well for a few decades, and I would submit there was absolutely nothing about him that one could characterize as either hip or cool. Huncke, a more deceptive and perhaps intriguing person, was another matter.

Cool dies when it becomes a fashion adjective. If your blue suede shoes seem cool today, they may be smudged tomorrow. To the extent that hip could become a commodity, sold as a style in the 1970s by merchandisers who could caricature, imitate, and package, it began to vitiate as a cultural force. O'Brien cheerfully admits that he was introduced to this subculture as a twelve-year-old by television, watching Maynard G. Krebs in *The Many Loves of Dobie Gillis*. The degradation of hip begins with such cartoon parody and is sustained by a magazine culture and the ad agencies that control it. The ad courtiers of corporate culture, the Don Drapers of television, tried to situate hip as glamorous or somehow appealing, so Burroughs appears in a Nike advertisement and Ginsberg and Kerouac end up wearing chinos for the Gap. At the still center of hip is an existential anguish ignored in such depictions.

CHAPTER 8

THE TRAVELING WRITER
BEAT MEXICO

*Who disappeared into the volcanoes of Mexico
leaving behind nothing but the shadows of
dungarees and the ash and lava of poetry.*
—Allen Ginsberg, "Howl"

I. Murder and Morphine

In the immediate aftermath of World War II, there were a few young people with literary ambitions full of a bottled eagerness to tell their stories, people who would later be identified as "beat"—that is, politically unaffiliated, suspicious of institutional ties, organizational structures, and establishment values, vaguely bohemian, animated by youthful nonconforming impulses. Simultaneously, some of the members of this small group suffered from an existential, psychic exhaustion, a sense of being beaten down spiritually by what seemed to them the regimented and oppressive patterns of American life. Living in a historical period of what seemed like stasis to them, their immediate priority became movement.

If the key figures in the Beat Generation—William Burroughs, Jack Kerouac, and Allen Ginsberg—would become known as transgressive innovators who crossed boundaries with what were then taboo subjects like drugs and the sort of sadomasochistic sexuality dramatized in Burroughs's *Naked Lunch*, they were also driven to cross national boundaries from Latin America to North Africa and Asia. Deeply, on some inchoate, intuitive level, they felt they needed to leave their own culture in order to see it and themselves more clearly, and early circumstances drew them almost magnetically to Mexico.

One register of the transformative, opening impact of Mexico for the Beats—the opportunity to "learn ourselves"—occurs near the end of *On the Road* when Jack Kerouac announces "the earth is an Indian thing." After a series of recklessly rollicking cross-country trips, his protagonists finally reach Mexico. Kerouac's narrator, Sal Paradise, is driving "alone in my eternity at the wheel" and declares in a line of sweeping significance: "Not like driving across Carolina, or Texas, or

Arizona, or Illinois; but like driving across the world and into the places where we would finally learn ourselves among the Fellaheen Indians of the world, the essential strain of the basic, primitive, wailing humanity that stretches in a belt around the equatorial belly of the world."

In 1944, seven years before Kerouac wrote those lines, William Burroughs had collaborated with Kerouac on *And the Hippos Were Boiled in Their Tanks*, the novel they based on Lucian Carr's murder of David Kammarer. Carr was a key figure in the Beat circle because he had introduced Ginsberg, whom he had met in the Columbia dormitories, and Kerouac to Burroughs. Eight years older than Kerouac and twelve years older than Ginsberg, Burroughs had already received a B.A. from Harvard and had done graduate work there as well. He had traveled in Europe and had lived in Vienna as a medical student in 1937. His sophistication was partly a function of caste—his paternal grandfather had perfected the adding machine that led to the creation of the Burroughs Corporation, a Fortune 500 company with skyscrapers in several cities. He had read a good deal more of modern literature than his new friends had—Kafka and T. S. Eliot, for example—and he introduced them to Oswald Spengler's *Decline and Fall of the West*, which was influential.

Herbert Huncke's morphine initiation, however, may have been more dangerous than the Spengler. Though neither Kerouac nor Ginsberg would become addicted, Burroughs did, along with his companion in the apartment, a married young woman with an infant daughter named Joan Vollmer Adams, whose husband was away fighting on the European front. Joan Vollmer developed a fatal attraction for Burroughs and would conceive a son by him in a common-law union in 1947.

By then, Burroughs, Joan, and her infant daughter Julie Adams had left the 115th Street apartment. Burroughs had been apprehended forging a medical prescription and, although his family helped provide legal counsel, he became too paranoid to stay in New York. Instead, he purchased a ninety-acre spread in bayou country near New Waverly, Texas, fifty miles north of Houston. Between rows of cotton and alfalfa, he managed to grow and harvest a crop of poor-quality marijuana, which he transported to Times Square and sold.

Again nervous because of traffic infractions and police visits—the neighbors, a mile away, complained of incessant shooting at Burroughs's farm—he moved to Algiers, a community just outside New Orleans that provided access to drugs on which both he and Joan Vollmer had become dependent. When the New Orleans police raided the Burroughs household—tipped off by the New Waverly authorities—they discovered a cache of drugs and weapons. Unfortunately, they had failed to secure a proper warrant, so the search was legally compromised. In the meantime, Burroughs and his family—Joan, her daughter, and a son who had been born in New Waverly—fled to Mexico City.

II. Why Mexico?

Lâchez tout—abandon everything—the surrealist theoretician Andre Breton had advised his cohort in Paris in the early 1920s. Breton's radical prescription responded to what the French called "ennui," a quality of spiritual exhaustion comparable to what some of the Beats in New York felt after World War II. In a repeated image, the novelist Henry Miller called *lâchez tout* the "blind leap into the dark." It required the folly of a peculiar kind of courage, the drastic ability to depart suddenly from one's country as Miller had in 1929, sacrificing family, career, routine expectations, domestic security, and comfort. In Breton's surrealist circle, voyage to a fundamentally different culture—Melville in the Marquesas Islands in 1842 or Antonin Artaud with the Tarahumara in Mexico nearly a century later—was considered a vital ingredient in any writer's sensibility that could lead to the freedom of an avant-garde perspective.

At first, Burroughs's intention was to open a bar on the Mexican side of the border—he had worked as a bartender in Chicago and Manhattan, but surely he would have been the only bartender in Mexico with a Harvard degree. He had, however, conceived of the notion of buying land in Mexico to grow opium, which he had tried but failed to grow in Texas because the climate north of the Rio Grande was unsuitable. His ambition points to his transgressive nature, an extreme, unorthodox response to the settled complacency of American life in the 1950s.

The legality of this project did not trouble him. In letters to Allen Ginsberg written in November and December 1948, he explained that as a farmer in Texas, he had observed that the largest farmers were allowed to violate the law by importing seasonal Mexican labor—called "wetbacks" because they were often required to wade across the Rio Grande at night—frequently maintained in conditions of virtual slavery. The law, he rationalized, was only relative to the power of money that ultimately determined it. Burroughs maintained that there was more pretense, dissimulation, and misrepresentation in acceptable business practices like advertising, television, and public relations (a field that his uncle, Ivy Lee, pioneered) than in the sale of drugs.

Unfortunately for Burroughs, as a result of the Mexican War and what American politicians called "Manifest Destiny" and the subsequent annexation of most of the American Southwest, Mexicans had made it very difficult for U.S. citizens to own property in their own names. Usually, a Mexican attorney would secure a deed in his name and the American client might occupy the property, which would work out well with a villa in a tourist resort like Acapulco but seemed much less feasible if the plan was to purchase land to farm opium. Burroughs found an attorney and applied to formally obtain Mexican citizenship. After considerable expense, he became frustrated when the Mexican bureaucrats mysteriously lost his file.

Settling in Mexico City, Burroughs began classes in Mayan and Aztec archeology and civilization at Mexico City College, fascinated by the absolute control systems maintained by priestly castes over a millennium. Burroughs was taking advantage of available veterans' educational stipends, a monthly allowance of $75.00 plus books and tuition. He had been drafted during the war and summarily declared unfit for service, probably because of a history of psychoanalytic treatment. Supported by a modest family allowance, he did not depend on the federal benefit, but, as he advised Kerouac with typical laconic acidity in a letter written on January 22, 1950, "I always say keep your snout in the public trough."

At first, Burroughs was happy in Mexico. He had seen a tripling of the federal bureaucracy in the United States after the end of World War II and had chafed under agricultural controls when he was farming. In a letter to Kerouac in June 1949, which contained a libertarian seed metaphor for *Naked Lunch*, he had complained that the officials who determined government agricultural quotas were a germinal "cancer on the political body of this country which no longer belongs to its citizens." In Mexico, there seemed to be less state control and governmental interference with daily activity. Even illegal drugs, needles, and syringes to inject them, for example, were available for very little money; doctors could be easily convinced to write prescriptions for morphine, and he could satisfy his heroin addiction for about a dollar a day.

Near the end of *Junky*, the first novel he would write in Mexico, Burroughs remarked that he felt safe there from the antinarcotics propaganda that had been manufactured by American politicians and government officials: "Initial symptoms of nationwide hysteria were clear. Louisiana passed a law making it a crime to be a drug addict. Since . . . the term addict is not clearly defined, no proof is necessary or even relevant under a law so formulated. No proof, and consequently, no trial. This is police-state legislation penalizing a state of being." The absence of regulation was evident in the omnipresence of guns in Mexico City where, if a policeman found a weapon, Burroughs observed, the worst that would probably happen is that he would seize it for resale. In his second novel, *Queer*, Burroughs argued that Mexican police were as respected as streetcar conductors and were always susceptible to *mordida*—the bribe they took to supplement their meager salary. He was particularly pleased when, for a modest fee, he obtained a permit to carry a pistol. According to Burroughs, life in Mexico was somewhat analogous to life on the American frontier as late as the 1880s.

In October 1949, when Burroughs arrived in Mexico City, its population was approximately a million, and the air seemed clean with "a special shade of blue that goes so well with circling vultures" as he noticed in his 1985 introduction to *Queer*. He would associate the ominous and particularly subjective detail of circling vultures with Mexico and compound it several years later after fleeing Mexico, writing the beginning of *Naked Lunch*:

> Something falls off you when you cross the border into Mexico, and suddenly the landscape hits you straight with nothing between you and it, deserts and mountains and vultures; little wheeling specks and others so close you can hear wings cut the air (a dry husking sound), and when they spot something they pour out of the blue sky, that shattering bloody blue sky of Mexico, down in a black funnel.

"A single man lives high here including all the alcohol he wants to drink for $100 a month," Burroughs wrote to Kerouac in January 1950, enticing him to visit. In fact, as Burroughs would later learn when searching for the psychedelic vine ayahuasca (yage) on the Putumayo River border region between Columbia and Peru, the closer the traveler came to the equator, the less costly living expenses became, almost in direct proportion to the hazards for human existence. In Mexico in 1950, compared to costs north of the Rio Grande, life was remarkably inexpensive: one could find a good hotel for eight dollars a month, cigarettes cost six cents a pack, a quart of tequila was forty cents, one could buy a water glass of tequila for a penny, a gallon of Cuban rum for a dollar, filet mignon was available for sixty cents a pound, a dozen oysters for thirty-five cents, and encounters with young boys could be arranged for forty cents.

Burroughs's impression—and we may wonder whether it was a self-fulfilling fantasy—was that generally the Mexican people minded their own business, and this created an atmosphere of tolerance that extended to the expatriate community. His friends were not bohemian or intellectual, he advised Ginsberg in a December 1951 letter, but former U.S. military, merchant seamen, bartenders, farmers, telephone linemen, retired policemen, and "a sprinkling of inactive criminals."

Burroughs's attitude toward Mexico began to change drastically just before the Christmas holiday of 1950 when an immigration inspector—responding to a neighbor's complaints about excessive drinking and drug use—threatened arrest and demanded a bribe. Burroughs had already begun what he called *Junk*, a narrative account of his own drug habit and the peculiarities of its demimonde.

The idea to record his experiences as in a diary had been suggested to him by his St. Louis childhood friend Kells Elvins, with whom he had shared a house in 1938 while doing graduate work at Harvard. Elvins descended from the same social register set as Burroughs; his father was a congressman and the family had a town named after them. At Harvard, Elvins had collaborated with Burroughs on an early but paradigmatic story, "Twilight's Last Gleamings," about the sinking of the Titanic.

In the story, which was mostly written by Burroughs, the ship's captain, disguised in a woman's wig and gown, boards the first lifeboat after looting the safety-deposit boxes in the purser's cabin. All through the story, Burroughs quoted fragments of patriotic songs like "The Star Spangled Banner" as an ironic commentary on the abuses of authority. The story was abruptly rejected by *Esquire*, causing the recurrence of a serious writing block that for years had prevented Burroughs from writing. Lacking confidence, he had been encouraged by Kerouac in 1944 and had been able to collaborate with him on *And the Hippos Were Boiled in Their Tanks*, but had not been able to find a subject or an authentic voice since then.

He began the *Junky* manuscript in Mexico City in the spring of 1950 and completed a first draft by the end of the year. He added what he called the "Mexican section" in March 1951 and continued to make alterations until his manuscript was accepted by A. A. Wyn, a mass-market publisher of last resort whose Ace Books imprint specialized in paperback crime novels that were sold primarily in drugstores rather than bookstores.

Junky was also affected by the tortured disintegration of Burroughs's union with Joan Vollmer. Their incompatibility began with Burroughs's preference for male sexual partners, but it was compounded by their respective choice of drugs. Joan was addicted to Benzedrine, an amphetamine that quickens the pace of events, and Burroughs to morphine derivatives like heroin, which slow everything down. When Joan complained late in the summer of 1950 that Burroughs's heroin use made him boring, Burroughs slapped her in the face. That fall, she attempted to file divorce papers although she had become too irresolute to follow through—Mexican tequila and amphetamines had drained her. She looked haggard, her face bleary, lined, and paunchy. She had gained weight and she limped as the result of a bout with polio. The limp was a subtle indication of how disabled she had become.

The critical factor, however, was Burroughs's infatuation with a gawky twenty-one-year-old American named Lewis Marker, a thin young man with a look of surprised innocence that belied his military training who would accompany him on the trip to Ecuador that forms the narrative center of *Queer*. In August 1951, when Ginsberg visited Mexico City for the first time, Burroughs was traveling with Marker and Ginsberg saw the desperation in Joan, who seemed barely able to care for her two children.

Burroughs returned just after Ginsberg's departure. Both he and Joan were depressed, baiting, belittling, and goading each other. Late on the afternoon of September 7, Burroughs brought a Star .380 automatic pistol (which he knew fired in a low trajectory) to a friend's house to sell. Burroughs, Joan, and several expatriate companions including Lewis Marker were drinking gin—there were several empty bottles on the floor. Known as a marksman, Burroughs was seated nine feet away when Joan dramatically placed her empty glass on her head and challenged Burroughs to shoot it off. The bullet struck her high in her forehead, just at the hairline.

Police were summoned, and the story was garbled in sensational newspaper headlines. Burroughs's family hired a slick attorney named Bernabé Jurado, known for his corrupt practices, who persuaded the witnesses to testify that Burroughs had dropped the loaded gun, which misfired. Burroughs was released on bail. The trial dragged on for almost year, during which period Burroughs was obligated to appear before prison authorities every Monday morning at 8 a.m. When two weeks before his sentencing he heard his attorney had killed a man, Burroughs fled Mexico. He had begun *Queer* earlier in the spring of 1952 while still awaiting his verdict and hosting Kerouac, who was visiting. Written after the shooting, when Burroughs was psychically stunned by the gravity of what he had done, *Queer* is weaker as a novel than *Junky*.

In *Queer*, Burroughs anticipates what he called his "routines"—tall stories told with a bizarrely ironic, almost vicious or aberrant edge—which perform so brilliantly autonomous a role in *Naked Lunch*. Still, *Queer* does not quite cohere as a novel and, like *Junky*, exists as what we might consider a laboratory text—a way of experimenting with the postmodernist techniques that would transform the possibilities for contemporary fiction in *Naked Lunch*. The "routines" are digressive, unsettling; they exist almost as rude distractions, but they fulfill Burroughs's key raconteur ability, what initially attracted Kerouac and made him predict that Burroughs would be a writer. The story he was telling, his masochistic pursuit of Marker, was not as compelling as the focused depiction of the addicted life in *Junky* and lacked its unified flow. In a sense, he was trying to restage in a more exotic South American neighborhood the ingredients of *And the Hippos Were Boiled in Their Tanks*—an older man obsessed with a younger one who isn't willing to reciprocate.

What is most surprising about *Queer*, and it is true of its predecessor *Junky* as well, is the novelist's refusal to be drawn into the exotic, to attend to the recognizable local color characteristics of Mexico City or Latin American life in the early 1950s. In fact, what he omits, deliberately it would seem, he highlights at the beginning of his 1985 introduction to the novel:

> The city appealed to me. The slum areas compared favorably with anything in Asia for sheer filth and poverty. People would shit all over then lie down and sleep in it with the flies crawling in and out of their mouths. Entrepreneurs, not infrequently lepers, built fires on street corners and cooked up hideous, stinking, nameless messes of food which they dispensed to passers-by. Drunks slept right on the sidewalks of the main drag, and no cops bothered them.

In *Junky*, Burroughs argued that most travel books failed to represent what was important to him: the salient political conditions governing human behavior. So he tends to omit the visceral details that a writer like Kerouac would systematically register. *Queer* was not published until thirty-three years after Burroughs wrote it, a history that might suggest it was practically an abortive attempt. At the end of the novel Burroughs includes a dream of returning to Mexico City, which he characterizes as a "terminal of space-time travel, a waiting room where you grab a quick drink while you wait for your train." The image of the transitional anonymity of the waiting room reflects Burroughs's use of Mexico in his fiction, but it also suggests a writer who had been so traumatized by his own action—shooting Joan—that now he was prepared only to occupy a recess so interior that outside events and conditions could be minimized.

In the beginning of *Queer*, Burroughs remembered "a silence peculiar to Mexico seeped into the room, a vibrating, soundless hum." The silence occupies his protagonist's body whose face is described as going "slack and blank. The effect was curiously spectral, as though you could see through his face." The effect of Mexico and the unspecified, implicit terrors of an alien culture envelop *Queer* with an almost sentient, mystical vibration or hum. Analogous in effect to the miasma around Roderick Usher's mansion, this "vibrating, soundless hum" is the register of Mexico on Burroughs, which had to be deeply associated with the shooting he always claimed was both accidental and determined by a haunting, occupying, malevolent force he called the "ugly spirit."

The most extraordinary aspect of *Queer* is the commentary Burroughs contributed to the 1985 edition. When he began his piece, he acknowledged he was "paralyzed with a heavy reluctance, a writer's block like a straitjacket" because the poison of his past was still threatening and seemed too difficult to remember. *Queer*, he wrote in 1985, "was motivated and formed by an event which is never mentioned, in fact is carefully avoided: the accidental shooting death of my wife, Joan, in September, 1951." He then claims: "I am forced to the appalling conclusion that I would never have become a writer but for Joan's death."

The claim may be considered hyperbolic since he had already written most of *Junky* prior to the shooting. *Junky*—the publishers felt *Junk*, Burroughs's proposed title, made the book sound as if its subject were garbage—is a linear narrative account of Burroughs's southward migration from Manhattan, to Texas, to New Orleans, and then to Mexico.

Unlike most travel writing, "which never gives the information I want," Burroughs observed in *Junky*, the real territorial objective of the novel is the landscape of the drug culture, the "invisible mouth" that influenced Burroughs's worldview. Written, as Oliver Harris has noted in his cogent introduction to the fiftieth anniversary edition, almost like an "ethnographic field report," Burroughs describes his sensational subject from a calm, ordered clinician's perspective, very differently from Nelson Algren's National Book Award–winning bestseller of 1950, *The Man with the Golden Arm*.

The topography and actual culture of Mexico seem tangential or even incidental as far as Burroughs's deeper purposes. "In Mexico, your wishes have a dream power," he states in the novel, and the quality of dream as drug nightmare informs his novel in a contrapuntal dance with the more factual, sociological observations on the conditions of addiction. When he reaches Mexico in the last section of *Junky*, it seems more sinisterly dangerous for the American gringo than any place north of the border, with the threat of violence or corruption more Kafkaesque, normative, acceptable, and expected.

One scene, in a cantina he names Lola's, seems characteristic of the sort of fear he would later magnify as he did with the Mayan and Aztec torture rituals in *Naked Lunch*. Burroughs is reading a newspaper when he overhears someone talking about lobotomy. At another table, two young men are flirting with two giggling Mexican girls. Burroughs situates them in Samuel Beckett's hell: "The conversations had a nightmare flatness, talking dice spilled in the tube metal chairs, human aggregates disintegrating in cosmic inanity, random events in a dying universe where everything is exactly what it appears to be, and no other relation than juxtaposition is possible." The "talking dice" image suggests the absurd science fiction imagery of Burroughs's masterpiece, *Naked Lunch*. The omniscient perspective of *Junky* is always informative, unlike the kaleidoscopic and fluidly discontinuous fragmentation that would inform the more cinematic presentation of *Naked Lunch*. In *Junky*, for example, Burroughs offers a history of a three-hundred-pound junk merchant named Lupita who "pays off to operate wide open, like she was running a grocery store," and ultimately monopolizes the heroin market with an inferior product.

Near the beginning of *Naked Lunch*, Lupita reappears in a fragment, as an inexplicable totemistic, ceremonial figure, a warning as Burroughs, driven by an unidentified female, approaches Mexico City "where Lupita sits like an Aztec earth goddess doling out her little papers of lousy shit." Like the view of Mexico that is filtered through *Naked Lunch*, Lupita flashes by the reader in a mysteriously jarring appearance. Her name, with its lupine connotations, is elliptical, an ominously menacing reflection of Burroughs's changing view of Mexico.

III. Beyond Darwin's Chain

"I know you will enjoy Mexico, since you can really relax here and save money," Burroughs wrote to Kerouac in March 1950. Burroughs believed, erroneously, that Kerouac would have money to spend and to save because of royalties from his first novel.

An aspiring novelist, Kerouac's origins were lower working class. Kerouac had been raised in Lowell, Massachusetts, a mill town that provided poorly paid jobs for immigrants; the Merrimack River flowing through it afforded cheap electric power. As a child living in a French Canadian ghetto, Kerouac spoke a creole called Joual, a spoken rather than written dialect. His father had a small print shop, destroyed when the Merrimac River flooded its banks at the height of the Depression in 1936. Kerouac played football in high school and was able to attend Columbia University on an athletic scholarship, which was discontinued when he refused to continue playing after an injury. Instead, patriotic in wartime, he shipped out on dangerous merchant marine bomb runs transporting munitions to the European theater during the war.

After Burroughs and Joan Vollmer left the communal apartment on 115th Street, Kerouac lived mostly with his parents in Ozone Park, Queens, where he completed his first novel, *The Town and the City*, a sprawling, traditional bildungsroman based on his Lowell childhood, an apprentice work, but good enough to be published by Harcourt Brace in the early spring of 1950.

Though the novel's publication was certainly confirmation of his talents, its mixed reception and poor sales were discouraging. His novel had been quickly forgotten, he complained in a letter, and he was afflicted with "the curse of Melville." He was struggling to find a new form for a novel based on a series of road trips he had taken with a new friend named Neal Cassady, a wild firebrand carouser who fascinated him.

That summer, he was driven to Mexico City by Cassady, who was seeking to divorce his wife Carolyn—divorces were much easier to arrange in Mexico. While visiting Joan and Burroughs, Kerouac developed a severe case of dysentery. They nursed him back to health on a curious diet of daily quantities of marijuana and some morphine. Recovered, Kerouac was as intoxicated by wandering the streets of Mexico City, a disoriented flaneur in a region he somehow connected to the fraternal camaraderie of the immigrant communities of his Lowell childhood. Returning by train to Laredo, Texas, he crossed the border in August "with a kilo of cured shit round waist in a silk scarf" as he confessed in his journal *Windblown World*. The "shit" was slang code for marijuana, properly aged, and the diary entry itself an admission of how profoundly the experience of Mexico had affected him.

Always more romantic and rhapsodic than the more cynical Burroughs, Kerouac's idealizations of Mexican life irritated Burroughs. Five months before shooting Joan, Burroughs reacted harshly, in a letter written in May 1951, to Kerouac's comparison of Mexico to his Lowell childhood: "Mexico is not simple or gay or idyllic. It is nothing like a French-Canadian naborhood [sic]. It is an Oriental country that reflects 2000 years of disease and poverty and degradation and stupidity and slavery and brutality and psychic and physical terrorism. Mexico is sinister and gloomy and chaotic with the special chaos of a dream. I like it myself, but it isn't everybody's taste."

Kerouac believed that one of his eighteenth-century Breton ancestors had settled in Quebec with a Mohawk wife, so he was particularly willing to identify with indigenous cultures. One reason for Kerouac's attraction to Mexico was the vitality and color of what he called the Mexican fellaheen, the surviving remnants of the pre-Columbian cultures that descended from the Mayan and Aztec empires. In an undated sequence in his journal *Windblown World* he called "A Tarahumare Afternoon," he admired what he imagined as a pastoral idyll:

> I go across sad railroad plazas of dust to Juarez Bridge and cross for two cents into the blissful peace of the Fellaheen village at hot sun noon—smells of tortilla, drowse of children & dogs, heat, little long streets—I go clear out of town to river levee and squat on ground and see on this side an Indian mother kneeling at the river washing clothes with little baby son clinging lovingly to her back—Thought, "If my mother was only simple as to do her wash at the river."
> —Felt happiness.

In the spring of 1952, Kerouac returned to Mexico, again to visit Burroughs in Mexico City—"a mad genius in littered rooms." *Junky* was awaiting publication; Burroughs was writing *Queer* and attending his trial for the shooting of Joan. Kerouac was working on an extension of *On the Road* called *Visions of Cody* and on *Doctor Sax*, a story based on his Lowell childhood. The apartment was too small for two writers, so Kerouac often had to work in a small hallway bathroom. Because of both the trial and the difficulties Burroughs was having with his own manuscript, Burroughs was irascible and Kerouac's lack of money did not help alleviate the tension.

In a long letter to Ginsberg, written on May 10, 1952, Kerouac described his trip from California to Mexico City. Neal Cassady, with his wife Carolyn and their babies "all gypsied and happy," had deposited him at the Mexican border. In Sonora, Arizona, he purchased a second-class bus ticket on a high, narrow bus with wooden benches, singing children, and goats on its roof that stopped in Culiacán, which he called the opium center of the world: "I ate tortillas and carne in African stick huts in the jungle with pigs rubbing against my legs; I drank pure pulque from a pail, fresh from the field, from the plant, unfermented, pure milk of pulque makes you get the giggles, is the greatest drink in the world. I ate strange new fruit, erenos, mangoes, all kinds. In the back of the bus, drinking mescal, I sang bop for the Mexican singers." Smoking joints laced with opium, he is celebrating, exultant, "beyond Darwin's chain." Later in the letter he reminds Ginsberg that his genealogy is partly Indian and that with his French Canadian mind he can understand everything his new Indian companions say, "digging everything, all of it, almost perfectly" even when one of them declares in Spanish that "the earth is an Indian thing"—a line he would transpose with a sacramental insistence to *On the Road*.

Kerouac returned to Mexico in 1955 and 1956, living in a rooftop stone hovel and working on *Tristessa*, a novel about a tortured love affair he had with a Mexican junkie prostitute named Esperanza Villanueva. The relationship was particularly dangerous because Esperanza was also sleeping with the police chief of Mexico City who could order assassinations with impunity. Practically living as a vagrant on pennies a day, he was torn by the despair he felt at the inability to get *On the Road* published. Trying to resolve his depression with an intense exploration of Buddhism, he was now more fully prepared to describe the poverty of Mexico.

This included aspects of urban Mexico like Tristessa's tenement shack with the rain-stained pornography on the kitchen walls, with the rooster, chickens, and dove pecking at garbage in the kitchen—the kind of authentic detail that Burroughs seems to have ignored. In the streets outside, a phantasmagoria lit by candles, dim bulbs and lanterns, Kerouac walks "with one quick Walt Whitman look" past the hundreds of whores with crooking fingers on Panama Street, over giant mud puddles and five-foot ditches, past half a mile of food stands "devouring whole mouthloads of fire."

The joyous discovery that animates Kerouac's view of Mexico is the energy that fuels his driven rhythms, the reason Sal Paradise finds the backbreaking labor of picking cotton with his Mexican lover Terry in *On the Road* so glorious, or the African American Denver ghetto so harmonious a community. Near the end of *On the Road*, Dean and Sal, Kerouac's feckless protagonists, finally reach a town called Sabinas Hidalgo in Mexico.

Dean, the yea-sayer, speculates that its inhabitants are without suspicion, soft and subdued: "the people here are straight and kind and don't put down any bull." The undeveloped frontier bustle of the town has its appeal: "The main street was muddy and full of holes. On each side were dirty broken-down adobe fronts. Burros walked in the streets with packs. Barefoot women watched us from dark doorways. The street was crowded with people on foot." Even the subsequent sordid disorder of the culminating Mexican brothel scene cannot cancel Kerouac's love for Mexico. As he had declared earlier in the novel when picking cotton with his Mexican lover, Terry, the landowners who hired him "thought I was Mexican, of course, and in a way I am." This empathy and the romantic emphasis that reinforces it determine his view. It seems quite deliberately innocent, not mindlessly myopic as the more mean-spirited Burroughs might have seen it, almost an unconscious spiritual counter to a profoundly debilitating despair and guilt that afflicted him and that he battled with Buddhism in the 1950s and booze until his early death in 1969.

IV. Into the Volcano

Twelve years younger than Burroughs, and four years younger than Kerouac, Ginsberg finally graduated from Columbia University in 1947. For many years afterward he had been trapped in stasis in an emotional dead end. He was ambivalent about his homosexual desires, which he related to an inability to discover his own individual voice as a poet, perhaps despite the brilliance of his undergraduate imitations of sixteenth- and seventeenth-century poetry.

When Kerouac's first novel was published in 1950, unhappy that his poems were not getting published, Ginsberg returned to his hometown of Paterson, New Jersey. Encouraged by Kerouac, he began an informal tutorial in the virtues of natural speech and a less self-consciously literary diction with an older poet, William Carlos Williams. This friendship became a turning point for him.

In December 1953 Ginsberg hitchhiked south to Florida, visiting Burroughs's former lover Lewis Marker in Jacksonville and Burroughs's parents in Palm Beach. Then he took a plane to Havana, and another to Yucatán. He would spend the next six months in Mexico. Kerouac had informed Ginsberg that he was going to a place where he could find himself in an encircling timelessness. Though this could lead to potential terrors, it could also become a route to freedom from one's conditioned expectations.

He experienced a glimmer of such freedom at the eleventh-century pyramid ruins of Chichén Itzá: "Stars over pyramids—tropic nite, forest of chirruping insects ... great stone relief of unknown perceptions, half a thousand years old—and earlier in day saw stone cocks a thousand years old grown over with moss and batshit dripping in vaulted room of stone stuck in the wall." While there were frustrations for Ginsberg caused by both his lack of money and fluency in Spanish, there were some gratifying encounters, particularly one in which he was invited to participate in a New Year's celebration in Mérida and, wandering into a bar for a tequila a few days later, met the "brilliant Spaniard"—as he eulogized him in "Howl"—"to talk about America and Eternity."

From Mérida Ginsberg traveled by train and bus to Chiapas in the extreme south of Mexico, part of the Mayan region that the Mexicans had seized from Guatemala, its smaller neighbor to its south, after the United States defeated them in the Mexican War and annexed the Southwest. At the edge of an inaccessible forest jungle, the temple ruins of Palenque had been smothered by trees and impenetrable vines, invisible for over a thousand years, reclaimed as it were by nature. Camping at the ruins in Palenque, he was stunned by the archaic resonance he felt in the seventh-century remnants of Mayan civilization, which for him emphasized the transience of human existence. While living in an archeologists' camp he met Karena Shields, an amateur archeologist. When Ginsberg complained that he was quickly running out of money, she generously invited him to stay at her cocoa plantation, and she proved to be an able exponent of Mayan history, symbolism, and metaphysics. Playfully, he called her his "white goddess."

He was living communally on tortillas and frijoles, he wrote to Kerouac on February 14, 1954. Tasting fried grasshoppers and roasted monkey, sleeping in a hammock under a thatched roof on an open platform without side walls, Ginsberg felt liberated—he was playing drums several hours daily on ceiba logs in the Mayan fashion. Early mornings, or late afternoons when the sun was descending, he would work in the banana groves, or in the cocoa groves, cutting, washing, fermenting, and drying the cocoa. Shields's finca was practically in the jungle, which added to the exoticism and uninhibited freedom Ginsberg experienced there. Midday he would walk naked, ankle, waist, or neck deep up a rocky clear stream, lush with plantains, lianas, and giant mahogany trees filled with monkeys.

Ginsberg was entering a new spaciousness not often available to young men raised in a suburban middle-class setting. This cosmic kind of loafing indolence Whitman was accused of is reflected in the second stanza of the poem Ginsberg was writing while at the finca, a poem he dedicated to Karena Shields:

> —One could pass valuable months
> and years perhaps a lifetime
> doing nothing but lying in a hammock
> reading prose with the white doves
> copulating underneath
> and monkeys barking in the interior
> of the mountain
> and I have succumbed to this temptation—

Although the form of "Siesta in Xbalba" still showed the formal influence of his mentor William Carlos Williams's triadic meter, variable foot, and short line, the long poem also revealed a breakthrough in consciousness for Ginsberg. Conflating what he had seen at Chichén Itzá, Uxmal, and Palenque with the mummified corpses in the catacombs that he had seen at Guanajuato, Ginsberg seemed intent on deciphering the "hieroglyphs of Eternity" while preparing for a crucial moment when ego could disappear or at least diminish:

> My soul might shatter
> At one primal moment's
> Sensation of the vast
> Movement of divinity.

Near the end of his stay at Karena Shields's finca, Ginsberg felt earthquake tremors and heard the rumors of disappearing villages. He was able to reach Yajalón, near the reputed epicenter, a small town surrounded by mountains, partly by getting a ride in a small 1914 biplane (which crashed several weeks later) and partly by mule. Joining an expedition of local tribesmen to determine whether there had been a volcanic fissure on the top of Mount Acavalna, he was again plunged into an authentic Mexico with bamboo drums in a church at night, women lighting candles in front of an altar decorated with old German religious paintings, and dolls representing bearded black Indian figures with Jesus. After an explosive boom, the entire mountain began to shake.

On the next day he accompanied another group of white-robed Indians from a neighboring village who wanted to see whether a sacred cave on the other side of the mountain had been sealed by the quake. As Ginsberg entered its "stupendous" mouth, he saw that part of the cave ceiling had collapsed; huge rocks, rubble, and trees lay scattered. There were several more booms and trembles. The cave was open, he wrote Kerouac on April 4, 1954, "like some awful dream vision, that big you know—and full of pulpit formations, and naves and arches, like a Piranesi drawing don't you know, pilasters and arks and giant dark religious formations."

In a region where the indigenous population spoke not Spanish but the Mayan language Tzeltal, Ginsberg was introduced to a part of Mexico that did seem "beyond Darwin's chain" as Kerouac had promised. The effect was transformative. A little over a year later he would compose "Howl," a poem that would alter the direction of American poetry and become the first clarion call of the Beat Generation.

v. Impact

Burroughs, the glacial iceberg of the Beat group, could seem unaffected by what he called in a moment of characteristic political incorrectness the "oriental" quality of Mexico, with the drunks sleeping soundly on streets where lepers prepared and sold food. The sinister "vibrating, soundless hum" he imagined and equated with Mexico was the metaphor he invented for a sense of evil catastrophe that haunted him. That hum was an isolating factor, an invisible wall that inevitably separated him from his surroundings, preventing him from any identification that was not ironic. Whether it was the drugs he was using or the absurdity he felt in daily Mexican life, or more probably a combination of the two, the experience was enough to trigger the writing of his first two novels, and to leave an indelible imprint on *Naked Lunch*.

Usually free of irony, Kerouac in Mexico comes closest to connecting with what he called "wailing humanity," seeing its poverty and consequent disease compassionately and not naturalistically. Like some Whitman in lower Manhattan a century earlier, he exists in willful denial of his own enormous vulnerability as the gringo from a culture than had swallowed half of Mexico before the middle of the nineteenth century. Instead, he projects a state of immunity, freedom, and fraternity, an ecstatic camaraderie reaching out to those who cannot understand his language or the bop songs he sings in the bus outside Culiacán. The result is the kind of transport characteristically associated with Kerouac.

"Something that you feel will find its own form" Kerouac predicted in his "List of Essentials," and the new direction this precept suggested represented a new direction for American writing in the 1950s. Kerouac's Mexican journeys, particularly as imagined in *Tristessa*, became a trigger for that release of feeling, a counter for a historical period marked by apathy and conformity.

Of the three writers under consideration here, however, Ginsberg may have been the most affected by Mexico, perhaps because in the southern and unchanged parts of Chiapas he could experience an even more profound sense of the "encircling timelessness" Kerouac promised. As he deciphered what he called the "hieroglyphs of Eternity" around him, and measured signs of the transience of human effort, he began to understand how his own pronounced sense of ego might interfere with the flow that could result in poetry. Mexico was seminal for him and "Howl" became his immediate horizon.

VI. My Mexican Journey

At the end of *On the Road*, Sal and Dean drive south in a banged-up 1937 Ford sedan, "flying down to the curve of the world" to a "magic land" for a "lonely exile gallop into the unknown." In 1974, after I had spent several years examining the Ginsberg deposit at Columbia University and all the Kerouac letters I could find in private hands and at the Harry Ransom Center in Austin, Texas, I only had a glimmer of the importance of Mexico.

I knew enough to apply for a National Endowment for the Humanities fellowship that I fortunately received in 1974. I had already been teaching at Queens College for a decade, but I could not continue while benefiting from the fellowship. What I needed to do was write *Naked Angels*. I felt some pressure because I knew there were others planning their own interpretations, some of them with big budgets and research assistants, and I understood the importance of being first.

I had been interviewing many of the figures in the Beat Generation, Burroughs, Ginsberg, Herbert Huncke, Carl Solomon, John Clellon Holmes, and a panoply of others. I admit that at first I had some apprehensions: Carr had murdered his friend, Burroughs his wife, and Ginsberg had been given a psychiatric sentence. I felt the danger of sensationalizing and the guilt of being associated, even as a literary critic, with a group that had consorted with criminals and used drugs. On one of the occasions when I was visiting Allen Ginsberg at his lower East Side tenement flat—the key tossed to me in an old sock from his window four flights up—Ginsberg calmly explained that I would not fully understand his companions unless I spent some time in Mexico.

My grant money, I soon realized, would not go very far where I lived, in Manhattan, which was already becoming too expensive. My money would be more than sufficient in Mexico, especially because Mellon decided to stay in Manhattan, continuing her career in fashion, rock, and editorial photography. As soon as my spring semester ended, I flew to Mexico City, which seemed densely overpopulated and vibrantly loud.

I only spent a few days there, trying to visit Burroughs's apartment on Orizaba Street where he had written *Junky* and Kerouac *Doctor Sax*, but now it was occupied by the pandemonium of half a dozen small children and their mother. Burroughs had described the air of Mexico City two decades earlier as clean and blue, but my disquieting impression was that it had a yellowish, brown coloration, smelled like diesel or sulfur, and was so turgid one inhaled its polluted particles with every breath.

Recalling Kerouac's trip to Culiacán, I took the bus to the city of Oaxaca, a twelve-hour ride to the south. The name "Oaxaca" had an alien, fiercely clashing, and almost sinister sound to my ear. I had read Malcolm Lowry's ominous characterization of it in *Under the Volcano*: "The word was like a breaking heart, a sudden peal of stifled bells in a gale, the last syllables of one dying of thirst in the desert."

The bus was modern and air-conditioned, not the rickety vehicle of Kerouac's trip. The Pensión Suiza had been recommended to me by a friend who advised that it was a quiet, modest place where one could do some writing. It was owned by Doña Luisa, a scowling, skeletal woman in her eighties who supervised everything from her wheelchair. Although she spoke little English, she informed me that breakfast was included but that if requested in advance, I could also have lunch or dinner in the dining room.

A ten-minute walk from the zocalo, the square in the center of most Mexican towns, the Suiza was an old hacienda with only a half dozen simply furnished rooms on its second floor above a lush interior courtyard. My room was oblong, with three narrow cots in a file and a small window, so it seemed like a military barracks. All the rooms bordered a circular terrace, partially shaded by a porch, looking over the courtyard garden. This flowering terrace was where I planned to work. Its fragrance of red frangipani and white honeysuckle was an extension of the garden below and offered a surfeit of seclusion, the privacy afforded by swaying palm fronds and huge banana plants.

In another terrace nook, steadily typing, was a rotund, white-haired gentleman named Ross Parmenter, a retired music critic who had worked for the *New York Times*. Invariably affable and cheery, Ross was writing a book on Oaxaca in the early 1920s when the Welsh novelist D. H. Lawrence lived in Oaxaca and made it his setting for *The Plumed Serpent*. Ross was a determined figure, and the sober diligence of his daily industry was a good model for me. He also had more than passing interest in the Beats—one of his former colleagues, Gilbert Millstein, had written the rave review of *On the Road* that catapulted Kerouac's novel into a best seller and was the trigger for his fame.

During the summer and fall of 1974, I had few companions in Oaxaca. The Suiza was too basic in its accommodations to attract many tourists, and Oaxaca was too far to the south to attract many of them anyway. On the terrace, I worked on my manuscript, sent letters to my wife, and dispatched chapters to my editor in New York City. Two of the residents of the Suiza became friends of the road, as Kerouac might have put it.

Kodiak Rose and Peggy were young Alaskan women in search of heat and celebration. They had earned good money in fisheries and saved enough of it to live in Mexico for an extended period.

Rose was a short, stout irrepressible lass who often had a beer in her hand. No matter the time of the day, she always appeared with her sunrise smile, which I suspect was the result of marijuana. Sometimes, late in the afternoon, when I was still at my typewriter, she would offer to share a few puffs with me in one of the more secluded, vegetative sections of the terrace. Cautiously, I would usually suggest that we retreat to the safety of my military room. Fearless herself, one evening she found a scorpion under one of the cots and, bending in one rapid movement, scooped it up in her hand and threw it out of my door.

Wild Peggy, her companion, was the generous source of the grass. A leggy, brassy blonde who only wore the shortest shorts, Peggy had been warned not to drink the water and seemed intent on compensating with all the wine, beer, and tequila she could find in Oaxaca. More properly though, the actual source of the marijuana was Peggy's boyfriend Juan. William Burroughs had warned me about the perils of purchasing marijuana in Mexico, that for Americans it could often result in a shakedown in which one might lose everything.

Juan, however, inspired confidence. A tall, lithe, exceptionally beautiful descendant of the Mayans, with gleaming shoulder-length ebony hair, Juan looked like a dancer but had the gravity and decorum that sharply contrasted with Peggy's bubbling enthusiasm. Kerouac, who claimed he was part Mohawk and Iroquois Indian himself, had expressed his admiration in *On the Road* for the indigenous inhabitants of Mexico like Juan "with high cheekbones, slanted eyes, and soft ways."

When my Spanish began to improve, Juan escorted me to Monte Albán, once a sacred Mayan temple complex, now a ruined Ozymandias destination. An imposing pyramid structure, it seemed to be one thousand steps high and over a thousand years old. Juan brought me to a plateau used as a ballfield where the losers were traditionally sacrificed. The seriousness of the contest, the screams of the vanquished and their bloody consequence would have fascinated Burroughs; for me the hushed silence of the place was spooky and ominous.

As a gift, one day Juan gave me some peyote buds. I knew Ginsberg had written the "Moloch" section of "Howl" after chewing peyote and that Native Americans had been ingesting the bitter juices of the plant for centuries as part of their ritual observance. Peyote can induce dangerous regurgitation that can blur or delay any hallucinogenic effect, but Juan had instructed me to fast for a day preceding.

I spent my high marveling through the morning in the great market of Oaxaca. Then, the market dominated the center of the town with the pungent smells of flowers and fruits, the fermenting odors of bananas and peaches in heat. The small, squat, soft pastel orange and yellow sun-blistered concrete buildings were set in the sprawl of hundreds of produce stands: giant piles of lettuce, tomatoes, cucumbers, mounds of red, green, and orange chilies, racks of inexpensive clothing, sandals, sombreros, straw mats, clay pottery, woven blankets, hardware, and household implements. The colors, especially of the produce, seemed so vividly illuminating, glowing in the aftermath of the peyote. I seemed to have glided for several hours for block after block, able, I thought, to suddenly comprehend—as confused as Kerouac who had the same empathetic identification—the fragments of Spanish or Nahuatl I overheard.

Walking for hours, I felt entirely safe, buoyant in my illusion and in my admiration for the bustling harmony around me. Although my personal circumstances were entirely different, the sheer radiance of the market that morning and its warmth reminded me of a similar spectacle of brilliance despite the surrounding poverty in Kerouac's Mexican novel, *Tristessa*.

I managed to see a much less romantic side of Mexico later that summer when Juan invited Peggy, Rose, and me to accompany him to his mountain village, five hours' drive west of Oaxaca, on the way to the Pacific Coast. We were driven by Chip, a bossy, big-boned blonde American with a Chevy International Harvester truck whom we had met in the Suiza and who had suddenly assumed a proprietary interest in Peggy.

Our gang reached Juan's village just before sunset. We left the truck off the highway, hiking several thousand feet up a narrow, steep, twisting footpath cutting through terraced fields to join Juan's family. Juan had informed Chip that he was expected to leave a *mordida*, a gift for the village headman, to insure the protection of his vehicle, but Chip had refused, outraged at the prospect of paying for parking.

It was quite dark when we arrived. Not one of the seven members of Juan's family spoke any English, but we smoked some *sensemilla*—more potent than the marijuana I had tried because cultivated at a very high elevation—and communicated without polite euphemisms. Rice and beans were prepared over a campfire by Juan's wizened mother, and we shared pulque from a cracked brown jug.

The crickets were humming loudly and it seemed as if there was a palpable energy field vibrating around us. I could not sleep at all that night. We were almost ten thousand feet high, lying on straw mats in thatched huts built of bamboo saplings so we could see the glittering stars. It was an intensely hot night with "no air, no breeze, no dew, but the same Tropic of Cancer heaviness held us all pinned to earth, where we belonged and tingled" that Kerouac describes in *On the Road*.

When we returned to the truck the next morning, its tires and everything inside from the radio to the instrument dials had been stripped. Nervous, I returned to Oaxaca by bus with the excuse of my writing, leaving Chip and Juan to negotiate with the police. Peggy and Rose hitched to Puerto Angel on the coast where Peggy was bitten on her foot by a scorpion.

The longer I remained in Mexico, the more I began to appreciate its dangers, the sinister edge of which is so present in *Junky*. Mellon joined me before Christmas on assignment from the *Magazine of Natural History* to photograph the Indians of the Oaxaca Valley, and their irrigation system and flower cultivation. She contacted the Oaxacan Water Authority, which provided a car and driver. We spent a week visiting colonial irrigation systems until one evening at dusk we stopped in a remote, isolated area so that Mellon could photograph a modern dam. From out of nowhere, two armed men approached the car and asked our driver whether the gringos wanted marijuana. We returned to the car immediately and our driver took off, convinced the men were banditos. They took a few shots at us too as the departing car careened through a dry riverbed at high speed. We were all bounced around a bit, safe enough, though terrified.

On New Year's Day 1975, Mellon and I took a crowded bus south to Guatemala. Unlike the modern bus that had brought me to Oaxaca from Mexico City, this bus had been built before World War Two and its suspension was shot. It was full of diesel fumes, crammed with market produce, and piled high with cardboard boxes on its roof, fastened with ropes. Struggling goats and pigs were tied to that hot roof too. All the other passengers were Indian, many of them carrying children or bamboo cases containing chickens. Some of them were on a religious pilgrimage, squeezing up and down the narrow aisle with a large wooden crucifix, singing psalms while the bus lurched around precipitous hairpin mountain curves.

The bus arrived in Panajachel on Lake Atitlán, a large body of water framed by three volcanoes. Panajachel was our destination, known on the hippie trail through South America for its dramatic beauty. As soon as we descended we saw Kodiak Rose seated at a curb, smiling as if she were expecting us as part of some Magical Mystery Tour. It seemed like a manifestation of the kind of lasting communion that had sustained Kerouac and Ginsberg, and, sure enough, Rose found us a room to rent in Peggy's house on the water where we spent a recuperative month, sleeping in a wool blanket decorated with quetzals, cooking fresh fish from the lake, and gorging on enormous saffron-colored papayas. With a completed manuscript, I looked forward to returning to New York.

CHAPTER 9

KEROUAC'S MUSIC

I troop forth replenished with supreme power, one of an average unending procession,
We walk the roads of Ohio and Massachusetts and Virginia and Wisconsin and New York and New Orleans and Texas and Montreal and San Francisco and Charleston and Savannah and Mexico,
Inland and by the seacoast and boundary lines . . . and we pass the boundary lines.
—Whitman, "Song of Myself"

My people go back to Breton France, first North American ancestor Baron Alexandre Louis Lebris de Kérouac of Cornwall, Brittany, 1750 or so, was granted land along the Rivière du Loup after victory of Wolfe over Montcalm.
—Kerouac, Preface to Lonesome Traveller

I. A Holy Ghost

A few years ago, the Bosnian American writer Aleksandar Hemon used Kerouac's name as a verb in the *New Yorker*, explaining that he had immigrated because he "thought it might be fun to Kerouac about in America for a while." While that remark illustrates the international pop appeal—like Walter Salles's film version of *On the Road* or its twenty-two foreign editions—it doesn't guarantee the literary respectability for which Kerouac yearned.

Recently, a professorial poet-pal whose company I've enjoyed for many years invited me to a cramped slice of a bar below ground level on Houston Street to hear a piano player who was becoming his accompanist. The jazz-inflected poetry my friend writes and performs is the result of a fusion form, one advanced largely by Kerouac, in the 1950s when he was an unknown, in Greenwich Village clubs such as the Figaro and the Village Vanguard. As we were leaving, I told him I was working on a piece on Kerouac in Mexico, circa 1950 to 1955. His response seemed curt and cutting: as a writer, my friend grumbled, "Kerouac was only suitable for adolescents." I wonder now whether he would offer the same evaluation to Mark Twain after reading *Huckleberry Finn*, or perhaps he might even snobbishly extend it to Hemingway because of the Nick Adams stories? Hemingway, infamously, probably would have laid him out with an uppercut, which I agree would have been an angry, adolescent response.

The notion of Kerouac as a facile phenomenon may stem from Truman Capote's maliciously dismissive quip that *On the Road* wasn't writing but merely typewriting, a jab at Kerouac's boast that he wrote the novel in three weeks, typing up to ninety words a minute for twenty hours straight, night and day. When the novel was published in 1957, the *New York Times* reviewer saw it as the sign of a new generation and compared it to Hemingway's *The Sun Also Rises*. Capote's *Breakfast at Tiffany's* was scheduled to appear a year later and he was jealous.

Actually, the novel had been written six years earlier, in the spring of 1951, on a scroll of pages taped together. When it was completed, virtually in the rush of one long, haphazardly punctuated sentence, Kerouac had used the real names of his friends who were its characters, which would have made any publisher susceptible to libel suits. Kerouac had been a fullback at Columbia University, and he compared his scroll to the length of a football field. He understood that with his novel he had created an epic announcement about the changes occurring in American life in the postwar period.

I have already alluded to the time when—in the flush of his enthusiasm—Kerouac displayed his sprawling scroll on his editor's desk. Surprised by the unconventional presentation, Robert Giroux immediately raised the issue of revision. Feeling rejected, always uncomfortable with authority, Kerouac stalked out of the office, saying that his story had been dictated to him by the Holy Ghost. Though similar contentions can be connected to the origins of some of the world's most prominent religions, it does seem preposterous in this more secular context. The implication, of course, was that revision would be blasphemous, but Kerouac's abrupt departure was also a radical revocation of the symbiotic relationship between writers and their editors. He was spurning the sacred cow of the literary experience. It was the beginning of his problematic publication history.

Kerouac knew that with *On the Road* he had reached a pinnacle of "peak maturity," that in 1951 he had been "blowing such mad poetry and literature that I'll look back years later with amazement and chagrin that I can't do it anymore." During the six years that Kerouac had to wait for *On the Road* to appear, he wrote another dozen books, sometimes living with his mother in Queens but sometimes on pennies a day in skid row San Francisco or in a rooftop stone hovel in Mexico. These unpublishable books were evidence of a writer's stubborn faith in his own capacities or the sign that he was helpless to stop, caught in the compulsion to record his feelings even if only for a singular audience composed of himself and a few friends like Allen Ginsberg.

In 1955, the critic and Lost Generation writer Malcolm Cowley intervened and persuaded Viking to reconsider the novel. Kerouac understood that unless his novel was published, he had little chance of any future success, so he allowed the Viking editors to conventionalize the manuscript with paragraphs and punctuation. When *On the Road* became a best seller, a number of the books he had written from 1951 to 1957 began to appear; others, like his masterpiece *Visions of Cody*, would only appear posthumously.

II. The Voice Is All

In the past quarter century, there has probably been more biographical interest in Jack Kerouac than in any other modern American novelist. On my bookshelf, I have an excellent oral biography by Barry Gifford and Lawrence Lee, a half dozen memoirs by former wives or lovers, some written with cudgels and sharpened axes, and eight biographies. The biographies are mostly flawed attempts, limited either by estate prohibitions or inadequate access, haphazard writing skills, faulty judgment, an undeveloped sense of literary history, or the inability to distinguish the actual from literary legend or self-perpetuated myth.

Kerouac's appeal can't be denied. The extraordinary monument dedicated to him in his hometown of Lowell, Massachusetts, with its eight ten-foot-high granite tablets, each engraved with a citation from another of his novels, dominates the town like a Stonehenge. The Christie's auction sale of the original scroll version of *On the Road* for $2.4 million to James Irsay, the owner of the Indianapolis Colts, was the highest price paid for any American literary manuscript. Now the scroll travels from museum to museum, and the scroll version has even been published exactly as Kerouac originally conceived it.

I suspect Americans respond to *On the Road* and Kerouac because of an irrepressible freshness that has everything to do with language. When Kerouac used exclamations like "Wow," or "Whooee," many of his critics cringed and proclaimed the barbarians were storming the gates. Like his predecessors Whitman and Twain, Kerouac could hear what I like to call "natural speech."

As Joyce Johnson, his most capable and most recent biographer, maintains in *The Voice Is All* (Viking, 2012), Kerouac's linguistic freedom may have much to do with the fact that his first language was Joual, a French Canadian dialect spoken in the ghetto of Pawtucketville in Lowell where he spent his childhood. An unwritten language, Joual was musical and infinitely various due to its lack of codification.

Kerouac's compassion for African Americans, for American Indians, often denigrated as evidence of his sentimentality, is also a function of his own early experience as part of a shunted minority, and his belief that in the eighteenth century his Quebecois ancestors, poor potato farmers who subsisted on potato skin soup and vodka to dull their hunger pains, had intermarried with Mohawk Indians.

Most biographers are capable only of wooden prose. It is rare to find one who writes with the style and imagination Johnson exhibits in her perceptively entitled book. She has had the advantage (and duress) of examining the huge Kerouac archive deposited in the Berg Collection of the New York Public Library, and she explores it with a discrimination displayed by no previous biographer. She made me, for example, want to immediately read all of Box 73, folders 10 to 12, labeled "Love Letters Written to Jack Kerouac." As a novelist herself, she has a genuine interest in creative process, and she has lived with this subject for over a half a century, enough time for the distance any biographer needs. She was Kerouac's lover when *On the Road* was originally published in 1957, and her intimate account of that friendship, *Minor Characters*, won the National Book Critics Circle award for memoir in 1983.

I asked her why she wrote this biography when so many attempts had preceded hers:

> Because I had the unique experience of being with Jack a half-century ago as *On the Road* set in motion a tremendous shift in American culture, and because I saw how Jack suffered from distortions of his views by the media and the lack of understanding, even among his fans and scholars, of what he had achieved in his body of work, I have always felt the obligation to try to set the record straight. It is time to cut Jack loose from the public's fixation

on the Beat Generation and the misleading creation myth attached to the writing of *On the Road* and take his measure as a classic American writer.

The Voice Is All is written with a poised balance between narrative and literary analysis, with the most nuanced view so far of Kerouac's volatile moodiness and considerable complexities. Fusing lots of intuition with personal observation, Johnson is able to identify Kerouac's emotional dynamics with more sympathy than any of her predecessors: "By nature, he was silent, and when he was sober, he probably kept most of his angry, unacceptable ideas to himself. When he was drunk enough, he would express them with the alcohol-ignited vehemence of someone dangerously certain that he alone sees the truth." Unable to tolerate routine (with football practice, the military, the notion of a steady job or marriage), his duality was only compounded by a simultaneous desire for irreconcilables: the alienated, introverted observer who searches for camaraderie, the man with a fundamentally melancholy nature who was so quickly surprised by his own inexplicable enthusiasms. Like Dostoevsky's Underground Man, Kerouac had a secret, isolating conviction of his difference; his friends, however, were drawn to his shyness, his warmth, his childlike, appealing naïveté.

Kerouac's parents were victims of what has been derisively called the Canuck sensibility, a fatalistic stoicism that accepted a frozen lower-class status. In New England, the region to which many French Canadians and Jean-Baptiste, Kerouac's grandfather, immigrated, they were called "les Negres Blancs" because of their reputation for taking any work to survive. Kerouac's father, Leo, was a printer who found it difficult during the Depression to support his family. He also lost money gambling, which contributed to matrimonial tension in a household utterly dominated by his wife, Gabrielle Ange, who worked in the shoe factories of Lowell. Her controlling influence only increased when Jack Kerouac's older brother Gerard—the family saint!—died of rheumatic fever at the age of nine, leaving Kerouac at four years old with a share of survivor's guilt and a haunting fear of death.

Kerouac ran track in high school and played football, which got him a scholarship to Columbia University. Relying on his speed to score touchdowns, he was hardly a team player and resented his coach for not using him enough. At Columbia, he set a record cutting classes because he was up all night at Minton's Playhouse, a jazz club in Harlem where a new musical mode was being announced by Dizzy Gillespie, Lester Young, Charlie Parker, Thelonius Monk, and a small group of other musicians. At Minton's, Kerouac was a white blip in an entirely African American setting. He may have missed many of his early morning classes at Columbia because Lester Young was bringing him to jam sessions after Minton's, but he understood that these musicians were stridently agitating with sound for the end of the harmonious dance music that had dominated jazz before the war with what was called swing—big bands led mostly by white orchestra leaders including the Dorsey brothers, Artie Shaw, and Benny Goodman. The jagged, edgy, asymmetrical, and sometimes ragged and raw dissonance of bebop, its inclination to veer into unprecedented directions and push against the conventional boundaries of what the jazz ear had been taught to accept, would profoundly affect Kerouac's own prose rhythms, his eagerness to improvise, his willingness to defy literary tradition.

Furthermore, the opportunity to watch and associate with musicians like Gillespie, who named a song "Kerouac," Lester Young, Monk, or Charlie Parker, the most rebelliously experimental figure in the jazz world, would subtly affect his own view of his own future possibilities. Parker was "whistling us to eternity" he would write in a poem, and Kerouac would remember his manic mood shifts and extemporaneous dexterity in *On the Road* and the time at Minton's "when he was flipped and walked around in a circle while playing." He would eulogize his friend Lester Young, an iconic figure in the history of jazz because of his smooth, velvety sound and the ability to lift his saxophone upward while playing, by comparing him in an extended riff in *Visions of Cody* to the magnificent flow of the Mississippi River.

After Pearl Harbor, Kerouac joined the navy only to be studied by naval psychiatrists as a "schizoid personality with angel tendencies" and discharged. He then began shipping out as a merchant seaman on six "bomb runs"—delivering munitions to England in waters patrolled by German submarines. He later recaptured the drama and boredom of those profoundly dangerous voyages in a piece called "Slobs of the Kitchen Sea."

By 1944, living with his parents in their tiny apartment in Queens, he was sleeping on the living-room couch and typing all day on a miniscule kitchen table. His mother was working in a shoe factory and the only job his father could get was setting type from midnight to dawn on Canal Street in Manhattan. When his father was afflicted with cancer of the spleen, Kerouac did not show up for the seventh merchant voyage he had signed on for, declaring that he wanted to care for his father. A German torpedo sank the ship and all hands were lost.

During this period, Kerouac was also sharing the apartment near Columbia with Burroughs and Ginsberg. Maintaining that "the only possible ethic is to do what one wants to do," Burroughs subjected Ginsberg to an amateur lay psychoanalysis, and led what Joyce Johnson calls "the libertine circle" in experiments with various drugs. Kerouac, with his deep filial connection to family, was less influenced by Burroughs than Ginsberg was.

For Kerouac, this was a moment of great creative growth as he attempted to purge his youthful excessiveness, to overcome an early tendency to use turgid symbolism, a voluptuous though uncontrolled lyricism, and an initial reluctance to write autobiographically. Kerouac was dissatisfied with the traditional form of his first novel, *The Town and the City*. In December 1946, when he was still writing *The Town and the City*, he would meet Neal Cassady, who would become a galvanizing subject for him as well as Allen Ginsberg.

A reform-school kid who read Proust and wanted to learn how to write, the "secret hero" of Ginsberg's poem "Howl," Cassady spoke in rapid discontinuities with a raw vernacular sound that Kerouac heard as a new energy for his fiction. "Neal's unique boplike way of speaking," as Johnson explains, "veering off his initial subject or the narrative line of an anecdote into a series of riffs or even riffs upon riffs, punctuated by percussive exclamations" excited Kerouac. When Kerouac read a twelve-thousand-word letter from Neal Cassady recounting some of his sexual exploits, he sensed the rush of energy that he would later exaggerate with such momentum and mythic resonance in *On the Road*.

In the Berg archive, Johnson found a kind of bridge between *The Town and the City* and *On the Road*, a fifty-seven-page manuscript written in a plain Joual about a forthright, ingenuous protagonist named Michel Bretagne. Kerouac believed his Celtic forbears came from Brittany—in Cornwall, right across the English Channel, some of them spoke a dialect called Kernouak—and Johnson identifies the voice Kerouac invents for Bretagne as the source of the style he employed with such power in *On the Road*.

The strong heart of *The Voice Is All* is Johnson's exploration of years of aborted attempts, Kerouac's struggle to find the voice and form he felt he needed for *On the Road*. "Something that you feel will find its own form," Kerouac predicted in his "List of Essentials," and his sheer release of emotion became an end in itself in a historical period marked by silence, apathy, and conformity. Ginsberg had this succinct recommendation and the other eighteen advisements on Kerouac's list on the headboard above his bed when he wrote "Howl" in 1955 because the notion represented a new direction for writing in the 1950s.

III. Listening

The critic Ann Douglas, reviewing Kerouac's *Selected Letters* in the *New York Times Book Review*, observed that "Kerouac's work represents the most extensive experiment in language and literary form undertaken by an American writer of his generation." That high praise is deserved.

The experimental adventurousness of *Visions of Cody*, a novel with Proustian and Joycean dimension, or even a more minor effort like *Doctor Sax*, or the bizarre love stories, *Tristessa* and *The Subterraneans*, illustrate the reach of Kerouac's imagination, one that was forever pursuing the limits of form so that no two of his fictions are really alike even as the voice remains characteristically Kerouac's: romantic, ebullient, despairing sometimes, underlined by the surging rhythmic urgency that governed his music.

The singer Tom Waits has explained that the reason so many musicians gravitate to Kerouac is that he is such a musical writer. The musical sounds of Kerouac's sentences, influenced by the bebop that Kerouac first heard in Minton's Playhouse in Harlem when he was a student at Columbia, are the key to Kerouac's accomplishment, and the passages I would have you hear from *On the Road*, *Visions of Cody*, *Desolation Angels*, or a half dozen of Kerouac's other novels would fill an anthology.

One soaring instance of the remarkable flights of language that Kerouac could create occurs near the end of part 2 of *On the Road*. Sal Paradise, his narrator, has just spent "the beatest time of my life" in San Francisco. He claims he is delirious, is out of money and without genuine friends, and like some vagrant is reduced to picking up cigarette butts on Market Street to empty into his pipe. As he passes a fish-and-chips eatery, its proprietress gives him a terrified look. He stops abruptly, "frozen with ecstasy," believing he had encountered the Dickinsian mother of a previous existence:

> And just for a moment I had reached the point of ecstasy that I always wanted to reach, which was the complete step across chronological time into timeless shadows, and wonderment in the bleakness of the mortal realm, and the sensation of death kicking at my heels to move on, with a phantom dogging its own heels, and myself hurrying to a plank where all the angels dove off and flew into the holy void of uncreated emptiness, the potent and inconceivable radiancies shining in bright Mind Essence, innumerable lotus-lands falling open in the magic mothswarm of heaven.

In an essay called "The Mystery of the Universe," Ginsberg saw Kerouac as "swimming in a sea of sound," intoxicated poetically by the ramifications and reverberations of language. The rhapsodic sweep and cascading momentum of this very long line that almost seems endless is characteristically Kerouac in its visionary spirituality and its central image of flying angels diving into a "holy void of uncreated emptiness."

Henry Miller, in his generous introduction to *The Subterraneans*, understood that Kerouac was always able to hear the "idiomatic lingo of his time—the swing, the beat, the disjunctive metaphoric rhythm which comes so fast, so wild, so scrimmaged, so unbelievably albeit delectably mad." The "magic mothswarm of heaven" passage is written with that extemporaneous idiomatic freedom that Miller praises while expressing the fundamentally religious pilgrimage of his journey.

The passage, with its relentless enjambment of eight clauses, can also be compared to the seething restless experimentalism of a virtuoso Lester Young on the saxophone providing one improvisational twist after another when accompanying Billie Holiday on "Lady Be Good." I would note here that although Kerouac's ideal was the jazz musician's spontaneity and the saxophonist's ability to extend the note with a prolonged breath, the second part of this line, after the diving angels, is not in the original 1951 scroll manuscript but added subsequently and clearly influenced by his study of Buddhism.

Kerouac had a remarkable memory and a phenomenal ear, and knew that listening is as important a function for the novelist as observation. When I was interviewing subjects for a documentary film on Kerouac in the early 1980s, I spoke to Paul Gleason, a former right fielder for the

Saint Petersburg Cardinals, a minor league team in Saint Petersburg, Florida, where Kerouac was living with his third wife and his mother in 1968. It was the end of a series of abrupt relocations—signs of a profound unhappiness.

Though writing was no longer pleasurable for him, Kerouac was working on a short novel about an African American runaway kid he named Pic. Gleason told me he was disturbed by the daily presence of a white man with a small notebook in the segregated bleacher section. He invited him for a drink after the game and offered him a season's pass to a seat behind the home team dugout. The white man—it was Jack Kerouac—refused, saying that he wasn't really watching the game, but listening to the dialectal qualities and intonations in the speech patterns of the people in the stands.

The story has a poignant resonance for me: Kerouac was far past his prime, like an athlete who has stayed in the game too long. But he was still intent on doing the work of the writer—*listening* to continue the music.

IV. Last Years

Kerouac once complained to his friend Neal Cassady that he had inherited the "curse of Melville." Always subject to drastic mood swings, as a young man of twenty-five, on New Year's Day 1948, he noted in a journal entry that he had reread his first novel, *The Town and the City*, and his opinion of it was similar to his view of himself: "Gleeful and affectionate one day, black with disgust the next." Nearly a decade later, the publication of *On the Road* and the controversy surrounding its reception marked a turning point for Kerouac, the beginning of a steep, downward trajectory.

When *On the Road* appeared, Kerouac was thirty-five; he would live for only another twelve years of alcoholism, precipitous decline, and diminution of his writing powers. Consuming over a quart of brandy a day for a decade, he had the honesty to record the nature of his addictions and what had become a poisonous paranoia in one his last novels, *Big Sur*, which was published in 1963.

In his last years of life, Kerouac never stopped writing, but it became more and more difficult. In 1956, the year before the publication of *On the Road*, Kerouac spent two months in total isolation working as a lookout on Desolation Peak in the Mount Baker National Forest in Washington, just south of the Canadian border. It is possible that some of the former resilience that once had allowed him to recover from his despair was dissipated by the terrors he imagined during his solitary vigil, terrors he would revisit powerfully in a late novel, *Desolation Angels*.

A few weeks before the publication of *On the Road* in 1957, Kerouac took a four-day bus trip with his mother to Orlando, Florida, and rented for forty-five dollars a month a small first-floor apartment in a weather-beaten cottage on Clouser Street with a backyard containing grapefruit and orange trees. It is coincidental, but the name of the street seems allegorical, a signal of closure: that like Stephen Crane, Nathaniel West, Scott Fitzgerald, or Sylvia Plath, Kerouac, too, would become one of the early casualties of American literature.

He lived at 1418 Clouser for much of the fall of 1957, working on the galleys of *The Subterraneans*, resisting the changes being proposed by his editor at Grove. He was writing poems on a new Royal standard typewriter and working on *The Dharma Bums*, a novel about his discovery of Buddhism, his friendship with the poet Gary Snyder, and their hikes into the Sierra Mountains.

With some of the money he had earned with *On the Road* he bought a house in Northport, Long Island, in 1958. There seems to have been a pronounced change in his consciousness after he was badly beaten when he had been "stumbling drunk" outside a Greenwich Village bar. He suffered a broken nose and a concussion, and he told Allen Ginsberg that he might have incurred some "brain damage . . . with the kindness valve clogged by injury." It is conjecture, of course, but this may have been the culminating blow to a body that had been once battered on the football field as a young man, and subsequently drained by vagrancy and excess.

Some of the fictions he had written during his years of literary anonymity were beginning to appear to a torrent of negative reception that troubled him as much as it was damaging. The establishment view was that Kerouac celebrated brutal instincts, and some critics used the minor thefts in *On the Road* as evidence of his sympathy for delinquency. David Dempsey, in the *New York Times*, claimed *The Subterraneans* "seeps out like sludge from a leaky drain pipe," and, in the same newspaper, the influential columnist J. Donald Adams dismissed Kerouac's sentences as "slaver" and said he was reminded of an "insistent and garrulous barroom drunk." The ultimate insult came from *Time* magazine, which pronounced Kerouac the "latrine laureate of hobohemia."

Kerouac began to rely on Dexamyl to write and asked friends for Benzedrine. He described what he called the "joyous disease" in a letter to Ginsberg of August 28, 1958, "My real problem is drinking. I drink alone and sometimes too much even alone." In the same letter he offered what seems like a crucial clue when he confessed that there was "no more fun in writing for me."

In the summer of 1960, Kerouac had an alcoholic breakdown in Big Sur, California, in his friend Lawrence Ferlinghetti's Bixby Canyon shack, which he would later describe in his novel *Big Sur*. In 1962, he confessed in a letter that "I am a hopeless paralyzed drunken mess and I don't know how long I am going to live, if I keep on like this." Photographs taken at this time document the way Kerouac was losing his former rugged look of bruised vulnerability and dark intensity, a Montgomery Clift movie star handsomeness. He began to put on weight, a distended unbroken belly beginning in his upper chest, jowls in his cheeks, and a fog in his eyes.

In the 1960s, he began making late-night desperate calls to former friends full of paranoid and delusional remarks. He was drinking a quart of brandy daily, and the equivalent of another quart in wine and beer chasers. He also began a series of peripatetic dislocations, a strange echo of the whirlwind journeys he had once made with Neal Cassady that revealed his restless dissatisfaction. In 1961, he moved back to Orlando to write *Big Sur*, and then back to Northport the next year after a relative tried to exploit him financially. In 1963 his paranoia and depression increased, and by 1964 he moved with his mother to Saint Petersburg, Florida.

In 1966, he moved to Hyannis, on Cape Cod, ending what he called his "southern sleep," and then back to his hometown of Lowell. He married for the third time, this time to a nurse named Stella Sampas, the younger sister of a childhood friend who had died in combat in World War II. He may have feared that he would predecease his mother and wanted to be sure someone would care for her.

The publication of Kerouac's final novel, *Vanity of Duluoz*, showed how drastically Kerouac's skills had declined. With his wife and mother, he moved yet again to Saint Petersburg in 1968. A year later, late in

October 1969, the small capillaries in his abdomen began to collapse and the bleeding could not be contained.

He was still writing at the end. Characteristically, when he felt the blood gurgling in his throat just before the ambulance arrived, he was sketching an observation into one of the little notebooks he always carried, practicing his craft to the end.

v. A Note on Walter Salles's Film

I've had very limited experience with the film world, but enough to realize that the writer is only initiating a process, that the screenplay will ultimately be revised by a committee, that actors may misinterpret your meaning, that the final product will emerge from the editing room. In 1980, a young West Coast filmmaker named John Antonelli asked me to write a screenplay for a documentary film on Jack Kerouac. I thought I could learn something about the medium and get paid for my efforts. I was also happy to hear that Antonelli had been born in Lowell and had a long interest in Kerouac.

When Allen Ginsberg invited me to participate in a weeklong celebration of the twenty-fifth anniversary of the publication of *On the Road* in Boulder, Colorado, I called Antonelli and asked him to bring his crew. The project could save a lot of time and money if we could shoot the interviews I had planned in Boulder, where many of those who had known Kerouac best would be assembled.

My script was too scrupulous, too anxious to account for too much, too complicated by a narrative flow and details more appropriate to the printed page, and Antonelli helped me to simplify and condense. I did most of the interviews in Boulder.

Then I left for Paris where I had been invited to teach a course on the Beats at a branch of the Sorbonne. Université Paris 8 was located in the working-class suburb of Saint-Denis, a remote dilapidated outpost with filthy facilities and students who were so liberated by the spirit of 1968 that they didn't need to attend classes or even receive academic grades. On four occasions, riding the metro to the university, however, I saw young people reading *Sur la Route*. I heard that a ninety-minute cut of Antonelli's film had been shown as a feature for weeks at an art house in Manhattan, the Bleecker Street Cinema, and that there had been long lines. Nationwide, it was featured in over a hundred other movie theaters.

When I returned to New York, I saw the film and was shocked. Without informing me, Antonelli had hired actors to play Kerouac, Cassady, and Ginsberg, and hammed the film into a docudrama. The worst scene sensationalized Lucien Carr's stabbing of David Kammarer with repeated, exaggerated thrusts, enough to fricassee a chicken. It wasn't Quentin Tarantino but it made me squirm.

I would never have signed on to collaborate on a docudrama, a form that to me only suggested television soap opera. Although I had been paid, however modestly, I might add, I felt somehow exploited. Many of the people I interviewed had been reluctant to talk on camera, but spoke because they had some trust in me. Was that now forfeited?

Eventually, when the shorter version of the film went to television and video, I realized that Antonelli's instincts might have been correct, that his film reached a large audience because of the corn—the acting was amateur, but there was a convincing voiceover provided by Peter Coyote. I believe that Antonelli's movie was the first on Kerouac; Lewis MacAdams's shorter, more traditional documentary followed. I learned a lot about the necessity of compression, how a filmed interview that lasted fifteen minutes could be edited into a succinct moment of highly distilled accuracy.

Walter Salles's film arrives after a long legacy of botched attempts to even begin a film. When *On the Road* was published in 1957 to the noise of a few favorable reviews and mostly angry denunciations by literary critics, Warner Brothers offered to option the novel for $110,000, and their offer included the opportunity for Kerouac to play Sal. The slick producer Jerry Wald had interested Twentieth Century Fox but wanted to incorporate the story of James Dean's mythic death in a car crash in an unlikely plot resolution about angry war veterans on a cross-country rampage. Wald's version might have confirmed Norman Podhoretz's malicious contention in an infamous *Partisan Review* piece called "The Know-Nothing Bohemians" that alleged that Kerouac couldn't write and that his interest was in "the poisonous glorification of the adolescent in American popular culture."

The actor Marlon Brando expressed interest in another version financed by Paramount but had just gotten married and never even took the trouble to read the novel. Kerouac's agent, Sterling Lord, made the mistake of prematurely rejecting the Warner Brothers offer, hoping to receive more from Twentieth Century Fox or Paramount. Kerouac could not accept Wald's violent distortion of his novel, and the often phlegmatic Brando was never genuinely in the mix. Subsequently, there was a proposal by the documentarian D. A. Pennebaker that never got financed. In 1978, after the success of *Apocalypse Now*, Francis Ford Coppola optioned the rights and over the ensuing decades tried to adapt the novel himself, and then commissioned screenplays by Barry Gifford, who had edited a valuable oral biography of Kerouac, and the novelist Russell Banks, who had met Kerouac in 1967.

Walter Salles's version has very little of Kerouac's music. His claim that "I had to betray the book in order to be faithful to it" is self-serving, a convenient rationalization in an age conditioned by the porn available to ten-year-olds after breakfast on their computers. His film presents us with a foggy surfeit of weed, cigarette smoke and booze, jazz and spastic dancing, at least six scenes that use Proust's *Swann's Way* as a pretentious prop, almost a joke, and lots of grunting, squealing fornication. The one virtue of the film is Eric Gautier's lyrical cinematography, in an almost improvisatory fluid manner shooting long drives through gorgeously panoramic vistas, past rushing streams, mountains, and swamps in quaint old cars, Hudsons, Studebakers, and Plymouths with curved backs.

There are cameos featuring Ginsberg as a gawky inquisitive geek and a remote Burroughs full of scorn, but little of the cascading rhythms of Kerouac's prose.

Some of the cameos of the figures Sal and Dean encounter—like the one of the "fag Plymouth" driver played with a smarmy brilliance by Steve Buscemi—seem dropped jerkily like Punch and Judy puppets into the narrative, desperate attempts to cover the high points of the novel in two hours.

José Rivera, the screenwriter, who may be projecting here, has Dean, in exchange for gas and food money, taking the male lead in a sexual encounter of torrid, pounding anal penetration with the effeminate driver of the Plymouth. Rivera is relying on the original scroll rather than the version of the novel actually published in 1957. It is a scene for which mainstream American publishing was unprepared at that time. Had the scroll version been published in 1951 when Kerouac submitted it to his editor, Robert Giroux, it would have probably had little success and at best only a cult following. Admirers of Proust and Joyce might have responded, but few readers were prepared for so experimental a fiction.

While Salles and Rivera can claim that, by relying on the scroll, they remain true to Kerouac's intentions, it is also a signal that the filmmakers, somewhat anachronistically, wanted to create their own jumbled story, using the novel as a sort of vague outline for their project.

Actually, it is this kind of invention that points to the dimensions of Salles's "betrayal" of Kerouac's intentions. Kerouac tended not to describe his characters' sexual encounters with the graphic and often unsettling insistence of William Burroughs. Indeed, Kerouac can be accused of a sweet coyness, a sentimental avoidance of the "Love has pitched its mansion in / The place of excrement" of Yeats's Crazy Jane. Kerouac sanitizes sex and alludes to it euphemistically. When Sal is intimate with a woman, nothing is usually described; instead, he follows most sexual conjunctions with an impossible metaphysical inquiry into its meaning, which may not be exactly what his partner desires to hear at that point. Like an orgy that has gone on much too long, Salles's film overcompensates for this shyness (an attribute of Kerouac's personality) with a relentlessness that becomes numbing and seems shallow.

I can't blame the actors who do the best they can. With the highly oversimplified screenplay they have to work with, like newspaper headlines without a supporting story, they exist in an atmosphere too thin to support life. I liked Viggo Mortensen, who captures Burroughs's acidic dryness; I think Kristen Stewart is better suited for vampire movies, but all she had to offer here was frequent moaning and a repeated sex squeal of porcine delight.

There is a fundamental difference between the medium of film, which rushes past the viewer on its own lurid terms, and the printed page where the reader can slow down, pause, reread, and reconsider. Come to think of it, almost every filmed version I've ever seen of a novel I loved fails to capture its magic and leaves me with a feeling of shallow flatness, a loss of dimension.

One of the worst examples I can recall is the Hollywood version of William Faulkner's *The Sound and the Fury* where a German actress (who was probably sleeping with the producer) with a thick Teutonic accent could not convince me that she was Quentin Compson's mother, a Southern aristocrat with a characteristic pronunciation, accent, and drawl. An even better example would be the sordid Hollywood version of Kerouac's *The Subterraneans*, a novel about his love affair with an African American woman that was quite radical as subject matter when he wrote it in 1953, when antimiscegenation laws existed in over half the country. In 1960, Metro-Goldwyn-Mayer optioned the novel for fifteen thousand dollars, money Kerouac used to purchase the house in Northport, Long Island, for his mother. The filmmakers treated the novel as an opportunity for caricature, casting Leslie Caron posing as a very white French girl to play Kerouac's lover in a film that only displayed the Beats as caught between sensational self-indulgence and twisted despair. Salles's film, though not nearly as cartoonish or gross, is similar. The shame of the film is that it exists only as a fulfillment of the media misrepresentation of the Beats as hedonistic escapists or even nihilists in a hurry to reach oblivion.

Readers of *On the Road* are often unable to see its traditional roots, a patterning as in the refrain of "everything is collapsing," the deliberate repetition of the color red or the words "ragged," "bent," "sad," or "zoom," or the suggestion of a loss of a former identity when Sal temporarily loses consciousness after a nap in a hotel in Des Moines early in the novel. The subtext of *On the Road* as a novel is a spiritual searching for a lost father alluded to in its final line, an ecstatic plunging into a mysteriously undefined "IT," a vision of deity in a time when existentialist philosophers were pronouncing the death of God.

With no sense of irony, Kerouac systematically uses religious terms throughout his novel, which is why he calls his narrator Sal Paradise. Dean is a "mad monk peering through the manuscript of snow"; the word "pilgrimage" recurs, as do "ghost," "vision," "angel," and "holy." Seen intermittently in the book, prophetic, wandering hobo types, such as Hyman Solomon in Testament, Virginia, or the tall old man with flowing white hair who suddenly appears at the end of the novel to poignantly "moan for man" and trudges off, all cohere to form what T. S. Eliot would have called the "objective correlative" of the novel, the images that implicitly render its thematic message. This pattern of religious imagery prepares us for the burning-bush spectacular view of God in the heavens that Sal sees in part 3 of the novel: "As we crossed the Colorado-Utah border I saw God in the sky in the form of huge gold sunburning clouds above the desert that seemed to point a finger at me and say, "Pass here, and go on, you're on the road to heaven." The scene, one of a number of moments when the issue of God is raised in the novel, flashes by, making it less explicit. Sal tells us he is in a car being driven by two pimps, and he is as fascinated by the passing scenery of desert detritus, rotting old covered wagons and an abandoned Coca-Cola stand, as he is in the subjective mystery of this annunciation. In its way, the scene and Sal's peering into the desert are reflections of what Kerouac once described as a "special spirituality" infusing his characters.

The recurrent pattern of a search for some significance in life, the yearning for the comfort of some divine connection is one Kerouac would continue with his study of Buddhism and his popularization of its values in *The Dharma Bums*, and it might even seem anomalous in an era when news of the Holocaust was being released. Nothing in the film captures the agony of this spiritual dimension. Instead, the frenetic self-destructiveness and rollicking glee of these flatly portrayed figures seems destined for removed voyeurs picking the popcorn from their teeth. The film is basically a travelogue on the surface, an exploration of the vast spaces and majestic natural landscapes of the United States, so it probably will not even serve to extend the audience for Kerouac's novel, which already—like John Steinbeck's *The Grapes of Wrath*—inevitably begins to seem dated, tied to the concerns of its particular historical moment.

CHAPTER 10　　**GINSBERG TODAY**

who passed through universities with radiant cool eyes hallucinating Arkansas and Blake-light tragedy among the scholars of war, who were expelled from the academies for crazy & publishing obscene odes on the windows of the skull.
—Allen Ginsberg, "Howl"

I. Geniusville

For the literary biographer or the historian, journals or diaries, letters, early photographs, and manuscripts all are potentially invaluable resources that can help determine the origins or evolutionary path of an artist. An arrangement of diary entries, dream records, early attempts at poems, brief essays, ambitious reading lists, and letters to mentors and friends, Allen Ginsberg's *The Book of Martyrdom and Artifice: First Journals and Poems, 1937–1952* is a young man's miscellany that demonstrates an anxiously probing unveiling of the self.

Ginsberg was, perhaps, the best-known American poet since Robert Frost, and his journal is replete with surprising observations, what Norman Mailer once called "advertisements," the nascent writer announcing himself to an unconcerned world: "If some future historian or biographer wants to know what the genius thought and did in his tender years, here it is. I'll be a genius of some kind or other, probably in literature. I really believe it. Either I'm a genius, I'm egocentric, or I'm slightly schizophrenic. Probably the first two." That astonishing prediction was written on May 22, 1941, when Ginsberg was almost fifteen, a ninety-five-pound adolescent living with his poet/schoolteacher father Louis in Paterson, New Jersey, and his mother Naomi, who was shuttling between "a dark room curtain closed soundless half year" and a series of painful psychiatric confinements at Greystone Park State Hospital.

Ginsberg's comment bears some comparison to Ezra Pound's presumptuous resolution that by the age of fifteen "I would know more about poetry than any man living." Pound, incidentally, was called the "professor" by his teasing prep school classmates. The first word of Ginsberg's Eastside High School yearbook description is "professor," followed by the boasting designation: "philosopher and genius of the class." Many years later, in the 1960s, Ginsberg would visit the older poet in Venice, Italy, to play for him on a tape recorder the music of Bob Dylan and John Lennon. It was then, ending the lock of his famous decade of silence, that Pound apologized for his "stupid, suburban prejudice of anti-Semitism."

The comparison between Pound, the midwife and manufacturer of modernism, and Ginsberg, the connective link of the Beat Generation, may be cogent when considering the enormous flair of which each poet was capable. Both had the impulsive capacity for theatrical gesture—Ginsberg on the railroad tracks in Rocky Flats, Colorado, blocking a shipment of plutonium, or participating in an exorcism on the grave of Senator Joseph McCarthy. Both Pound and Ginsberg could propose the defining existential semaphore that detractors would condemn as ego projection and beneficiaries would proclaim as inspired vision.

Ginsberg gives us very little record of his early years in his journal—there is much more by implication in his great elegy for Naomi, "Kaddish." Most of *The Book of Martyrdom and Artifice* is devoted to the formative Columbia University period during the Second World War and immediately after when the Beat Generation coalesced as a small underground band bent on replacing the stuffiness of literature with more immediate confessional concerns. Ginsberg provides an extensive character analysis of his new classmate Lucien Carr, who feels a desperate need to prove his own genius though he is short of the requisite talent. Carr introduces Ginsberg to William S. Burroughs, living on Bedford Street in the Village and working as a bartender, who advises Ginsberg with his typically acidic cynicism that "art is just a three letter word."

His new friend Jack Kerouac, a fullback on the Columbia University football team, sees Burroughs as "an authentic devil," an observation (among others) entered in Ginsberg's journal in Kerouac's own hand. However, when Carr murders Burroughs's childhood friend David Kammerer, Burroughs, Kerouac, and Ginsberg, separately and collaboratively, tried to make art of it.

If the word "art" is linguistically related to the "artifice" of Ginsberg's somewhat ponderous title, the masochism of "martyrdom" is probed in one of the little moral assays that punctuate the journal of youthful decadence and experimentation and in a little poem called "Gang Bang" in which he recalls a threesome with Kerouac and "Dionysiac Lucy" who "coyly giggles in the night." Frequently, he thinks about Arthur Rimbaud, though more for his political posture than his willful disequilibrium.

At the same time he records his own initiations with Wilhelm Reich's orgone box and with drugs like marijuana and Benzedrine. Almost casually, he notes that he has injected heroin for six consecutive nights with Burroughs, explaining that at least in his case it had not become addictive. Characteristically, all this is related in a charming manner though incongruously juxtaposed to how he had "begun to work up a liking for Dryden," a typical English major's reflection as if some literature were medicinal or potentially nourishing, bran flakes for the soul. If anything, the journal reveals just how literary and self-conscious the studious young Ginsberg was.

One key element that may not be fully visible in *The Book of Martyrs*, though, is the extent to which Ginsberg was struggling to overcome the shell of conventional respectability, the model provided by his father, who taught classes and expressed himself as a poet with decorously neo-Victorian rhymes and iambics. In his 1977 introduction to Burroughs's *Junky*, Ginsberg noted that he was "at the time a nice Jewish boy with one foot in the middle-class, writing careful revised rhymed metaphysical verse." Then he adds a subversive "—not quite" as if to punctuate the extent of his own conflict between family expectation and the new directions he would pursue.

In the *New Yorker*, I saw a photograph of the Ginsberg family taken decades later by Richard Avedon on the occasion of the publication of a book of Louis Ginsberg's poems. There are five men, including Ginsberg, on the far right side of the black-and-white photograph. They are holding desert plates and coffee. They look related and very similar: his father, his older brother Eugene, and two uncles are all in eyeglasses with rapidly receding hairlines, all wearing dark suits, white shirts, and ties. They could be Wall Street brokers or attorneys like Eugene. Allen's bow tie is the only sign of nonconformity though it isn't exactly subversive. With his arm around Eugene, Allen is wearing the uniform dark suit, tie, and white shirt, though his suit seems baggier than the others and he probably purchased all of his garments at the Salvation Army where he always got his clothing. Allen, however, looks different: he has a full beard and his curly hair is uncut, flowing down to his shoulders. He is also wearing mandala beads, the Buddhist equivalent of the rosary, a clear sign of how much he had departed from the straight path of his kin. *The Book of Martyrdom and Artifice* provides the early glimmers of that divergence.

The element of martyrdom was less a function of letters than life. As Ginsberg declares in a poem called "Kerouac in the Hospital," "there always / Is a wound."

For the Beats in general, as unknown voyagers in W. H. Auden's more polished Age of Anxiety, the issue of martyrdom may have had a ritual and mythic dimension. In the kind of formulation Edmund Wilson proposed in his "The Wound and the Bow" essay on Philoctetes, where the artist's incapacity leads to cultural discovery or resource, Ginsberg's understanding—he was only twenty-one—was that "as life wounds us, so art must wound us." Later, this would be confirmed by Kerouac, who saw that Naomi was the profound source of Ginsberg's "wound," a subterranean creative urge that found its ultimate expression in a poem like "Kaddish."

But in the context of Ginsberg's undergraduate years, the immediate peril of martyrdom as a hyperromantic dead end was best exemplified by his obsessive pursuit of Neal Cassady in the winter of 1947. As a reform-school delinquent from Denver with enormous masculine charisma, a highly pitched sex drive and a sixteen-year-old wife, Lu Anne, Cassady would become Kerouac's subject in *On the Road* and *Visions of Cody* and represented a whirling antiliterary dynamism that galvanized Kerouac and Ginsberg.

As uncertain of his own sexuality as he was unsure of his poetic capacities, Ginsberg embroiled himself in a very carnal liaison with Cassady, whose heat and doldrums are typical of the energies of the journal, as the entry for February 1948 suggests: "It is unfortunate that as yet I am unable to woo him with my speech, but, in bed, merely discuss things with earnestness. Try him laying me again; try breast to breast position. Try 69 again, coming both at once. Try sitting on his chest and making him blow me. Try laying his mouth." The earnestness reminds us of the awkwardness of youth and it seems absurd given the graphic and confessional quality of the passage, which continues and speaks directly to the transgressive and transformational goals of the Beats. Like the surrealists in France, they saw *amour fou*, mad or crazy love reached through the cultivation of audacious sexual behavior, as a route to a transporting delirium that could transcend conditioning and lead to change.

Ginsberg and Cassady may have been the two great talkers of their generation—and Kerouac alludes to that rapturous excitement with the elated conversations of Carlo Marx and Dean Moriarty early in *On the Road*—but Cassady's inclinations, insofar as Ginsberg was concerned, grew more from a desire for manipulation and curiosity than ardor. The two young men travel on a "sacramental honeymoon" to New Waverly, Texas, where Burroughs was shooting his weapons daily and busy growing marijuana secreted between rows of alfalfa. Rejected in Texas as a lover, Ginsberg shipped out on a merchant marine vessel to Dakar.

The dance of desire and disappointment with Cassady forms the lustful crescendo of Ginsberg's journal, though there are other peaks that follow: the Blake visions that inspired Ginsberg to believe that he belonged to a prophetic, bardic tradition; the troubles caused by his friendship with Herbert Huncke, another catalyst underworld figure, that landed Ginsberg in a psychiatric hospital for a year; the mentorship with William Carlos Williams, who responded to Ginsberg's prose notebooks and saw the latent poems in them.

One might wonder, with all the self-revelation and exposure in this diary, why Ginsberg does not allow more than a glimmer of Burroughs's lay psychoanalysis of him in 1944, or any view of their sexual mingling and subsequent incompatibility. Nakedness, for the Beats, was part of the process of self-discovery, but Ginsberg was only twenty-two in 1944 when he lived with Burroughs and Kerouac in Joan Vollmer's apartment on 115th Street and Broadway, which is one sign of why the journal is such a remarkable accomplishment.

II. A Literary Excursus

Writers become known as much for what they see and say as their manner—the way they find to express their visions. What we call the writer's "voice," that singular sound as individual as a fingerprint and as particular as a snowflake, is rarely a birthright. Usually it results from a gestatory and sometimes an imitative period that can take years; or decades in the case of writers like Conrad, Henry Miller, or Burroughs.

For the critic Harold Bloom, the influence of the past is often as much a source of anxiety as inspiration, and an unconscious or deliberate "misreading" of the past serves both to wean the artist from the dependence of imitation and to yoke the past into a more usable, renewable present. One illustration of this dynamic is Ezra Pound, who begins his career with a vicious denunciation of Whitman "who seems to be conferring a philanthropic complacency on the race." Pound would resolve his detestation of Whitman's romantic affirmation and offer his amends in an early poem, "A Pact," at the end of which he declares:

> I come to you as a grown child
> Who has had a pig-headed father;
> I am old enough now to make friends.
> It was you that broke the new wood,
> Now is a time for carving.

Though his motto was "Make It New," Pound assiduously studied the past, particularly Confucius, twelfth-century Provencal poetry, and such poets of the Italian Renaissance as Cavalcanti. It may be fashionable to deny it, but most artists seem umbilically connected to the past. As T.S. Eliot, who was Pound's first acolyte, stipulated it so eloquently in his essay "Tradition and the Individual Talent," the writer selects a personal canon of preceding figures whom the artist admires and from whom he or she has learned some essential element of technique or spiritual quality. In "The Waste Land," Eliot would quote without attribution certain of the writers he most admired such as Spenser, John Donne, Shakespeare, and Andrew Marvell, whose heroic line "But at my back I always hear / Time's wingèd chariot hurrying near" Eliot would twist to "But at my back in a cold blast I hear / The rattle of the bones, and chuckle spread from ear to ear." "Immature poets imitate," Eliot famously declared, but "mature poets steal"—though his poem was more an illustration of ironic reinterpretation than literary theft or plagiarism. Pound, the dedicatee of the poem, declared it was "about enough to make the rest of us shut up shop."

Ginsberg was aware of the enormous impact of "The Waste Land" as one of the signifying touchstones of Anglo-American modernism, though like Kerouac he found Eliot's fear and deliberate avoidance of emotional release desiccating. For Ginsberg, the crucial predecessor was Walt Whitman.

Whenever I visited Ginsberg in his tenement flat on East Twelfth Street in lower Manhattan, I commented on the portrait of Whitman hanging on the bedstead like an old friend. Whitman made many appearances in Ginsberg's poems: in "A Supermarket in California," one of the poems in his breakthrough book, *Howl*, Ginsberg warmly imagines he sees Whitman in the supermarket's meat section poking through the refrigerator while eyeing the grocery boys. Poignantly, he addresses Whitman as his father, his "lonely old courage-teacher." In a letter to his own Columbia University mentor, Mark Van Doren, he acknowledged that Whitman was a "vast mountain so big I never saw him before." In a notebook draft version of "America," another poem in *Howl*, he wrote, "I Allen Ginsberg Bard out of New Jersey take up the laurel tree cudgel from Walt Whitman." In a letter to Kerouac, he buoyantly declared that his purpose was to "go rewrite Whitman for the entire universe" and the first step occurs in the poem "Howl."

"Howl" was written in 1955, when Ginsberg was twenty-nine years old. Except for editing the Columbia University undergraduate literary review, winning the support of Mark Van Doren and the poet William Carlos Williams, who lived in Ginsberg's hometown, Ginsberg was unknown and completely unsuccessful in finding any audience for his work or getting published.

Whitman's situation had been similar. An autodidact from a poor family who had been forced to leave the charity school in Brooklyn when he was eleven, he had been a messenger, learned to set type as an apprentice in the printing trade, taught school, spent a decade as a newspaper reporter. He reached a pinnacle of his profession as editor of the *Brooklyn Daily Eagle*, one of the largest newspapers in the country. Suddenly disillusioned, he abandoned his career, moved back into the family home in Brooklyn, and began working as a part-time carpenter. In 1853, at the age of thirty-four, he also began writing a long poem of 1,336 lines, which he divided into fifty-two sections, like a secular bible for each week of the year.

In the spring of 1855, he set the type for the poem on a borrowed hand press, ran off 795 copies, and, with a horse and cart, brought them to the bindery. He spent the next three decades promoting the poem he later called "Song of Myself" and the rest of his growing body of work. In the summer of 1855, when he sent "Song of Myself" to Emerson in Concord, Massachusetts, Emerson replied that he found it "the most extraordinary piece of wit & wisdom that America has yet contributed."

This high praise was virtually the only recognition Whitman would receive; most of the reviewers reviled the poem. One of them, John Greenleaf Whittier, puritanically threw it into his fireplace in disgust; another advised suicide. The literary minister Rufus Griswold, who had defamed Edgar Allan Poe, declared Whitman's poem "a mass of stupid filth" in the high-toned *New York Criterion*. Charles A. Dana found the poem full of "grotesque and uncouth" thoughts. James Russell Lowell, at Harvard, denounced the poem as "solemn humbug" and did his best to keep it off the university shelves. The poet Thomas Bailey Aldrich called Whitman "a charlatan" and predicted that his poem would never survive unless preserved in "a quart of spirits in an anatomical museum." In Boston, the critic for the *Intelligencer* determined that Whitman was a brute and a lunatic, capable only of bombastic egotism and vulgarity. Whitman anticipated such negative responses. In his own pseudonymous review of his own poem he acknowledged that while it would appear as devilish to some, it would be seen as divine by others. During his life, Whitman had only a small cult following, mostly in London, and his fame would grow posthumously.

In 1955, exactly a century after Whitman self-published "Song of Myself" on the Fourth of July, Ginsberg wrote "Howl," and its initial appearance in San Francisco was in an impression of twenty-five mimeographed copies. Ginsberg's poem was a response to Whitman, not homage as much as reinterpretation for a very different age. Whitman could still believe in progress and the myth of the "American Dream." Almost daily, when he was writing his poem in 1854, he journeyed from Brooklyn by ferry and horse-drawn cart to midtown Manhattan to what was called the Crystal Palace, a giant display of such American inventiveness as the Otis elevator. Whitman understood and accepted how the elevator would transform the city he loved into a place of towering vertical spires. For Ginsberg the city would become "robot apartments" with "a thousand blind windows"—his views were less positive, infected by what he saw as a coming ecological disaster, systematic entropy, and a materialistic craving that would ultimately corrupt goodwill.

Yet the correspondences between the poems are evident: both poets use free verse rather than any conventionally acceptable metrical arrangement, and a line so long it approached the density of prose; both repeat the initial word of a line relentlessly, an Old Testament device creating a rhythm that did not depend on end rhyme; most significantly, both poets had the epic intention to explain a nation to itself and the world.

The differences are also evident in Ginsberg's angrier tone: instead of celebrating himself, as Whitman announced in his provocative first line, Ginsberg would record the suffering and magnanimity of his generation "destroyed by madness, starving hysterical naked." Ginsberg would frequently invert, telescope, or magnify a quality he found in Whitman, who presented himself as "hankering, gross, mystical, nude," certainly a weird enough image for his nineteenth-century readers.

In Whitman's time, poetry was a genteel art. Poets did not use the diminutive "Walt" instead of Walter, and in fact most of them required at least three names—like Alfred Lord Tennyson who published *Maud* in England in 1855, or Henry Wadsworth Longfellow who published *Hiawatha* in the same year. Longfellow's middle name, incidentally, testified to his stature as a descendant of a very established American family, wealthy enough to have endowed our first museum in Hartford, Connecticut. Married to an heiress, Longfellow enjoyed a sinecure at Harvard.

Poets like Longfellow usually wore a jacket, vest, and tie, not the workingman's coarse attire and brazen Quaker hat displayed in the daguerreotype prefacing Whitman's poem. The image suggests insolent provocation and Whitman could have been predicting Ginsberg's more turbulent arrival when he declared in one of his self-admiring moments, "What living and buried speech is always vibrating here . . . what howls restrained by decorum." The violation of convention and what was considered poetic propriety was a key consideration in both "Song of Myself" and "Howl."

Whitman's line appears near the end of the eighth part of the poem, one of the first catalogs he presents with so panoramically expansive a lens, a listing of what he saw in the dirt streets of Manhattan, including suicides, prostitutes, and the victims of venereal disease, and much of what Victorian England and America would not allow as suitable subject matter for poetry. What is considered distasteful is subject to condemnation as impropriety. The notion of what is proper, however, is often a function of the word "property," which comes from the same root. So established authority determines the dress code as well as the subject matter of poetic discourse.

Less dandified than Baudelaire's flaneur but also promenading, more like a reporter recording, Whitman observes the variety and procession of American life with empathy and amplitude, merging with everyone he encounters, whether the runaway slave, the immigrants on the wharf, the carpenter whose plane "whistles its wild ascending lisp." Although Ginsberg panoptically employs Whitman's sweeping antihierarchical perspective, and the first part of "Howl" is a catalog, what he relates is more desperately driven, shattering, and despairing, and what he discovers is taboo; the outcast and self-exiled pariahs with whom he sympathizes are his friends and "best minds."

The velocity of Ginsberg's lines, however, and the ensuing momentum, represents yet another point of connection to Whitman: "Myself moving forward then and now and forever / Gathering and showing more always and with velocity. . . ." Whitman often uses the present tense and the participial case "Speeding through space . . . speeding through heaven and stars" because like a dervish of poetry "the whirling and whirling is elemental within me." Throughout his poem, Ginsberg echoes this rapid movement: "yacketayakking screaming vomiting whispering facts. . . ." "Rocking and rolling in the midnight solitude. . . ." Ginsberg suggests a similar excitement, which is heightened by a mutual reliance on exclamation points.

One of the themes implicit in Whitman's poem is the aspiration for a cultural opening, crossing social and moral boundaries when they were restrictive, relying less on the formality of Victorian manners, rigid hierarchical values, and the separations caused by social class and more on the spontaneity of intuition, qualities suggested by the lines from "Song of Myself" that Ginsberg proposed as a general epigraph for his collection: "Unscrew the locks from the doors! / Unscrew the doors themselves from their jambs!" Whitman promised to "sound my barbaric yawp over the roofs of the world" while in Ginsberg's poem we are surprised by his drugged, angelheaded hipsters "floating across the tops of cities." Early in Whitman's poem we see him responding to a universal imperative to "urge and urge and urge" while Ginsberg's hobo visionaries find themselves hurtling across the country whose geographical expanse Whitman so admired in "boxcars, boxcars, boxcars."

The parallels become more pronounced when we consider the sexuality in each poem, both unprecedented for their eras. Though both poets write in a vernacular, natural voice, understanding Emerson's notion that "language is fossil poetry," Whitman, necessarily, is more veiled in his ambiguity and homoerotic undertones as in the poem where a woman secretly admires a group of male bathers. While he admits that forbidden voices of sex and lust speak through his poem, references like the "soft tickling genitals" of the wind, the "soprano who convulses me like the climax of my lovegrip," or even the "spirit of my own seminal wet" will seem timid to us, unless we realize such references would have been regarded as at best indelicate, improper, and even obscene in the middle of the nineteenth century.

Although there are sequences that seem to mix masturbation with the beauty of the sunrise, and in section twenty-eight of his poem Whitman seems assaulted by licentiously "prurient provokers" leaving him helpless before a "red marauder" and his "floodgates" are released, such allusions pale before Ginsberg's graphic accounts of sodomizing motorcyclists, a sexuality that conflagrates "with dreams, with drugs, with waking nightmares, alcohol and cock and endless balls."

While such moments caused the public trial of Ginsberg's poem for obscenity in San Francisco in 1956, the spiritual parallels between the two poems may be as threatening. Whitman claims his own armpits exude a scent more effective than prayer, that copulation seems no more rank to him than death, that his own head and semen are worth "more than churches or bibles or creeds." Sacrilegiously, he proclaims his own divinity, making "holy whatever I touch or am touched from." Such extreme sentiments connect with Ginsberg's even more outrageous assertions, particularly in the prayerlike "Footnote to Howl" where he repeats the word "holy" seventy-three times with a chanting, at times ranting, rhapsodic, and exclamatory extravagance.

Whitman, a perfect transcendentalist, suggests he sees God in every object, but for Ginsberg the madman, the bum, and the "unknown buggared and suffering beggars" are as holy as the seraphim, those child angels surrounding the throne of the Old Testament God of the Jews. Whitman maintains that no part of his body, "not an inch or a particle of an inch is vile," but for Ginsberg even the "tongue and cock and hand and asshole holy." Surely such equations are the most excessive claims any poet has ever made?

Lawrence Ferlinghetti was in the audience when Ginsberg first read "Howl" and immediately wrote to him, offering to publish it and paraphrasing Emerson's famous letter to Whitman: "I greet you at the beginning of a great career." Ferlinghetti had the poem printed in England and two thousand copies were seized by San Francisco Customs police. The *Howl* trial was the trigger that publicized the Beat Generation and declared it as an active presence in American culture. I don't agree with Lawrence Ferlinghetti's assertion that the ideas of the poem were so in the air that had Ginsberg not written it, someone else would have, but what is clear is that it led the way for *On the Road*.

There is historical irony in the recognition that Whitman was the source. Though Whitman never had a large following during his lifetime, late in the nineteenth century he was the subject of censorious pressures because of the homosexual implications in some of his poems. His collection, *Leaves of Grass*, was attacked by Anthony Comstock, whose Society for the Suppression of Vice seized thousands of books and was responsible for the 1873 Comstock Law that gave the Post Office the power to ban and seize whatever they regarded as indecent. Comstock denounced Whitman's work as the attempt to "clothe the most sensual thoughts with the flowers and fancy of poetry, making the lascivious conception only more insidious and demoralizing." Such attacks only made readers curious and extended Whitman's audience.

III. Epistles of Fame

"Is there a great mad wave of fame crashing over our ears?" Allen Ginsberg asked Jack Kerouac after the publication of *On the Road* in a letter from Amsterdam in the fall of 1957. The query was prescient; the image apt. Ginsberg would learn how to surf the wave his image evokes while Kerouac would capsize and drown.

The publication of *Jack Kerouac and Allen Ginsberg: The Letters* is a signal literary event. Most authors' letters are never published, not even by university presses, so the fact that as large a commercial enterprise as Viking Press undertook this project reflects broad interest. The twenty-year dialogue the collection represents is often elated with aspiration, extravagant, even hyperbolic with language that can soar for its own sake, but other times plunges into bleak despair—"God knows what oblivion we'll wind up in like unpopular Melvilles," Ginsberg ponders.

The letters begin at the time the two young men met as undergraduates at Columbia University during the Second World War and continue until a few years before Kerouac's death in Saint Petersburg, Florida, in 1969. Probing, always candid, they are often composed with an elegant studious manner as if the muse were peering over the writer's shoulder; sometimes they explode with the rash, irrepressible vigor of "Wow!" vernacular that the early critics of *On the Road* deplored. The Beats had been greeted by American media as the barbarous buffoons at the cultural gates, but the letters demonstrate a committed literary perspective: allusions to Melville and Whitman, Balzac and Dostoyevsky, Pound and Eliot, Joyce and Henry Miller serve to establish the tradition they continue.

Some of the letters present the daring literary ambitions of unknowns quite convinced of their potential, especially Ginsberg's attempts to win recognition for friends such as William Burroughs. Other letters, written from Mexico in the early 1950s, reveal how their views were deepened by living in a country "beyond Darwin's chain," as Kerouac put it. Fortified with tequila and peyote, Kerouac emphasized the pastoral Mexico, and both men saw it as a foil to an American obsession with acquisition and consumption. Occasionally, the letters crawl with the ballast of Buddhist theory; inevitably, they race again with reports of the latest recklessness of friends such as Neal Cassady and Gregory Corso. Later letters, more dangerously, are full of the hysteria that overwhelmed Kerouac after the notoriety of *On the Road*. As he reported to Ginsberg, with some of the cascading presumption that galvanized his prose, repeating what he had announced in a television interview: "I am waiting for God to show his face."

The Letters are one register of a cluster of recent Beat tributes: the compelling exhibition at the New Museum in lower Manhattan of Brion Gysin's (Burroughs's "cut-up" collaborator) artwork, the exposition of Ginsberg's photographs at the National Gallery in Washington, and the biopic about the public trial of Ginsberg's *Howl*, a censorship spectacle that identified the Beat Generation at the time of the publication of *On the Road*.

That Ginsberg seems situated in the center of this attention is not surprising. With *Howl* he exploded the claustrophobia of convention in American poetry so that even Robert Lowell turned from the elite formalism of *Lord Weary's Castle* to the more confessional direction of *Life Studies*. But Ginsberg's work had an even broader impact with regard to propriety, abandoning the polite timidities of writing for an audience of the genteel few for the most overt social commentary since Whitman. In *Howl* and other works, he changed the nature of American poetry and our expectations of what a poet could do. And he didn't just write poetry, he performed it with a dramatic presence, a sheer vocal power and exuberance we had not heard or seen since Dylan Thomas. His dynamic rhythmic momentum and his insistence on performing with musicians were factors leading to rap and hip-hop.

Some of his influence has clearly been extraliterary, such as his prolonged involvement with the principles and practices of Tibetan Buddhism, or as exemplified by the famous early 1960s Avedon photograph of Ginsberg and his lover, Peter Orlovsky, in a nude embrace that was posted all over the streetlamps of San Francisco and became a trigger for the gay rights movement. It is no wonder that there continues to be such sustained interest in his poems.

"I would call that man poet," Henry Miller once declared, "who is capable of profoundly altering the world." Ginsberg put his "queer shoulder to the wheel," as he promised in his poem "America," to do his best to better the world. Believing that things could change, that no authority was absolute, he was a main organizer of the counterculture. Our principal spokesperson for candor in an age of secrecy, deceit, and denial, he would offer his remarks on censorship or psychedelics to congressional committees or *People* magazine. "Well, while I'm here I'll do the work," he wrote in "Memory Gardens," his elegy for Kerouac:

> And what's the work?
> To ease the pain of living.
> everything else, drunken
> dumbshow.

Ginsberg's engagement with what Whitman called the "procreant urge of the world" was central, continuing, consuming—and it made him a zeitgeist phenomenon.

IV. Totemic Moments

Ginsberg documented his life with pictures as well as words. The National Gallery of Art show was curated by Sarah Greenough, who introduces its catalog, *Beat Memories*, with a comprehensive account of Ginsberg's place in the Beat Generation and his fascination with photography. His first pictures were taken with a box camera at the age of fifteen of his mother, Naomi, in Greystone Park Psychiatric Hospital in New Jersey.

His photographs of his friends—his "funny, family photos," as he called them—are absorbed with warm intimacy. The early 1950s shots, such as the one taken of William Burroughs standing next to a sphinx at the Metropolitan Museum of Art, or the classic brooding shot of Kerouac with a railroad brakeman's manual sticking out of his pocket on a fire escape outside Ginsberg's window on East Seventh Street on the Lower East Side of Manhattan, were drugstore prints taken with a Kodak Retina camera purchased for thirteen dollars in a pawn shop. Probably the best portraits of the Beats (who have been, after all, the most frequently photographed of American writers), they exist as what Ginsberg called "totemic moments": "when you notice something clearly and see it vividly." The objects in each photograph, sphinx and brakeman's manual, serve to illuminate some mysterious quality in the subject.

Ginsberg's photographs illustrate the Beat priority on spontaneity, the expression of feeling with autobiographical immediacy. As Greenough so cogently observes, they are "as natural as talking or writing" like the lyrical moment when Ginsberg captured his companion, Peter Orlovsky, in a naked handstand in the fields at their old farm in Cherry Valley, New York. Ginsberg's snapshot poetic is based on what he has termed an "unpremeditated awareness," influenced by the mentorial relationship he had with his friend, the photographer Robert Frank and resulting in a casual unselfconsciousness, a trust in chance, a belief that there is grace in the ordinary, even if convention sees it as ugly, a sympathetic acceptance of the human condition without judgment, pose, or artifice. The touchingly nude self-portraits he took near the end of his life exemplify this.

His purpose as poet and photographer began with the sharpest focus on a moment in time, "a little shiver of eternal space." "The poignancy of a photograph comes from looking back to a fleeting moment in a floating world," Ginsberg wrote in a previous collection published by Twelvetrees Press in 1990. Mutability is so often the poet's saddest subject. So the poignancy expresses a haunting yearning for what would otherwise be irrecoverable, or at best a memory blurred by time, and his comment underlines his belief that ordinary experience has a sacred quality to be cherished because life is so transient.

Another, deeper dimension was achieved after 1983 when Ginsberg began using Robert Frank's printer Sid Kaplan and writing on the bottom of the prints. Frank would say that a photograph was only paper, and he would write over some of his prints as well. Ginsberg had discovered this means of expanding the significance of a photograph by visiting with photographer Berenice Abbott, but in his hand the words, as Sarah Greenough notes, "seemed to tumble over one another with rich exuberance." Often, a phrase leaps out of his scrawled commentary with the shock of epiphany: for example, the note for a 1953 photograph of a homeless man on East Seventh Street whom he characterizes as a "shopping cart prophet" (in the same spirit as Kerouac who would idealize the hoboes in *On the Road* as the opposites of careerists). On other photographs, Ginsberg's squeezed comment is definitively informational, such as the note on an iconic late shot of Kerouac in 1964 where Kerouac, at the age of forty-three, looks absolutely ravaged by time though the reason for his harried, drawn appearance, Ginsberg tells us, is DMT.

v. A Hollywood Holiness

Some of Ginsberg's photographs—such as the one of Carl Solomon, the dedicatee of "Howl," in only a white shirt and tie, grinning gleefully and absurdly bare below the waist and sitting cross-legged on a bed—are used to add a layer of authenticity to Rob Epstein and Jeffrey Friedman's film about "Howl" that features James Franco as Ginsberg and a sexy male favorite, Jon Hamm (Don Draper of *Mad Men*). I must admit Hollywood biopics are hardly my favorite genre, but such enterprises sometimes serve to extend any audience. The vulgarity of the genre is oversimplification, sanctimoniousness, and the desperate housewives' stress on sensationalism to the extent that ideas often seem parodied or genuine concerns seem trivial.

This film is ambitious and valiantly heartfelt in its attempt to recreate the creative context for the most important long poem written by an American since "The Waste Land." Its structure mixes four tracks. The first shows James Franco as Ginsberg talking about how he writes and key events in his past such as his internment in the psychiatric hospital where he met Solomon or his aborted love affair with the firebrand Neal Cassady presented with the lurid compression film affords. Most of this track is actual—that is, drawn from Ginsberg's interviews, letters, and journals.

I confess to being quite partial to Franco when I learned he was studying for a Ph.D. in literature at Yale and writing short stories himself. These are hardly the usual prerequisites for a Hollywood career.

The second track depicts the notorious court trial of Lawrence Ferlinghetti for publishing and selling an obscene poem—his small press, City Lights, published *Howl and Other Poems* as a small, sixty-page pamphlet in 1956. The steely, cool Jon Hamm plays Ferlinghetti's defense attorney with resolute sincerity. Mary Louise Parker is quite believable in a cameo role as a puritanical schoolteacher who dismisses the poem with disgust, and Bob Balaban is the prim though judicially proper Judge Clayton Horn, whose ruling exonerated the poem and helped to inform a national audience of its radical nature.

A third track restages the famous Gallery Six first public reading of "Howl" to its enthusiastic audience in San Francisco in 1955, a subterranean event with Kerouac passing out jugs of cheap wine in a former dirt-floor garage turned hip art gallery that literary historians acknowledge changed American poetry. Ginsberg remembered the event as "amateur and goofy" but the reading itself "was such a violent and beautiful expression of revolutionary individuality (a quality bypassed in American poetry since the formulations of Whitman), conducted with such surprising abandon and delight" that the audience was left stunned. The film recreations seem quaint and don't really suggest the impact of the reading, the "brilliant shock" of the performance, as Gregory Corso once put it. Some of the other poets sharing the stage with Ginsberg that night immediately recognized the reach and power of "Howl."

Michael McClure realized that Ginsberg's performance "left us standing in wonder, or cheering and wondering, but knowing at the deepest level that a barrier had been broken, that a human voice and body had been hurled against the harsh wall of America." Gary Snyder, who also read that evening, remembered walking away afterward saying, "'Poetry will never be the same. It is going to change everything.' Everyone who attended was set back. It was the power of 'Howl.' He got right into the quandaries and complexities of the Eisenhower era. The personal lives of those who were marginalized and often in pain, and brought those voices forward. It was the beginning of the Beat Generation and, in a sense, the defining moment in all our literary careers."

Some historians, however, might quibble that, contrary to what the film pretends, at the Gallery Six reading Ginsberg did not recite the "everything is holy" "Footnote"—the fourth part of a poem that took over twenty minutes for Ginsberg to read—because it had not yet been written. The distortion may have been so tempting because the "Holy, holy, holy" rant exists as one of the most powerful conclusions of any poem, so who can blame the filmmakers for ending with it?

The fourth track is the most experimental feature of the film, an animation illustrating the poem. I suspect Ginsberg might have welcomed this aspect of the film because of his collaboration with Eric Drooker, who illustrated Ginsberg's *Illuminated Poems*. Despite the slick glamour of its technical sophistication, I think the animation deflates the poem, tempers its rage. Imagine, if you can, a cartoon version of Dante's *Inferno* or T. S. Eliot's "The Waste Land" that might be suitable for children but how can Homer Simpson ever substitute for King Lear? Drooker's animation is entertaining, it does alleviate the weighty despair of its subject, and it might be effective as a pedagogical device, but I'm not ready to share it with elementary school students. The animation just doesn't shed much light on Ginsberg's great poem, and it is a fundamentally different form of imagining than that afforded by the arrangement of words and sounds that constitutes a poem.

VI. A New Consciousness

The film maintains Ginsberg's centrality in the gestation and development of the Beat Generation, a position forwarded systematically by Bill Morgan in his history of how the Beats emerged, *The Typewriter Is Holy*, an inspired title drawn from one of the many repetitions of the word "holy" in the "Footnote" to "Howl." As Ginsberg's archivist, initially working with his photographs, Morgan was an intimate of Ginsberg's inner circle and so positioned to observe the ways Ginsberg advocated for the recognition of his friends. Ginsberg's detractors have accused him of self-promotion but, like Whitman or Pound before him, Ginsberg understood that unless the poet spoke on his own behalf, the world would safely ignore him.

Sober, meticulous, with the methodical persistence of the bibliographer, Morgan argues that the Beats were less of a movement than a gathering of friends gravitating around Ginsberg's orbit. This overstates the argument Burroughs maintained when I first interviewed him, that the Beats were more of a cultural force than a defined literary movement with shared principles like the surrealists.

There was considerable dissension and little unanimity among the surrealists, and a more contentious lot could not be imagined. Their titular leader, Andre Breton, like a little Lenin or Stalin, frequently exiled or excommunicated his followers. The Beats never seemed susceptible to that sort of internecine schism, though there were squabbles, especially when wives or girlfriends were appropriated as when Kerouac slept with Kenneth Rexroth's much younger wife in San Francisco just after the Gallery Six event.

Ginsberg would be the first to admit how much he learned from Burroughs and Kerouac. He shared Burroughs's perspective that life was as much about entropy as growth, that America was ecologically poisoning the planet with its uncontainable lust for gas and oil. Kerouac reaffirmed the importance for Ginsberg of the long line rhapsodic voice and was his first tutor in Buddhism.

What helped the Beats cohere over time were common values. Reacting to the stultifying repression of the postwar years, they shared an anarchist suspicion of governmental controls, they were socially transgressive and experimental as writers, and from their inception they were interested in a new consciousness.

Ginsberg was a key figure in promoting that consciousness. Unlike most American poets since Eliot, he enjoyed an international reputation and *Howl* was translated into twenty-five languages. Its unprecedented excess, the emotional juggernaut of its rhythm and language profoundly influenced American writers, musicians like Bob Dylan, John Lennon, Leonard Cohen and Patti Smith, and affected several generations of the young. With over a million copies printed in the United States, *Howl* is the most purchased book of poems by an American in our time.

When Ginsberg died in 1997, there were memorials all over the world: in Berlin, Barcelona, and Calcutta as well as in New York, Los Angeles, and San Francisco. After his death, in what amounted to a last-page editorial in the *New York Times Book Review*, its editor, Charles McGrath, asserted that Ginsberg had failed to match the genius of early works like "Howl" or "Kaddish," the epic elegy with its depths of anguished empathy he wrote to commemorate his mad mother, Naomi.

This has been the perennial establishment view of Ginsberg, a tired cliché of criticism that has been routinely applied to great poets from Wordsworth to Whitman. The attitude is condescendingly wrong, as silly as the claim that Whitman's only great poem was "Song of Myself." In poems such as "Wales Visitation," in a very late poem modeled on an eighteenth-century homiletic such as "Ballad of the Skeletons," in an outrageously priapic short outburst such as "Please Master," in the final "Death and Fame" that appeared on two pages of the *New Yorker* at the time of his departure, or in an earlier volume like *The Fall of America*, Ginsberg showed that he was always at the borders of poetry and beyond, inventing the new. His *Collected Poems* and the volumes that followed will stand among the monumental achievements of modern American letters.

It is good to be reminded of that. That's what the continuing interest in Ginsberg, in film, photographs, and print, accomplishes. Ginsberg resonates with our times because he helped create them. Rock 'n' roll will never die, and neither, apparently, will Allen Ginsberg.

CHAPTER 11 **THE OPPOSITIONAL WRITER**

I would not feel so all alone
Everybody must get stoned.
—Bob Dylan

I. American Samizdat

The study of any language is replete with confusing curiosities and obstacles, as illustrated by as fundamental a word as "insane," the word we use to measure social acceptability and compatibility. The familiar understanding of the preposition "in" ordinarily leads us to believe we are enclosed within a defined area; however, those determined to be insane are out of the space we collectively agree represents sane behavior. Logically, it might seem that the correct term for those who are called insane should be "outsane" except that in Latin the prefix "in" can often be used to negate what follows it, as in "inability," "insignificant," "inanimate," and "insane."

The term "counterculture," used in the 1960s to designate those who denounced the decade of American war with Vietnam, exists in a similarly confusing context. The "counter" part of the phrase implies negativity or militancy, which only applied to a frustrated fringe element such as the Weathermen and the Black Panthers, or events such as the Symbionese Liberation Army bank holdups and kidnapping of Patty Hearst. It would not apply to the elements of a much larger, more pacific populace who may have marched in civil rights and antiwar demonstrations but also began to practice yoga and meditation, join in food cooperatives and modify to a more vegetarian diet, study Buddhism, or decide to live off the grid, although that was another fringe element. In general, however, this group did not represent a counterattack on culture as much as an *alternative* view of its possibilities as a means of deemphasizing a gluttonous overconsumption, a systematic waste of resources, a mounting materialism reflected in obesity rates and oil dependence. The mostly young people who formed an alternative subculture were concerned with the quality of the water available and the air they would have to breathe in the future, the depletion of the soil and the reliance on chemicals. Though they didn't particularly believe in the old gods, their spiritual purpose seemed to be centered around the recovery of human virtues becoming rapidly diminished in a changing world.

Many young Americans in the early 1960s felt suffocated by the sexual inhibitions and political restrictions that had been imposed on them by a dominating cultural emphasis on uniformity and conformity since the end of World War II. During this period, when it was considered improper to refer to sexual practices publicly, an obscure scientist named Alfred Kinsey—who for decades had studied the mating habits of the gall wasp at Indiana University—decided to interview thousands of Americans about their sexual habits and preferences and published his findings in two volumes in 1947 and 1953. There were other early harbingers of resistance, such as when eight homosexual men in Los Angeles began to meet in 1950 to form the Mattachine Society, or when five years later in New York, the novelist Norman Mailer helped begin the *Village Voice*, and the literary scholar Irving Howe started *Dissent*. When a little known disc jockey named Allen Freed with a rhythm-and-blues format on his radio show began playing Bo Diddley, Little Richard, Fats Domino, Chuck Berry, and Elvis Presley, the sound of rock 'n' roll was disseminated. When Elvis swung his hips and pelvis on the Ed Sullivan television program in 1956, it was confirmed. As the poet Allen Ginsberg used to say, "When the mode of the music changes, the walls of the city begin to shake."

The trial of Allen Ginsberg's *Howl* in San Francisco in 1956 on grounds of obscenity and the subsequent vindication of Lawrence Ferlinghetti, its publisher, was as significant a sign that the judicial system was flexible enough to sustain reasonable change as *Brown v. Board of Education*, the Supreme Court decision that created the largest crack in the wall of apartheid culture in the American South since the Civil War. The long court battles in the early 1960s over Barney Rosset's right to publish and promulgate what Henry Miller had already published in Paris in 1934 as *Tropic of Cancer* only sustained such notions of change.

By 1960, the birth control pill would change everything. Young American women, for example, would no longer feel so pressured to get married that over half of them felt compelled to marry by the age of nineteen. One sign of reaction to an atmosphere that seemed so stifling to some was the ransacking of the papers of U.S. congressmen serving on the feared House Un-American Activities Committee in San Francisco in

1960. Later that fall, incredibly and outrageously at the Republican nominating convention, the director of the FBI, J. Edgar Hoover, declared in an appeal to the Old Guard that the greatest menace to America was "Communism, eggheads, and Beatniks." Perhaps Hoover was planning a trip to Siberia for scientists like Kinsey or poets like Ginsberg?

What I choose to call the oppositional writer is usually first discerned as a sort of whisper or faint trace on the social margins in part because of a message we won't consider. Even a loud and clear voice is often lost in an age of deep denial, and affluence tends to overwhelm critical thinking in any historical moment. One of the still relatively unknown oppositional figures of our time is Ed Sanders, a poet of considerable depth, talent, and historical concern, as reflected in his endlessly panoramic poem *America*. An early acolyte of the Beats, he had memorized "Howl" as an undergraduate at the University of Missouri.

The following lines from a recently published poem (in an underground venue called *House Organ* in the spring of 2012) reflect a continuing intransigence:

> The Pax Americana
> replete with land mines
> and coopted thises and that's
> replete with marksmen
> and quickly mopped-up mayhem
> all designed
> for riches, power and glory
> and of course
> the blood lust of a good part
> of the officer corps
> and of course
> more money to the already moneyed.

Sanders is one of our leading living exponents of what Russians prior to Gorbachev called *samizdat*. In the time when all publication was controlled by a state party apparatus, writing was circulated clandestinely in mimeograph format—that is, illegally and underground. The antecedent for this was the earliest handwritten newsletters in France in the eighteenth century, spreading the gossip of court scandals and then the news that led to a revolution: the French word for news, *nouvelle*, becomes our generic label for fiction.

The delicious gossip in Sanders's memoir, *Fug You: An Informal History of the Peace Eye Bookstore, the Fuck You Press, the Fugs, and Counterculture in the Lower East Side* leavens his serious intent: Janis Joplin introducing television journalist Dick Cavett to oral sex; actress Sharon Tate's reputed involvement (according to Dennis Hopper) in a sadomasochistic group before the Manson murders; Jack Kerouac characteristically jotting on a notepad at the moment before the blood began gurgling in his throat in 1969.

Fug You presents a record of the years from 1963 to 1969, a period during which Sanders subordinated poetry for the circus of rock 'n' roll and the principle of free speech. This is the era between the assassinations of the two Kennedy brothers when some Americans, perhaps romantically or at least much too optimistically, expected world values were actually changing as rapidly as technology and in a more progressive direction.

Born just at the beginning of World War II, Sanders was raised in Missouri farm country at a moment when farmers started selling their land to real estate developers who built the suburbs around Kansas City. In New York City he studied classics and Egyptian hieroglyphics at New York University. Its high tuition was waived because of his job in the purchasing department (NYU, ironically, was in the process of purchasing as much of lower Manhattan as it could acquire).

Married with an infant daughter, Sanders lived on the Lower East Side in a time of thirty dollar a month rentals in an apartment he painted black. There may have been a particular kind of downtown despair that motivated such a sable color scheme, and I know that the earlier Beat surrealist, Carl Solomon, also painted his apartment black in the same neighborhood. An "unself-confident egomaniac" (alluding to the opening lines of Kerouac's *The Subterraneans*), Sanders placed a small Speed-o-Print mimeograph machine on the porcelain cover of the kitchen washtub.

The process began with a typed stencil, with hand drawings illuminated from behind by a flashlight, and the tedious chemistry of correction fluid. Then he would print, collate, and hand staple hundreds of copies of each issue of a publication he flamboyantly called *Fuck You / A Magazine of the Arts*, which he gave away for free. So its cost was a matter of a writer's dedicated effort and passion, and that commitment would seem to be a signal of anomaly in a culture concerned primarily with acquisition and money.

An avant-garde voice of the underground, the motto of *FY* was William Burroughs's philosophy of "total assault on the culture." Sanders began sending it to Europeans like Beckett, Picasso, and Sartre, and to Charles Olson, Allen Ginsberg, Gary Snyder, and other American poets he admired. The enterprise suggests a perennial model for young writers: start a lively publication, keep it alive, and you may realize a life in print.

I lived on the Lower East Side in the early 1960s and was impressed by Sander's intentness when I saw him read at Café Metro and at the Living Theatre event to raise funds for the jailed poet Ray Bremser. Sanders looked like a Mark Twain cherub, a curlyhead standing so straight, stiff, a soldier of somber, self-contained anger. But *Fug You* is by the only "Beatnik who can yodel." It is full of a playfulness that also characterizes an era full of idiosyncratic absurdities—like Sanders's memory of filmmaker Ron Rice rushing into a party naked, flinging a cat at Tiny Tim singing with his high-pitched "skyscraper voice" while strumming his ukulele.

Fug You is organized chronologically, but often feels more like a scrapbook than a memoir with fully developed sequences; instead, Sanders presents us with fragmentary vignettes, the resume of an archive. Illustrated by snapshots, posters for poetry readings, press and book announcements, manifestos for legal marijuana and protests, clipped newsreel accounts of political events such as the trial of Lenny Bruce, the civil rights campaign in the South, and Johnson's war acceleration in Vietnam, the book has a jagged, nervous quality that fits the era it depicts.

Influenced by friendship with folklorist Harry Smith and filmmaker Jonas Mekas, Sanders bought a Bell and Howell camera and began a reportage on Lower East Side amphetamine culture. Another twenty-four-minute film focused on Andy Warhol's Factory with figures such as Burroughs, Frank O'Hara, painter Jim Rosenquist, and the film actress Jayne Mansfield in it. This film, and another ten thousand feet of footage, was subsequently confiscated by the New York City Police Department and never seen again.

The infamous raid, part of a police and FBI purge of coffeehouse culture, Jonas Mekas's Cinematheque, the Living Theatre, all exponents of what the squares saw as the unfathomable new manners of the 1960s, occurred because Sanders had opened the Peace Eye Bookstore—a former butcher shop with the "strictly kosher" legend written in Hebrew letters on the window—as a center for his publishing activities. One of Sanders's first publications was Burroughs's *Roosevelt after*

Inauguration, a viciously hilarious attack on the American political system (based on Roosevelt's ill-fated attempt to add new Supreme Court justices and push through his New Deal) in which Burroughs imagines a purple-assed baboon fornicating with the justices and later running for president.

The bookstore was located on Tenth Street, between Avenues B and C. A young poet named Tuli Kupferberg lived next door. Tuli was already legendary in Alphabet City because of a line in "Howl" that commemorated his attempt at suicide—jumping from the Brooklyn Bridge and miraculously surviving his fall. Looking like "an obscene Yeshiva student," as Elizabeth Hardwick described him in the *New York Review of Books*, the son of Hungarian orthodox Jews who worked in garment sweatshops, Tuli was the zaniest of anarchists with an ineffable sense of loony humor who sold his poetry magazine, *Birth*, on the streets.

In 1965, Sanders would create the weirdest of rock groups with Tuli. Think of the Mothers of Invention led by Harpo Marx on Ecstasy. Named after the euphemism for "Fuck" that Norman Mailer had been forced to use by his publishers in *The Naked and the Dead*, the Fugs were billed as the "freakiest singing group in the history of western civilization." These "children of Lenny Bruce" (as *New York Times* music critic Robert Shelton categorized them in favorable review of a Town Hall concert) lived up to their reputation of liberated wild men: throwing spaghetti at an audience and hitting Warhol among others, cutting up and scattering a very valuable Warhol silkscreen after another concert, playing at a legalize cunnilingus demonstration. After a tour to California, Sanders compared the impact of the group to "Albanian hillsmen storming Byzantine nunneries."

Performing songs like "Kill for Peace," "Slum Goddess," and "Group Grope" through the rest of the 1960s, they opened for other groups like the Velvet Underground and the Grateful Dead, and were featured in many venues such as the space above the Café Wha? (where Jimi Hendrix was discovered) on McDougal Street in the honky-tonk part of the Village where in 1966 they gave over seven hundred performances. Combining what critic Hardwick called "a schizophrenic sweetness and dirtiness," the group was more about agitprop parody or cabaret astringency than anything else, and depended more on bohemian shock, the épater les bourgeois of raw sound than musicianship. As Sanders acknowledges, the group specialized in an "atonal masochism, angst, metaphysical distress" that could result in a Blakean sweetness or noisy rejoicing, but often in a whining or caterwauling, a cymbal clash with harmony, a screaming, rancid, manic twist on the Living Theatre's "unspeakable cry."

The sound must have been strident enough, however, to get Sanders's face to illustrate the "other culture" on the cover of *Life*'s Happenings Issue in February 1967 with the magazine's enormous circulation of five million subscribers (and how many dental offices?). Sanders was interviewed by television's highbrow David Susskind and his more entertainingly puerile rival Johnny Carson.

From this high point of public recognition, Sanders's book careens into a history of bitter lifestyle protests on the Lower East Side in the crucible of antiwar protests, of how peace and love ideals collapsed in a sea of LSD and methamphetamine, of how the Free Store was plundered by owners of used clothing stores, of how Linda Fitzpatrick was raped, her head smashed with a brick, her lover Groovy murdered in a basement boiler neighborhood "Free Love" room.

The karmic poison was the war in Vietnam:

> All throughout the history of The Fugs in the '60's the war in Vietnam throbbed like an ever-seething soul sore. However much we partied, shouted our poetry, and strutted around like images of Bacchus, we could never get the war out of our minds. It was like that Dada poetry reading that Tristan Tzara gave in 1922 in Paris, with an alarm clock constantly ringing during the reading. The war was THE alarm clock of the late '60's.

By the spring of 1968, rioting began in Washington, D.C., Baltimore, Chicago, Detroit, Boston, and over a hundred smaller communities. The man who organized an exorcism of the Pentagon with two hundred thousand mourning marchers and a smaller one with Allen Ginsberg over the late Senator Joseph McCarthy's grave in Wisconsin was changed by the assassination of Robert Kennedy, which moved him in a direction he calls "scholarly activism."

Now, he defines himself as a democratic socialist, certainly a lonely position in the United States where only *one* member of Congress, Bernie Sanders, the junior senator from Vermont, can afford to identify himself in similar terms and hope to get reelected. In these United States, we, at least, can now identify two socialists—both coincidentally named Sanders. We must seem strange—quite unwilling to control greed—to our European allies, over half of whom are socialists.

Sanders may have lost more faith in American political processes when he witnessed the police riots in Lincoln and Grant Parks at the Chicago Democratic Convention at the end of August 1968, and heard Ginsberg lose his voice while chanting "Om" for hours. The book ends somewhat forlornly on this note, with a coda of the transcript of Sanders and Kerouac playing the drunken clown, a soused and soured W. C. Fields, on William Buckley's television program *Firing Line*. Although Sanders doesn't need to inform us, it was the end of an era.

II. A Communal Alternative

> *The real goods is to be a man like me who doesn't really know his next move, but his next move is anywhere.*
> —Gregory Corso

A close view of the lives and emotional hazards faced by oppositional writers is provided by Gordon Ball's *East Hill Farm: Seasons with Allen Ginsberg*, an account of the commune that clustered around Allen Ginsberg in the 1960s. It should provide no surprise that a poet like Ginsberg, whose death in 1997 was commemorated all over this country, in Europe and Asia, is the subject of another memoir. One danger for anyone writing about Ginsberg is the inability to measure the poet's historical guise as court jester—holy fool!—which is what limited the petty judgments of Sam Kashner in his acerbic, self-serving *When I Was Cool*.

Gordon Ball's *East Hill Farm* is much more than an account of two years managing Ginsberg's farm in Cherry Valley, New York, "of separate egos all fighting for their moment in Allen's sun," of a few nascent poets with radical sensibilities trying to redeem an abandoned farmhouse while raising vegetables in depleted soil. While it may not have the resonance of Peter Coyote's *Sleeping Where I Fall*, it will stand as a prime historical resource and as a fascinating record of late 1960s America, its agitation and aspiration.

A village of eight hundred inhabitants, Cherry Valley is located in upstate New York, near Cooperstown, the town named after the patrician family of James Fenimore Cooper and now home of baseball's Hall of Fame. The seventy-acre farm had no amenities: no electricity, no insulation, no heat other than a wood and coal Kalamazoo kitchen stove, and a broken outside hand-powered water pump.

Earlier, in New York City in the summer of 1967, Ball had been part of a group of experimental filmmakers who circled around Jonas Mekas's Cinematheque, where, in the boiling crucible of new discovery, he had been introduced to group sex and psychedelics, the initiations of an avant-garde intent on changing consciousness.

Inspired by the natural spectacle of America presented so lyrically in *On the Road*, Ball hitched cross-country with his lover, Candy O'Brien, and then down to Mexico, only to be arrested and incarcerated by Mexican federales in an arbitrary sweep of gringo hippies—a story Ball told previously in an earlier memoir called *66 Frames*.

The "black sheep son of a dour and distant banker," Ball had been raised in Tokyo, sheltered and socially inept. He was good-looking, passive but curious, caught by the sexual intoxications of youth that were particularly prevalent in that interval of liberation after the birth control pill in 1960 and before the AIDS virus. Both twenty-three years old, Ball and O'Brien were friends with filmmaker Barbara Rubin, who helped Ginsberg find the farm and joined his group of followers.

The best feature of Ball's narrative of the time he spent at East Hill Farm, from 1968 through 1969, is the vibrant portrait of its "lost battalion of pastoral conversationalists": Ginsberg, maintaining equanimity despite the unplatonic frustrations of communal living, dedicated to his own work and to the commune he was supporting with poetry readings around the country; his companion, poet Peter Orlovsky, in a sometimes scary amphetamine rush, abrupt, abrasive, often cockeyed with the "operatic absurdity" of his shouting character; Peter's brother, Julius, a catatonic schizophrenic who could go for days without sleeping or eating, a poignant slouching figure with a protruding belly and lowered chin who was once chastised for brushing his teeth in the dishwater, a brooding Bartleby solemn reminder of potential misfortune in the care of the communards; poet Gregory Corso with his perennial propensity for chaos and catastrophe, an idiot-savant mixture of Falstaff and Chaplin; and Herbert Huncke, "a swan gliding down a limpid stream," his chameleon grace, consideration, con-man heroin charm and suffering all displayed. Unlike Nathaniel Hawthorne at Brook Farm a century earlier, who mocked the ineptitudes of utopian transcendentalists in *The Blithedale Romance*, Ball admires his subjects, even as he charts some of their crippling disabilities.

Ball's record is crowded with other visitors, but as concerned with the mundane quotidian of communalism: building a woodshed, cleaning the well and, later, laying water pipes to the house, winterizing it, struggling with vehicles in giant snow accumulations. The journal is buoyed by Ball's observations of the farm menagerie: goats, geese, a kitten playing with a baby raccoon, the cow named after Bessie Smith (the singer Ginsberg often heard as a child), and Penny, the runaway horse that threw Ball, breaking his wrist badly.

The perspective is broadened to include extracts from Ginsberg's diaries, letters from others, the running news from the culture wars, and the explosive rage of those who hated the bombing of Vietnam—an anger, Ginsberg felt, that only served to prolong the conflict. Frequently, what Ball depicts is tinged with a touch of gentle incongruity as when the members of his group squeeze into a neighbor's tarpaper shack to watch the first American moon landing on a nine-inch, black-and-white, battery-powered television. There is a more emotional dimension in Ball's awareness of his own testing of sexual boundaries, and Ginsberg's paranoia about needle drugs and Peter's amphetamine abuse.

Generally, Ball is quite candid, unafraid of a more conventional dismissal of this group as depraved or demented. He is meticulous with detail, in describing settings and clothing. Some readers may find him too indefatigable, relentless even in the accumulation of events—unlike Thoreau, for example, who in *Walden* economically chose to condense two years into one.

I suspect this approaches an aesthetic choice Ball must have faced with his material. He seems absorbed (to the point of infatuation?) by all the activities at the farm and the behavior of some of its outrageous guests. His book must be based on regular diary notation, but Ball may have allowed the weight of those diaries to overwhelm the dramatic potential of memoir, a form that depends on brutal selectivity. Like a documentarian who is reluctant to edit and thus shade actual circumstance, Ball's inclusiveness is both a virtue and a test of the reader's patience.

III. Literature in the Fields

Mellon and I visited East Hill Farm for a week in the late summer of 1973. I doubt that I could have persuaded her to accompany me had she read Ball's account, and even without having read it, she was quite apprehensive. Usually intrepid, a photographer who had already gone down the Saramacca River in Suriname alone in a dugout canoe, she was afraid that visiting the farm might turn into an uncomfortable experience with a group of gay, misogynist men. She still maintains that Ginsberg had a blind spot as far as women were concerned and that it took him a decade to recognize her when she was not with me. Eventually, they became friends and fond of each other.

We drove there from Vermont in a beaten-up Austin Mini Cooper, a tiny, square breadbox of a car. I had purchased it new for $1,200—a dollar a pound I used to joke—when I started teaching at Queens College, and because I could park it on a dime. Its battle scars came from the neighborhood kids who had overturned it as a prank once and all the bigger American boats that rammed it when parking. The most severe damage had occurred years earlier when we were uptown retrieving wedding bands. Suddenly struck from behind at a red light, the Mini was propelled into oncoming Broadway traffic. We were married a few days later, but the car received a giant dent in its rear, which I festooned with thirteen American flag decals in variously skewed arrangements. I didn't know about Jasper Johns then, but it was like driving one of his paintings reinterpreted by R. Crumb, and it often got us stopped by curious police.

Allen and his companion Peter Orlovsky admired the uncommon brevity of the car. After a few moments, Ginsberg asked whether we had ever met previously. If there was a touch of suspicion in his query, I understood that it derived from an ancient antipathy between the artist and critic, who so often represents the betrayal of oversimplification, distortion, or sensationalism. I told him I had met him once years earlier in Stanley's Bar, a watering hole just north of Tompkins Square Park in the East Village, but that he had been surrounded by noisy admirers.

Peter showed us up a flight of stairs to our room with a bed that he had constructed for our visit. Peter was good with tools and with his hands. A shy, moody man, I felt an immediate connection when he told me that as a young man he had worked as a field laborer on some of the last farmland in Queens, just adjacent to the campus where I teach. That entire week, Peter roared around the farm in his tractor as he vigorously worked the land, mended fences, cut and stacked cords of wood, canned tomatoes, and pickled beets.

One of the reasons Ginsberg had purchased the farm was Peter's reliance on Methedrine, which he would score in the East Village. During the 1960s, Allen was constantly giving readings through the United States and Europe, and when he was away Peter could be tempted. The farm represented health and recovery, and on it Peter was an incarnation of masculine vitality.

Peter's intense silences reminded Mellon of sexy Mellors in *Lady Chatterley's Lover*, but he had a tender side underneath an exterior of macho gruffness. He wrote poems, many quite eccentric and erratically spelled. In his book, *Clean Asshole Poems & Smiling Vegetable Songs*, he includes one about his older schizophrenic brother Julius who "sits alone, lumpy / in a corner for hours." Poignantly mute, passive, bent, simultaneously ominous and innocent, a catatonic who seemed to be musing or daydreaming, we saw Julius every day, mostly a shadowy, hovering presence at meals in the kitchen though he never seemed to eat anything.

The kitchen was where I could interview Allen, and it was the communal center of the farm. Redolent with herbs and spices and the vegetables Peter was canning, it was a place of warmth and companionship. Allen himself was the mother hen, concerned about everyone's needs. He baked us an apple pie with apples gathered on the farm and the delicious winey odor permeated the house.

The week we spent at the farm was harvest time and some of my questions of Allen were answered in the fields as I was bending and stooping, picking vegetables with him. I had a little notebook in my back pocket in which I would scribble with dirty fingers while Allen resolved matters of Beat history or Burroughs's and Kerouac's fiction. He seemed as eager to talk about their work as his own. I felt more like an anthropologist than a biographer; instead of the cloistered sanctuary of the library archive, I could smell the earth and hear the birds sing as I learned.

IV. "I'm with You"

> ah, Carl, while you are not safe I am not safe,
> and now you're really in the total animal soup of time.
> —Ginsberg, "Howl"

Ginsberg's friend Carl Solomon was visiting East Hill Farm at the same time. Though he didn't really help much with the harvesting, he was loquacious and willing to talk about his past.

Carl Solomon is known as the dedicatee of "Howl," the most famous long poem written by an American since T. S. Eliot's "The Waste Land." Certain of his notorious actions are reflected early in the poem: an unsigned postcard of only a single word—"vanished"—or his throwing potato salad at a lecturer on Dadaism when he was an undergraduate. More memorably, he also was the subject of Ginsberg's compassion in the third part of the poem with its Whitmanesque ringing "I'm with you" refrain of solidarity.

In 1949, Solomon had been a patient in the New York Psychiatric Institute for two months when he met Allen Ginsberg, who had been remanded there in lieu of facing felony charges stemming from a fracas involving the crash of a stolen car in which he was a passenger. Absurdly and pathetically, Solomon was there for less felonious reasons after confessing that he had stolen a sandwich in the Brooklyn College cafeteria. Demanding a lobotomy, Solomon talked his way into treatment with threats of suicide.

Six years earlier, in 1943, he had been a student at City College, precociously beginning at the age of fifteen. Midway in his studies, he left when he became increasingly paranoid about leftist associations. He joined the merchant marine immediately after the war where he worked as a scullion. In 1947 he jumped ship and made his way to Paris searching for surrealists and existentialists. He began reading Henry Miller and one day saw Antonin Artaud giving a spontaneous, animated reading outside of a bookstore in San Germain-des-Prés. It was a branch point, an epiphanous moment. He became interested in Artaud's book, *Van Gogh: The Man Suicided by Society*, in which Artaud condemned all psychiatry, vilifying it as an agency of social conditioning, claiming that most mental patients were gifted with a lucidity that allowed them to see through social shams.

Returning to New York, he transferred to Brooklyn College but was in a very negative, nihilistic state when he stole the sandwich. Ginsberg and Solomon bonded in the psychiatric ward, writing letters to figures like T. S. Eliot, and Ginsberg began making notes on his new friend's surreal, aphoristic exclamations. In his journal, *The Book of Martyrdom and Artifice*, Ginsberg identifies him as a former "swish" who knew the hipsters in Greenwich Village and "a whole gang of Trotskyite intellectuals."

Ginsberg and Solomon were both released after a year of treatment and remained friends. Solomon married and went to work for an uncle who owned Ace Books, a small publishing firm that specialized in noir fiction and sensational exposés, inexpensive paperbound originals that were more likely to be found in a drugstore or magazine stand than a legitimate bookstore. Ginsberg brought Solomon the manuscript of William Burroughs's *Junky*, which Ace Books published with a series of cautionary notes and under a pseudonym. Solomon also turned down an early version of *On the Road*.

Solomon was writing book reviews for the *New Leader* and a series of pithy, humorous, eccentric, but often brilliant essays that would later be published by City Lights Press, Ginsberg's publisher, as *Mishaps, Perhaps* and *More Mishaps*. Aphoristic, witty, Carl had insight into his world and himself: "Every man lives by a set of rules to which he is the only exception," he once wrote. Called the "lunatic saint" by some of his friends, he was capable of a kind of Artaudian gesture, an acting out of the most impulsively emotional, extravagant positions, such as dissolving his marriage by painting the marital bedroom black and tossing the bed out the window. When he left Ace Books, unable to stand the strain of editing, he got a job with a company named Eskimo Ice selling ice cream in front of the United Nations, and suddenly decided to give away all of the ice cream in his truck.

Coincidentally, or karmically, this was exactly the time that "Howl" was written and then published on the West Coast. Carl was again committed, this time to a more serious facility, Pilgrim State Hospital on Long Island, which at that time accommodated twenty-five thousand patients. Ginsberg, whose mother Naomi had received a frontal lobotomy at the same hospital, has acknowledged that Carl's commitment triggered the composition of "Howl." Carl would spend six years at Pilgrim State and receive seventy-one insulin or electroshock treatments during his years of psychiatric confinement.

When he was released, he was regulated with Thorazine and Mellaril, and routine psychiatric evaluations, a diet for the rest of his life. He thought that most psychiatrists were desensitized by the intolerable anxieties of their patients, that professionally they had lost faith in the curative power of talking therapy and instead had become licensed dope dealers, field agents for pharmaceutical empires.

He lived with his mother in a housing project in the Bronx, sought comfort in fishing in a dinghy off City Island, and found menial jobs as a bookstore clerk and messenger. When I met him at the farm, he formed a persisting avuncular attachment. We would meet every other week or so for lunch or dinner in greasy spoon diners in the Village, and occasionally he visited me at home. My wife saw that he had been severely bent by life. She sympathized with his exacerbated nervousness but noticed he still had his wit and a subdued though subversive charm.

Carl began to rely on me as a counselor, a sort of lay therapist, almost a maternal figure, I suppose, although the only qualification I had was a small quantity of common sense. Maybe he thought I was a literary connection. One of his grudges was his feeling that Ginsberg had exploited him in "Howl." Perhaps it was irrational hypersensitivity, but I suspect Neal Cassady felt similarly after he read his depiction as Dean Moriarty in *On the Road*.

As an activating principle in Carl's life Artaud had been replaced by Franz Kafka, and Carl began to resemble the victimized, nameless central characters of *The Castle* and *The Trial*. By turns vehement, enraged, Carl could melt down suddenly into a cowering, apprehensive figure, somehow soiled, degraded, and dehumanized by his imagined terrors. In this he resembled certain of William Burroughs's unfortunate characters in *Naked Lunch*.

His suspicions and his outbursts could be frightening—once on the telephone, he exploded for fifteen minutes so vociferously I thought it wasn't really safe to see him. However, I was editing *American Book Review* and asked Carl to contribute. What he wrote on several occasions was sharp and penetrating. I saw that it gave Carl new life to be again writing his minimal, pointed, absurdist essays, and eventually I encouraged him to collect material for a new book. Carl had a lot to say about his world, and an illuminating though quite singular perspective. He was also still working as a messenger, not with a bicycle but with the subways and his feet, so I suggested that he call his new collection *Emergency Messages*.

Sometime late in the 1980s I was invited for lunch at the Harvard Club by Ken Stuart, an editor who admired my book *Naked Angels*. When I told him about Carl's book, he offered to consider it and eventually he published it. *Emergency Messages* may have been part of a healing process for Carl, and I was pleased to hear that Ken Stuart had hired him to help care for an ailing parent in Wilton, Connecticut, complete with salary, room, and board. It was an act of kind-hearted generosity. Carl, the chronic invalid, had become the nurse, and he was changed by these new responsibilities. I could not quite picture Carl pushing a wheelchair through the suburbs though I knew it would give him new, humorous material.

At our last lunch a couple of years later, Carl complained of a pain in his back, which he attributed to helping a friend move some books. Actually, it was an early sign of emphysema.

Once again, Carl raised the painful issue of his sensational appearance in "Howl." Harper and Row had published a facsimile edition of "Howl," an extraordinary oversized book in which Ginsberg generously annotated the lines of his own poem and probed their germination and historical contexts.

In a clear statement Ginsberg explained that he wrote the poem in the time of his own literary obscurity, a poem intended to be read aloud and without consideration of the possibility of publication. A few friends, excited by hearing the poem at the Gallery Six reading, printed a mimeographed version, and a year later, in 1956, Ferlinghetti published it with City Lights, at best a marginal, small publisher. Ginsberg added that he had no idea the poem "would make its way around the world and proclaim a private reference to public attention." He also admitted that he had used Carl's insanity and confinement as a masque of his own ambivalent feeling toward his own mother, Naomi, who spent years in the same institution as Carl.

On February 26, 1994, the day of the first attempt to bomb the World Trade Center, my wife Mellon accompanied Allen Ginsberg on the D train to the Bronx Veterans Hospital to visit Carl on his deathbed. Carl was getting oxygen and the mask covering his mouth and nose made him look alien, ready to embark on a long voyage to outer space. Calmly surrealistic, he claimed he was still thinking about sex even as he realized he was fading. Allen took copious notes and some photographs, and encouraged Mellon to use her camera as well.

At one point, Mellon told me that Allen cleaned Carl's glasses with affectionate warmth. Then, bending over him, Allen asked Carl's forgiveness for having put him in the spotlight and making him a sensational cipher for universal suffering in "Howl." The bond of life friendship had brought Allen to the dying man's bedside, and the plea seemed like a ritual of release. Carl died a few minutes later.

v. Burroughs's Last Words

At the beginning of his 1964 novel *Nova Express*, William Burroughs proposed in a famous cynicism that "To speak is to lie—To live is to collaborate." His experimental fictions of the 1950s and 1960s were partly motivated by his attempt to reveal the extent to which dishonesty is built into our linguistic conditioning. As a writer, Burroughs refused to "collaborate." Throughout his career, he embodied uncompromising honesty and possessed an uncanny ability to see into the future.

One of Burroughs's refrains was "dead fingers talk"—a cryptically harrowing image that applies not only to all past literature but to his own work as well since his death at eighty-three in 1997. His final book, *Last Words*, is a diary of the jottings, dream notations (lots on centipedes and other insects), diatribes, and recollections of his final year. The writing fingers are arthritic; he knows his mental and physical powers are failing because a heart valve needed replacement, and he knows his death is imminent. "The heart doc says I am leaking," he notes with typically mordant flatness in the second entry of the journal.

The inventor—along with such contemporaries as John Cage and Samuel Beckett—of postmodernism, Burroughs admits that any final statement will have to be part of "a jumble of fragments." In terms of literary structure, one could argue that surreal juxtaposition and fragmentation have defined his style since his early fiction. And while his entries may seem random, they are designed and deliberate, the final warnings of the ultimate, dissenting Outsider, the extremist plague artist of our time.

The initial entry is surprising given Burroughs's usually glacial exterior, his reputation for toughness and a complete lack of sentimentality. It records an "uncontrollable sobbing" caused by the death of one of the stray cats he had cared for in his final home in Lawrence, Kansas. His maternal grandfather had been a fire-and-brimstone preacher in Lawrence, and Burroughs had retired there because of a long companionship with a younger assistant, James Grauerholz.

Other cats die or their deaths are recalled during the course of his final year, occasions for a tenderness and pity conspicuously absent from Burroughs's earlier writing. There are human deaths as well. Allen Ginsberg calls him from Beth Israel Hospital early in April 1997 to report that he has been diagnosed with liver cancer. Sounding almost exhilarated instead of terrified, according to Burroughs, Ginsberg would die less than a week later.

The austerely moving reflections on Ginsberg, one of Burroughs's closest friends for over half a century, are a reminder that *Last Words* depends on an element of personal detail usually omitted in

Burroughs's writing. With the wry humor of a condemned man, he relishes the ordinary: eggs over medium, three slices of bacon, hash browns, white toast, and three cups of coffee after visiting the methadone clinic in Kansas City, and his cocktail hour repast of caviar chased with vodka and Coke. But among the daily pleasures are intimations of mortality: bleeding gums, a cataract operation for the sake of reading and the marksmanship he had always exhibited when shooting guns.

Some of these routine details are more unsettling, like the .38 Special he wears on his belt whenever his door is unlocked. Maintaining that a writer needs something to do with his hands to keep them fluent when he is not writing, Burroughs retrieves cat hairs and practices target shooting. There may be something fundamentally American about Burroughs's devotion to guns and self-defense. In Howard Brookner's documentary film, he displayed the array of weapons he kept secreted in his lower Manhattan Bowery loft when he lived there in the 1970s: a variety of guns long and short, a Bowie knife in a drawer, a blackjack that could crush or slice, all of which he demonstrates with an animated vicious glee.

In the least-characteristic reflection of his career, following a mild heart attack he suffered after Ginsberg's death, Burroughs admits a belief in God. This was unexpected, coming from a man who had blasphemously proclaimed in *Naked Lunch* that "we see God through our assholes in the flash bulb of orgasm." Was this a deathbed conversion, a culminating apostasy? The admission, however, is completely undeveloped, a perfunctory observation deliberately eliminating the possibility of either piety or platitude.

Considering the totality of Burroughs's work—more than twenty books by a writer who had suffered as much from writer's block as Joseph Conrad had—the acknowledgment of a God force in *Last Words* seems almost as incongruous as the book's conclusion: a Gnostic reflection on love as the most "natural painkiller." Years earlier, he had famously defined love as "a fraud perpetrated by the female sex" and had sardonically alleged that morphine was "God's Own Medicine" and that without it he would never have discovered his vocation.

Lest anyone imagine that Burroughs had become a domesticated sentimentalist just before he died, he delivers plenty of characteristically excoriating fulminations, often as stinging asides on politicians like the "Squeeker of the House" or that "vile salamander" Newt Gingrich. No writer since Jonathan Swift has managed such grotesquely macabre vitriol for what Burroughs calls the "Moron Majority." "People in the mainstream," he admonishes, "are actually getting stupider, under a deadly hail of lies and misinformation from those in power." His grim recommendations of cannibalism and legalized dueling for the problems of overpopulation and dwindling natural resources express the mess human beings have made of their planet.

To enlighten us, he considers some of his favorite writers: Conrad, Paul Bowles, Baudelaire, Céline. The task of those he enrolls in the Shakespeare Squadron (his personal literary pantheon) is to change reality by exposing the lies on which, he asserts, all governments and institutions depend. It is a sweeping theory, and its anarchist hyperbole animates Burroughs's radical rage.

Attempting to "expose the lies" himself one last time, Burroughs frequently becomes a homilist in *Last Words*, a priestly scribe—recalling his role in Gus Van Sant's film *Drugstore Cowboy*—offering spare but fierce opinions on issues ranging from the dropping of the atomic bomb on Hiroshima and Nagasaki to the emerging international police state administered under the guise of antiterrorism measures and narcotic laws. Such arguments, the very sound of intemperance itself, reveal what a singular voice he had.

VI. An Incarnate Outsider

When the fashion model Lauren Hutton introduced William Burroughs on *Saturday Night Live* in 1981 as "the greatest writer in America," she may not have been kidding. Burroughs's literary stature will be determined by a canonical critical process although his role as a pariah figure who denounced his own country and said it was cursed for having first used atomic weapons in Hiroshima and Nagasaki in 1945 surely makes him our most politically incorrect writer, a marginal man, an incarnate outsider.

There is a snapshot I like by Marcia Resnick of Mick Jagger and Andy Warhol having lunch at Burroughs's table in the "Bunker," the Bowery loft (a former YMCA locker room) he inhabited in the 1970s. The photograph suggests Burroughs's cultural importance, particularly because it was featured on the table of contents page of the *New York Times Sunday Magazine*. This was a recognition first signaled by other artists:

consider, for instance, Burroughs's distinctive appearance in the crowd on the jacket of the Beatles' *Sgt. Pepper's Lonely Hearts Club Band*.

Another musician who seems to have responded to his work is the composer John Adams, who in a recent memoir, *Hallelujah Junction*, recalls a high point of his undergraduate education at Berkeley when a classmate loaned him a copy of *Naked Lunch*:

> It was my initiation into the crazed intoxication of beat literature. The wild off-the-wall sexual and drug-laden fantasias of Dr. Benway and the surrounding cast of junkies, small-time crooks, and deadbeat cops were like a beat version of Rabelais, only better. More than any other writer of his era—more than Norman Mailer, or Allen Ginsberg, or Jean Genet—Burroughs was the voice of the anti-establishment. He was funny and morally shocking, and he was boldly experimental in what he did with literary form and structure.

Adams goes on to praise the brutal candor of Burroughs's parody of American pieties. His point about Burroughs's fundamentally antiestablishment perspective is accurate, but it does not reveal how surprising it is given his pedigree and early conditioning.

Burroughs's family was listed in the Social Register in New York and St. Louis. In his youth there were skyscrapers in major American cities bearing his name because his paternal grandfather had perfected the adding machine by introducing an oil cylinder which enabled a then unprecedented rapidity of calculation that every bank in America wanted. So the Burroughs name was a Fortune 500 stock. The legend had it that on his mother's side he was a descendent of Robert E. Lee, a fact that Burroughs minimized when I interviewed him in the Bunker in 1974, saying that many southerners stretched that claim. Not everyone, however, was the nephew of Ivy Lee (known as "poison Ivy") who had been John D. Rockefeller's publicist, who lived in his own townhouse on Fifth Avenue, and whose daughter, Burroughs's first cousin, made her debut at the Court of St. James in London.

I knew *Naked Lunch* was a classic when I first read it in the early 1960s—hilarious relief from a surfeit of the so-sobering Henry James I was immured in then. I had already read *Ulysses* so I had some experience with an encoded densely textured text, but even with Joyce I had the advantage of ponies like Gilbert Stuart's *The Making of Ulysses* to help me limp along.

Naked Lunch was the most arcane, allusive, elusively elliptical fiction since *Ulysses* and much of it seemed impervious to my probing, mysterious, resistant to intellectual explanation. Half a century later, for students of the perplexing dynamic of Burroughs's imagination, the nature of postmodernism, or colonial theory, the recent publication of *Naked Lunch @ 50* (Southern Illinois University Press, 2009) offers much relief, explication, and lots of contextual assistance.

If we consider the novel's almost fortuitous publishing history as well as its unorthodoxy, it is a wonder that *Naked Lunch* appeared at all. It began as letters to Ginsberg that Burroughs sent from Tangier where he was living when he left Mexico and the Amazon Putumayo region after 1953.

Living in a hotel in what was called the "native quarter" by the eight colonial powers that administered Tangier, he would begin his day with a vigorous hour of rowing while standing, Venetian style, in the choppy currents of the bay. Returning to his room, he would chew a ball of homemade *majoon*, a hashish confection, before beginning work on his typewriter. Later in the afternoon, he might inject something even more potent and continue to work.

He called the delirious, berserk, exaggerated sketches he was writing "routines," and Ginsberg, in New York, was so excited by them that he forwarded them to two students at the University of Chicago who were editing its literary magazine. Enthralled, they wanted to include Burroughs in the magazine but were denied permission by the university dean. Outraged, the students discontinued their studies to begin their own magazine, which they called *Big Table*—the name was provided by Kerouac—where excerpts from *Naked Lunch* appeared, only to cause the intervention of U.S. postal authorities.

Stunned by the censorship controversy that ensued, a reporter for the *Chicago Tribune* wrote an article that was syndicated internationally and read in Paris by Maurice Girodias, who had already rejected some of the material from the book that Burroughs had already proposed. Girodias had inherited the infamous Obelisk Press in Paris from his father Jack Kahane, who had published Henry Miller's *Tropic of Cancer* in 1934, even though he was bankrupt and had no funds to pay his printers. Girodias, who published a lot of pornography as his father had, maintained the same principle of annually selecting a novel for his list that was considered unpublishable by the rest of the world.

With a suitcase of disorganized manuscript material, Burroughs moved into a cheap hotel adjacent to Notre-Dame Cathedral. Working with an extremely tight schedule, Girodias gave his top editor, Sinclair Beiles, two weeks to help Burroughs assemble something publishable. Burroughs would read a routine to Beiles in his small hotel room, and if they both liked it sufficiently, they piled it on a table. After two weeks, when they had a pile big enough for a novel, Beiles began to gather the manuscript. When Burroughs protested, arguing that they had not ordered the chapters, that the selection was arbitrary and accidental, Beiles's response was that there was no time left. Girodias had told him he had to deliver the manuscript as it existed immediately.

When the novel appeared in 1959, Oliver Harris argues in *Naked Lunch @ 50*, it had been preceded by a mythology that turned "act into fiction, life and legend into a fast revolving door." Ginsberg's 1956 dedication of *Howl* to "William Seward Burroughs, author of *Naked Lunch*, an endless novel that will drive everybody mad" and Kerouac's enigmatic portrayal of Burroughs as Bull Lee in *On the Road* the following year launched a publicity campaign among the cognoscenti that helped to form an anticipatory audience. That audience would only be compounded by the censorship trials led by the attorney general in the State of Massachusetts who prosecuted the novel as perniciously vile.

Edited by Oliver Harris and Ian MacFadyen, and celebrating more than a half century of publication, *Naked Lunch @ 50* is a critical collection and the best source available for deciphering the spectacular hieroglyphics of Burroughs's novel, for mapping its intricately allegorical geography and discovering the roots of its landscape of nightmare in East Texas, South America, Tangier, and Paris. As far as the small library of Beat literature is concerned, I would compare its importance to the publication of the annotated facsimile edition of *Howl* by Harper and Row in 1986, or the Viking Penguin edition of the original scroll of *On the Road* in 2007.

Take, for instance, MacFadyen's assertion that "Burroughs' geographical references contain secret, hip connotations" complicating the embroidery of the novel in the manner of T. S. Eliot's allusions in "The Waste Land" or in the way Joyce's use of Greek myth adds a cohering, unifying dimension to *Ulysses*. Early in *Naked Lunch*, Burroughs's junky protagonist flees toward Mexico City on the Pan-American Highway with an unidentified female companion. They stop for a drug fix.

> "Thomas and Charley" I said.
> "What?"
> "That's the name of this town. Sea level. . . ."

MacFadyen's explication of this seemingly innocent, almost innocuous snatch of dialogue is representative of the relentless sort of probing that occurs in *Naked Lunch @ 50*:

> This mysterious, oblique exchange refers to the town Tamuzunchale, 220 miles north of Mexico City, pronounced "Thomas 'n' Charlie." But what is the significance of this name? Both "Thomas" and "Charlie" are slang expressions related to narcotics. Thomas comes from Tom Mix (signifying a fix), Tom becoming Thomas just as Charlie, a euphemism for cocaine ("C" for cocaine) became Charles in Britain. The two words also have sexual connotations, Charlie meaning cunt, derived from Cockney rhyming slang (Charlie Hunt is a "right cunt") while Tom means a prostitute, and the term was taken up by homosexuals to signify available trade through its reference to the penis (John Thomas=cock). The interlocutory "What?" is a double take, pointing to the hidden significance of these two words, their multiple coded meanings encapsulating in an extraordinary way the operations of slang in narcotics parlance and sexual euphemism.

MacFadyen's commentaries occur sporadically throughout the volume, a buckshot presentation (like Burroughs's paintings, which he used to shoot with a rifle when he thought they were finished). These commentaries are not consecutive but circular, swiftly moving around a perimeter of rapidly changing perspective like the kaleidoscopic presentation of *Naked Lunch* itself.

Many of the other essays in *Naked Lunch @ 50* provide an abundance of compelling curiosities, a plethora of esoteric instruction, and moments of considerable insight into the cultural contexts of Burroughs's writing and its processes. I especially liked Rob Johnson's account of a cracker barrel folkloristic element reflecting the time when Burroughs lived in East Texas (where he tried, unsuccessfully, to grow opium), particularly the lynching, the parodied but rancid racism, the grotesque versions of southern mob justice. Johnson alleviates a certain Eurocentric bias in the collection that reminds me that interest in Burroughs's fiction has always been more international than provincial.

I also liked both Allen Hibbard's and Kurt Hemmer's essays on the impact of a Tangier emerging from colonial occupation in the mid 1950s while Burroughs was working on *Naked Lunch*, distorting the nationalistic riots in the Arab neighborhoods into some of the hysterical pandemonium of the novel. I responded as well to Andrew Hussey's essay on the revolutionary praxis of Paris when Burroughs was living there in 1958 and 1959, in the wake of the Algerian War and avant-garde critical theory, and R. B. Morris's lively version of some of the cultural consequences of *Naked Lunch* (even affecting Bob Dylan's lyrics).

The critical question—which no one in *Naked Lunch @ 50* has the temerity to raise—is whether we should consider Burroughs a one-shot wonder, whether without his infernally combustible novel he would remembered at all as a literary figure except historically as a Beat collaborator, someone who rented an apartment on Henry Street on the Lower East Side of Manhattan so that he could observe, with the clinical detachment of an anthropologist, the activities of a few small-time thieves and addicts. A novel like Laurence Sterne's *Tristram Shandy*, however, if it serves to extend the borders of traditional fiction and open new vistas for it, is usually all it takes to qualify for some measure of literary greatness.

My guess is I've exposed several thousand undergraduate and graduate students to *Naked Lunch*, and they still seem to respond to the explosive violence of its bizarre fantasies, its sometimes morbid burlesque. When I read the bizarre "Talking Asshole" routine to them, enough of them laugh to convince me that Burroughs's savage vitriol will continue to find its audience, even outside *Saturday Night Live*. If I show them scenes from Howard Brookner's documentary, they often chuckle when Mortimer, Burroughs's older brother (incongruously wearing short pants in the film) testifies that the novel repels him, that its objectionable language and disgusting depiction exists just to shock. Mortimer's comment makes me wonder how much of the offensive nature of Burroughs's fiction and its sadistic brutality exists as an unconscious response to a familial propriety he found suffocating?

My own report from the Bunker is that *Naked Lunch* still continues to offend most of its readers, many of whom are left feeling queasy and uncertain because of the rapaciously transgressive sexuality. I take this as a sign of the novel's continuing vitality. Unlike *On the Road*, it will resist becoming dated. In another fifty years, another group of scholars will probably compile another volume of essays to praise it, to recognize that Burroughs understood the implications of the worldwide problem with drugs and that like a possessed Orwell warned us of the dangers of surveillance and a police state that used terrorism and narcotics as a rationalization for abusive, tyrannical control.

VII. The Art of Difficulty

> *How far can a writers' writer go?*
> —William Gaddis to Katherine Anne Porter, January 21, 1948

Since the brilliant leap of his first novel, *The Recognitions*, a 956-page masterpiece, William Gaddis has always been a writer with an endangered reputation. The length and complexity of Gaddis' narrative about Wyatt (why art?) Gwyon, an unrecognized painter who had turned to art forgery, made his appeal more evident to other writers than to any large audience. In his 1986 *Paris Review* interview, an unlikely event for Gaddis conducted in Budapest, he claimed his novel was a "pilgrimage toward salvation," but many readers found his proliferation of characters, the dazzle of reverberating motifs, and the thicket of his allusions too dense and demanding to be considered paradisiacal. The *Paris Review* formulation for Gaddis was that he was the "satiric chronicler of chaotic existence and entropic disintegration," which seemed closer to postmodernist hell than to any more ethereal possibility.

The subsequent fictions became even more complicated with unattributed dialogue, "word storms that rage for scores of pages," and "page long paragraphs in which oxygen was a premium," Jonathan Franzen complained in a long piece on Gaddis in the *New Yorker* in 2002. The complexity—which Franzen associates with T. S. Eliot but should be traced to Henry James's late period, from *The Awkward Age*, *The Sacred Fount*, and *The Golden Bowl*—prevented many hopeful readers from completing Gaddis's subsequent fictions such as *J R* or *A Frolic of His Own*.

Gaddis's numerous detractors may have felt he was frolicking in their claustrophobia. They accused him of prolixity, of logorrhea, rambling, and occasionally ranting, "constipated to the point of being unreadable," as Franzen so harshly put it. In his *Paris Review* interview, Gaddis confessed that when he wrote, he did not "think of the audience." His implicit purpose was to recruit the reader, whom he imagined "almost as a collaborator in creating the picture," a reader who shared the courage to face a relative universe that was purposeless and even senseless. That reader, however idealized, would have to be highly intelligent, perspicaciously disciplined and diligent, with sufficient patience to persevere and glean.

Gaddis's demands on the reader increased after *The Recognitions*, and it took him two decades to write his second novel, *J R*. That evolution is somewhat akin to Ezra Pound's turn from imagism as an end after the First World War when he spent forty years fabricating the labyrinthine density of *The Cantos*. Earlier, this was the direction Henry James had taken after he was booed in 1894 when he took his curtain call at the premiere of his hapless play *Guy Domville*. James's humiliation, and his consequent Flaubertian decision to write exclusively for himself, marked a point of demarcation for fiction in English that came with the promise of considerable risk for any writer who believed that the art of fiction trumped the necessity for entertainment. Though there is no reference to Henry James in *The Letters of William Gaddis*, there are over seventy evocations of Eliot, who with Pound, Conrad, and Ford Madox Ford formed part of a cult of admiring younger writers who revered James as "The Master."

Always urbane, *The Letters of William Gaddis* reflects James's fastidiousness with a meticulous concern for the architectural propriety of every sentence. However, the early pages, letters to his mother, Edith, who had separated from Gaddis's father when he was four, are more clipped than James, without the flair. Edith worked for an energy company in New York and sent her son to boarding school and to Harvard. These letters to Mom seem written without angst, almost perfunctory—with the tactful deference of a son to a supportive mother—and they mostly skim the surface of Gaddis's adventures branding cows in Arizona and taking classes at Harvard.

Gaddis must have used his experience contributing to the Harvard *Lampoon* to help him get a job as a fact checker at the *New Yorker* after the war. Living on Horatio Street in Greenwich Village, drinking at the San Remo on Bleecker Street (which he characterizes with a line in *The Recognitions* as being filled "with people all mentally and physically the wrong size"), he met a set of young writers like Chandler Brossard and Jack

Kerouac. The camaraderie that ensued was reflected as he became a character in Brossard's *Who Walk in Darkness* and a young novelist who had "acquired a strange grace" in Kerouac's *The Subterraneans*.

In March 1947, Gaddis set off for Mexico with a few friends in a Cord convertible leaking oil and water. His account of this road trip, as Stephen Moore, the assiduous and most capable editor of the letters points out, "reads like a comic outtake from Jack Kerouac's *On the Road*." Gaddis's descriptive and linguistic powers, as he details the picaresque perils of this rain-soaked journey, show signs of considerable maturation and the comic deftness associated with his fiction. In Mexico City in April, living on twenty-five cents a day for food, he conceives a fifty-thousand-word novel he intends to call *Blague*—French for kidding—that is the beginning of *The Recognitions*.

His project grows, now called *Some People Who Were Naked* and with a pronounced concern for vanity. Living in Panama and working on a crane in the Canal Zone, his ambitions as a writer seem to have clarified, as indicated by a letter he writes to Katherine Anne Porter about Gertrude Stein in which he wonders "how far can a writers' writer go?"

The novel he is writing "harrows me all the time." Any writer who projects so monumental an enterprise as *The Recognitions* requires an obsessive motivation as well as an awareness acute enough to keep all its internal permutations of character and reverberations of plot and image consistent. That is what allows any fiction to cohere.

"If I can't make a good novel, then I must keep running," he writes to Edith who faithfully sends him the income she gets by renting her home in Massapequa, Long Island. Gaddis goes to Costa Rica and participates in a civil war, and then to Spain for six months, which, he explains, "is not the kind of country you travel in; it is a country you flee across." He pauses long enough to buy cuff links and a hand-carved walking stick, and then to face "Paris' hard, dull, dreary, absurd, pretentious, stupid, tiresome indifference" for the next year and a half. His mother sends him the books he needs to continue work on *The Recognitions*: Frazer's *The Golden Bough*, Toynbee's *A Study of History*, Graves's *The White Goddess* among others. He visits Robert Graves on Mallorca and finds it easier to go swimming than to talk to the poet about "Recognitions, crucifixions, incarnations, saints."

The letters begin to reveal Gaddis's witty, marvelously focused, and defining considerations such as the times he had spent in Europe with a drinking companion: "A time usually spent between us in the standard American way (figuring out how to make a million dollars) or figuring a way to get back across the Atlantic Ocean—obviously we haven't managed either solution yet. Just winding up old men . . . our lost youth: lost somewhere between London and Tripoli—Lord! If you see us selling pencils in the Edgeware Road don't be surprised." Gaddis once said that he "came out of Mark Twain's vestpocket," and in the letters of the late 1940s, one begins to detect the signs of Gaddis's humor, self-deprecating at times, the mock astonishment, the barbed asides, smilingly acidic or caustically angry, the utter outrage. Often the wit is understated and occurs as the wry, astringent fiber at the core of his sentences: "My intestines have apparently decided that insurrection is to no avail, and have settled down to the right and reasonable acquittal of their duties."

His intestines may have been symptomatic of an internal struggle Gaddis was having trying to continue *The Recognitions*. Progress was slow and though he writes that he has constant pleasure when it goes well, he also feels "disgust and depression when I read it and it looks ridiculous, pretentious, sophomoric, imitative." He is still "scrabbling along," he writes his friend John Napper, with his "parade of megalomania." The evolving complexity of his manuscript made tracking his proliferating characters, incidents, and situations formidable. At one point Gaddis describes a village of confetti, bits of paper on which he has made notes that he has spent the entire afternoon trying to arrange.

Gaddis returned to New York in late spring of 1951 with almost one hundred thousand words (a quarter of the final version), and the resolve to continue. He got some writing assignments for a cultural magazine subsidized by the United States Information Agency, but he had more than enough time for his growing novel. Often, however, he was faced by "the usual horror of time scattering by, and little done."

In April 1952, an early section of his manuscript appeared in an influential place, *New American Writing*, which got him an agent and a contract with Harcourt Brace. Renting an empty suburban house on Long Island with everything functioning but the "immense television set which broke in protest of my moving in," the work went on for another year and a half and could sometimes seem like a "boring pretentious adolescent parade." Over ten pounds in weight and nearly a half million words, the novel would be almost a thousand pages of printed matter and would have to be priced accordingly, an issue that Gaddis realized would "assure it against anything so vulgar as a popular success."

About "dissolution and corruption of authority" in a time of confusion, Gaddis wrote to the physicist J. Robert Oppenheimer, *The Recognitions* was published in March 1955. Perhaps the most ambitious American fiction since *Moby Dick*, it was greeted as unenthusiastically as Melville had been by reviewers—"calmunists" Gaddis called them—who had not seemed to be able to read it, at least not with any generosity. Harcourt had published his book "surreptitiously," he confided to a friend, and treated him like a "posthumous author." He wouldn't even ask them "for air in a jug." Most of the reviews were "no-nothing" attempts. In the *New York Times*, the noted critic Granville Hicks blamed Gaddis for the ostentation of his effort, accusing him of "playing a game with such readers as he may be fortunate enough to have." The experience of being so misunderstood, Gaddis wrote, was like the first time one was "hauled into a police station." "The reception of a book," Gaddis would warn his friend David Markson, "can be plain water torture." Like Salinger, Pynchon, or Don DeLillo, Gaddis famously avoided his critics on the very Jamesian grounds he proposed in *The Recognitions*: "What's any artist but the dregs of his work? The human shambles that follows it around."

Although he conceived of *J R* in 1956, it only appeared in 1975. In the interim, he married, had two children, and wrote publicity and speeches for Pfizer Chemicals, Eastman Kodak, IBM, and the Ford Foundation to support his family. His own experiences in corporate America would become the basis for *J R*, which would be written at a snail's pace. Living "in a world of scrawled notes on the back of envelopes," made even more disorderly by the collapse of his first marriage, he continued to work on *J R* despite the "constant temptation to avoid it" and his own struggle with its "paralyzing effects."

That effort was rewarded with the National Book Award in 1976, and in his acceptance remarks Gaddis projected a standard for the invisible writer, the deliberately obscured figure whose ambition is to further the work without fostering any legend about its creator or the circumstance of its creation: "I feel like part of a vanishing breed that thinks a writer should be read and not heard, let alone seen. I think this because there seems so often today to be a tendency to put the person in the place of his or her work, to turn the creative artist into a performing one, to find what a writer says about writing somehow more valid, or more real, than the writing itself."

The Letters are a reminder of Gaddis's artistic seriousness as well of his clear moral center, the most traditional perspective for the novelist. Although he avoided interviews, he did give one to the English critic Malcolm Bradbury (who called Gaddis a writer without a biography) when his late novel *Carpenter's Gothic* came out. Trim, he seemed ill at ease, his jacket buttoned too tightly, with a constant cigarette and a pursed tension showing in his body, his hand over his mouth or supporting his own head as if the weight of what he had seen was too heavy to bear. His ancestors were Puritans who had come to Boston early in the seventeenth century and, to me, watching him years later on a bleached YouTube video, he resembled a modern version of Hawthorne's black veiled minister.

Many of the letters in the last part of this collection are about *Carpenter's Gothic* and *A Frolic of His Own*, the grit of literature, complaints and negotiations, thanks for awards like the MacArthur genius grant, the National Book Award, and others. In stark contrast are the letters to his children full of sound paternal advice and a rare humanity, such as the one he writes to his daughter Sarah in 1969 advising her that "a sense of humor is simply a sense of proportion." At least one of the letters is a comic gem, a four-page minute-by-minute account of a twelve-hour day in 1974 misspent avoiding his craft. Like some of his fiction, the letter is both excruciating and hilarious, and it reveals the enormous difficulty involved in writing prose that seems so natural and effortless.

CHAPTER 12

THE EDITOR AS MIDWIFE
WRITERS AND LITTLE MAGAZINES

[The critic's mission is] is to lend himself, to project himself, to feel and feel till he understands and to understand so well that he can say, to have perception at the pitch of passion and expression as embracing as the air, to be infinitely curious and incorrigibly patient, and yet plastic and inflammable and determinable, stooping to conquer and serving to direct—these are fine chances for an active mind, chances to add the idea of independent beauty to the conception of success.
—Henry James, New Review IV, 1891

In an essay simply called "Criticism," Henry James argued that the value of the critic depends on the degree to which he "reacts, reciprocates, and penetrates." For James, the act of criticism had to be as supple as it was sentient, as full of curiosity as sympathy for a perspective that might seem alien. A "torch-bearing outrider," to borrow James's compelling image, the critic, or editor, becomes the artist's "real helper," the midwife of a creative process.

While most critics may be concerned with abstruse theories sophisticated enough to force the work of art into a reductively Procrustean evaluation, others seek *value*. They see their function as introducing the new or recovering the forgotten that initially may have seemed either provocative or confusing. As the critic Walter Benjamin once observed, some works of art exist to confound tradition, to dissolve genre, to create something so new it defies our expectation of what art can become.

I would like to consider the careers of several editors in our time who have understood the receptivity James was describing, who have succeeded in finding a wider public for artists who otherwise might have been neglected or even ignored. These editors were acting critically, and Oscar Wilde could have been predicting their appearances in his essay "The Critic as Artist," when he decided that the central function of such discovery depended on comprehending new priorities and social changes the public is often too dense to ascertain.

Richard Seaver was a renowned editor at Grove Press in the 1960s who advocated for such writers as Henry Miller, Samuel Beckett, and William Burroughs. But his beginning was far more modest, joining the editorial staff of a precariously underfinanced little magazine named *Merlin* in Paris in the early 1950s. Like many editors, he was left with almost no time to write his own work. His posthumous memoir, *The Tender Hour of Twilight*, is an engaging account of the literary life in Paris in the 1950s and New York in the 1960s.

Seaver had no literary antecedents or personal connections, and was raised in anthracite country in northeastern Pennsylvania. At the University of North Carolina he wrote a senior thesis on Hemingway and began writing himself. After teaching Latin and starting a wrestling program at a prep school, he received an American Field Service fellowship to study at the Sorbonne.

Arriving in Paris in 1948, he was impressed by the gratitude the French felt for Americans while amused by their scorn for the English language. Short of funds, like James Joyce, he began teaching English at the Berlitz School for fifty cents an hour and to Air France flight stewardesses at Orly Airport, which he would reach by bicycle, an hour and a half of piston pumping wrestler's legs each way.

Life was incredibly inexpensive and food was still rationed: one could purchase a bottle of Algerian wine for twenty-five cents. His first hotel room, with its "hideous flowered wallpaper," was a former cramped maid's quarters and cost thirty cents a day. In exchange for watching an antique business for a few hours a week, he moved to a storage depot in what had been a fifteenth-century windmill in Saint-Germain-des-Prés.

Through a girlfriend, he encountered a purported diamond merchant who was actually a thief and whose promise to finance a literary magazine only got Seaver (and his friend, the painter Ellsworth Kelly) detained by police. Despite the opéra bouffe overtones of this, some of the people Seaver would encounter in Paris would help determine his future career as an editor. Writing film pieces for the English-language Paris *International Herald Tribune*, he met Orson Welles, which only led to conversational delight, and then a young "imperiously tall" Scottish writer, Alexander Trocchi, who spoke with a musical lilt and who had organized the first issue of a new magazine magically called *Merlin*.

Seaver would contribute one of the first intelligent assessments of the then barely known Samuel Beckett. He had been an early admirer of *Molloy* and *Malone meurt*. Seaver had read these stripped, minimal fictions in the uncut pages Beckett wrote in French as published by Editions de Minuit (which he tells us accommodated the neighborhood bordello before the war). Intrigued, he read an earlier novel, the bawdier more self-consciously Joycean *Murphy*, in English. The result was what Edmund Wilson once termed a "shock of recognition," compounded by the fact that no one in France seemed to have heard of Beckett.

After finding the reclusive Beckett through his French publisher, Seaver asked him to contribute to *Merlin*. On a night of pouring rain, a tall, gaunt, drenched man in a raincoat (Beckett himself) passed the unpublished manuscript of *Watt* to Seaver and strode off. Subsequently, in a repeated bonding ritual with red wine at La Coupole and the Dome, Seaver would translate into English, with Beckett's collaboration, a story called "La fin." In the process, Seaver became a first-name friend with some entry to Beckett's mysterious privacy. Beckett even described the sparseness of his furnishings—though he had a radio to satisfy his interest in sports—in his two-room cottage, his writer's retreat, in Ussy-sur-Marne, and the concrete wall he wanted built (at the cost of his view!) to protect him from the occasional glances of passersby. Still quite unknown, Beckett had been on the verge of discontinuing writing but was about to receive worldwide recognition because *Waiting for Godot* would be staged in Paris in 1954.

Jean-Paul Sartre had published "La fin" in his magazine, *Le Temps modernes*, so Seaver sought him out to suggest a publishing collaboration. A very short man with a disconcerting stare, one eye looking straight at his interlocutor while the other veered off to the side, Sartre encouraged Seaver to publish the former convict Jean Genet in *Merlin* as the uncloseted Genet was still too outrageous for the French.

By 1954, after six years in Paris, Seaver was tentatively entering the literary culture there. At the same time, he had met and married Jeannette Medina, a student of the violin at the Paris Conservatory and, with the assistance of a Fulbright fellowship, he was writing a doctoral dissertation at the Sorbonne on Joyce's use of interior monologue, where every virgule had to be fastidiously placed in its proper French order. In the high and often hilarious spirit of youth, Seaver describes the misadventures of financing a struggling underground literary venture, working as a translator for an American company building airbases in France to underwrite several issues. While *Merlin*'s success was complicated by Trocchi's propensity for heroin, the highlights of the experience were the opportunities to meet writers of distinction and perhaps to help discover other writers.

One of these was the aspiring Irish playwright Brendan Behan, a rotund bulldog of scotch and song, who sought him out for an introduction to his fellow Irishman, Beckett, and moved into Seaver's easy chair, pleading indigence and consuming all his scotch. Seaver met another playwright, Eugène Ionesco, a diminutive, balding, owlish man with a cherubic face and better manners, and translated one of his plays for *Merlin*.

A more consequential meeting was with the French publisher Maurice Girodias, who convinced *Merlin* to join forces to publish books, starting with Beckett's *Watt* and an English translation of Genet's *Thief's Journal*. Girodias had inherited the Olympia Press from his father, who had notoriously published Henry Miller's *Tropic of Cancer* in 1934. A dandy (with manicured fingers but very limited assets), Gerodias drove a dark blue Citroën, and always dressed in impeccable black suits, and like his father was determined to publish the most scandalously shocking and unpublishable works in the world.

Yet another publisher whom Seaver had met in Paris was Barney Rosset, the American son of a Chicago banker who had purchased a small firm on Grove Street in the Greenwich Village section of lower Manhattan. Initially, Rosset was interested in Beckett but eventually in Seaver. A few years later, after a tour in the navy and a stint administering a book club for the small New York publishing house of George Braziller, Seaver went to work for Grove Press.

Opinionated, irascible, brazen but smart, a gutsy dynamo, Rosset was a 130-pound bantamweight on amphetamines with a bear's loyal heart and stubbornness, a two-martini man who often forgot about the need for food to accompany his gin at lunch. In business for a decade in 1959 when Seaver became editor in chief, the house was publishing sixty to seventy titles annually though still condescended to by the larger uptown firms.

Rosset, who had written an undergraduate piece on Henry Miller at Swarthmore College in 1940, wanted to issue the first American edition of *Tropic of Cancer*, and decided to set a precedent by first bringing out the unexpurgated third version of D. H. Lawrence's *Lady Chatterley's Lover*, the Orioli edition that had been published in Italy in 1928. The court challenges, aided by the sympathetic testimony of witnesses such as critics Malcolm Cowley and Alfred Kazin, resulted in the sale of millions of copies of the book.

Rosset was willing to gamble the entire future of Grove Press on the dangers of publishing *Tropic of Cancer*, a book that had been banned as contraband in the United States since its original appearance in Paris in 1934. He offered Miller a huge advance of $50,000, an unheard of amount then. The problem was Miller was reluctant, living in Big Sur, California, with his fourth wife and children in genteel poverty, ambivalent about fame and a predictable court wrangle, and happy enough with his reputation as an "outlaw author" with the occasional sale of one of his watercolors for fifty dollars.

The ensuing court battles, which lasted two years—beginning with over sixty legal contentions all over the country—were ended by the Supreme Court, enlarging forever the notion of what one was free to write and publish. That decision of the Warren Court, like *Brown v. Board of Education*, an earlier one that ended a century of American apartheid, changed the face and future of America. No wonder Eisenhower regretted his nomination of Earl Warren to head the court. Although the costs of the legal process almost drained Rosset entirely, there was enough moxie and money left for the publication and defense in 1962 of William Burroughs's *Naked Lunch*, which would only be fully exonerated in the highest court of Massachusetts in 1966.

Barney Rosset sold his firm to Anne Getty of the oil fortune in the early 1970s, at which point Seaver left Grove to start his own imprint. At that time I met Rosset, who told me that his last act as a publisher—right before Getty fired him—had been to reprint *Naked Angels*. Grove succeeded in keeping my book in print for another few decades. I can testify that to the end of his long life Rosset still drank prodigiously, mostly rum and coke, and remained thin and lively, always interested in the new.

Properly, *The Tender Hour of Twilight* is much more devoted to the writers Seaver admired and helped sponsor than to the more modest details of his own life. Near its end, the memoir begins to lose momentum and become anecdotal. He reveals that he translated the sensational *The Story of O* into English for Grove, for instance, and how he took Beckett (who knew nothing about baseball) to a Mets doubleheader with Beckett insisting on staying for the second evening game despite his failing eyesight. The book ends with Seaver and his wife Jeannette escorting the gnomic Jean Genet to the seedy sides of Times Square in

1968 and to the Chicago Democratic political convention. By this point the narrative collapses entirely—Seaver was writing this fitfully over the final decade of his life—and his widow, who edited the book posthumously, adds trembling extracts from Seaver's diary accounts of the police riots terrorizing the protesters in Chicago.

I read the memoir wanting to learn more about the intricacies of the editorial process, but on this score I was disappointed. Seaver tells us how much he likes the smell of fresh print (which makes me sneeze). He does admit that his normal workday at Grove involved ten to twelve hours, for which he was never properly compensated. The book has a useful index, and my only qualm with *The Tender Hour of Twilight* (an allusion to Fitzgerald) is Seaver's systematic invention of dialogue he claims to have remembered. When he visits one of James Joyce's sisters in Ireland, he gives her the fluency of Richard Ellmann; at another point he repeats a five-hundred-word disquisition by Sartre on the reasons for his rupture with Camus, which would have required a hidden tape recorder to recall. While such passages may induce more narrative flow, they inevitably reduce authenticity, which always compromises history.

One key perception that Seaver offers, however, at least in the little magazine scene that *Merlin* occupied, is that there are always more ambitious writers than devoted readers. To that admonition I would add the advice that for any unknown writer—as Seaver was when he wrote about Beckett for *Merlin*—magazine or small-press publication represents an opportunity to establish credibility.

Working on a small magazine, for free probably and on whatever level, can become a possible entry to a literary life. Proximity often leads to possibilities, which may begin with a book review or an emergency assignment. When I began writing seriously I had no agent and no sure knowledge of how to go about getting my work published. In college, I wrote for the newspaper and edited a journal. My first soap-bubble essay, a far too enthusiastic discussion of a long-forgotten utopian novel by Austin Tappan Wright, *Islandia*, was published there.

In those heady days, I would go to the most literary bookstore in Manhattan, the Gotham Book Mart on Forty-Seventh Street, directly across the street from where my grandfather and father had their offices and traded diamonds. The Gotham was owned by Frances Steloff, a tiny, thin elderly lady whom I often saw musing near the front entrance. Innocently, I never realized she was keeping her eye open for book thieves. The small, narrow store had a good selection of poetry magazines and I rifled through them, mainly to get their addresses. I was writing poems then and, like some mole blinded by sunlight, I would submit to a dozen magazines simultaneously. A few accepted my poems. Pretty soon I was also doing book reviews for a magazine run by the Paulist fathers, the *Catholic World*, which would even pay me for my efforts. All this juvenilia would become credentials, printed matter I could show to others.

From Poe to Whitman to Hemingway, writers have learned much about their craft by working for magazines and newspapers. If you cannot find such an opportunity, an even better recourse would be to begin your own magazine as Ed Sanders did with *Fuck You / A Magazine of the Arts*. To some extent, the blog may seem as valid a medium as the magazine, though for me the printed word always conveys more authority. I realize this advice may sound old-fashioned in the new world of MFA programs and writing workshops on every university campus. And if you manage to excite a connected instructor, as Ken Kesey did when he wrote *One Flew over the Cuckoo's Nest* in Malcolm Cowley's workshop at Stanford University, your path may be facilitated.

Seaver began with France and *Merlin*. He did much more editing than writing himself. Curiously, another student from his generation attended the same university. The poet Lawrence Ferlinghetti had a literary career with parallel antecedents. Ferlinghetti had a rocky beginning in life: his father died six months before his birth and his mother was sent to an asylum a few months after. Fortunately, he was adopted by the daughter of the man who founded Sarah Lawrence College and was raised in Bronxville, an elite suburb north of New York City. He was sent to prep schools and at the University of North Carolina at Chapel Hill he wrote on sports for the *Daily Tarheel*, and contributed stories to the *Carolina Quarterly*, an excellent literary magazine.

Enlisting in the navy after Pearl Harbor, he served as an officer on subchasers, escort vessels that dropped explosives on German submarines. He participated in the invasion of Normandy, which was the beginning of the defeat of Germany, and visited Nagasaki six weeks after the atomic explosion that ended the war with Japan. On the GI Bill, he studied at Columbia University, and then went to France in 1947 to study at the Sorbonne where he received a doctorate in 1949. In San Francisco two years later, he began working with Peter Martin on his magazine, *City Lights Journal*, named after Chaplin's film and in which Ferlinghetti's first translations of Jacques Prévert appeared. Like Seaver, he began by translating and editing a little magazine.

With Martin, Ferlinghetti started a paperbound bookstore, a novel idea after the war as the book market was changing, located between North Beach and Chinatown. Called City Lights, it was intended as a place to foster intellectual inquiry and activity. He also created his press, which like Rosset and Seaver's Grove Press was based on the notion that freedom of speech needed advocacy. One of its focal points became Beat-related publications like *The Yage Letters*, an epistolary exchange between Burroughs and Ginsberg from the Amazon basin, and Neal Cassady's *The First Third*, a somewhat awkward, strained account of the Beat catalyst's early years. City Lights Press became the model for a small-press alternative in America. This was important at a time when bigger, more commercial publishers were selling their assets to Europeans, collapsing their trade divisions, consolidating, or disappearing.

Ferlinghetti wanted to publish poetry in an inexpensive format that could reach working classes rather than the more elite audience that patronized poetry. The Pocket Poets Series issued funny-looking little square paperbacks that could be easily slipped into a pocket. The first book he published in this series was his own *Pictures of the Gone World*, a mixture of elegy and optimism influenced by the innovativeness of Apollinaire, Prévert, and e. e. cummings. The fourth in the Pocket Poets Series was Ginsberg's *Howl and Other Poems* that changed the nature of American poetry.

Like Ginsberg's, Ferlinghetti's poetry was written as a reaction to academic formalism, and he seems inspired more by the street than the museum. Just as Ginsberg's *Howl* would be the best-selling book of poems in his generation, Ferlinghetti's own *A Coney Island of the Mind*, with its insouciant bravado and cheer, has passed the million sales mark, and probably has introduced more young Americans to the sphere of poetry than other living poet. New Directions recently published Ferlinghetti's *Time of Useful Consciousness*, the second part of a longer work in progress called *Americus*. What may be surprising about this latest book is Ferlinghetti's age: he is ninety-three but still as overtly political and progressive as ever.

Both Seaver and Ferlinghetti were leavening agents who were as open to the Beat sensibility as to other kinds of writing. I have often been asked, by students and journalists, about the successors to the

Beat movement, the writers in our culture who might be seen as having the same degree of cultural impact. Ferlinghetti is still alive, as are Gary Snyder and Judith Malina, among others, but soon we will reach a point with no first-generation Beats left. There was what we might call a flickering second generation, beginning with Burroughs's son who wrote three books before his early death; Kerouac's daughter, Jan, who wrote two novels; and Lucien Carr's son Caleb, who wrote the best-selling *The Alienist*. Others such as Ed Sanders or the poet Anne Waldman figure prominently in this succession.

Literary movements are quite rare, however, and no one expects much continuity. The Beats may be achieving canonical status because their work remains in print internationally, there has been a lot of posthumous publication and criticism, and they have a wide university audience. The road novel has become generic (with predecessors such as Mark Twain, Jack London, and John Steinbeck) but imitation often only shows unassimilated influence, and the faddishness of popular culture tends to co-opt and vitiate the real message. Singers such as Patti Smith and Tom Waits may offer nostalgic reminders, but these can only be shadow messages.

The Beats came together in Manhattan at a time when the artistic energy attracted by the city was at a high point. Between the two world wars, Paris had been the dominant center, until a seismic shift was revealed particularly with the emerging abstract expressionists like de Kooning and Pollock. De Kooning was Dutch and during the war a number of French surrealists and expressionists, such as Max Ernst, sought refuge in Manhattan. While artists were devastated by the war, it was a time to imagine something new. The Beats benefited from a moment of great reciprocity in the arts as well, which was nourishing and encouraging.

The Beat movement was constituted by a whole panoply of poets, novelists, playwrights, and visual artists that began in New York City and San Francisco and then spread around the country and the world. One neo-Beat whom I knew for years was the poet Ira Cohen, whose Lower East Side loft was like an artist's salon in the 1960s.

Ira's parents were deaf and as a child he was taught to communicate with them with signs. As a scholarship student, he went to Horace Mann, graduated at the age of sixteen, and then attended Cornell where he took a class with Vladimir Nabokov. He never completed his degree and by 1961 he was living in a room in Tangier for sixty cents a night where he met the novelist and composer Paul Bowles, Burroughs, and Burroughs's friend Brion Gysin, an artist who had a nightclub called the Thousand and One Nights. Cohen would spend the next four years in the "revolving dream machine of a Tangier fantasy not even Scheherazade could have imagined."

Later, staying at what was called the Beat Hotel near Notre-Dame in Paris, he saw Burroughs and Gysin again. Like Seaver with *Merlin* and Ferlinghetti with *City Lights Journal*, he began a literary magazine called *Gnaoua* where he published Burroughs and Gysin's essay on the exorcistic music and the trance rituals of a group of Moroccan Joujouka musicians. Gysin had introduced Burroughs to the "cut-up" technique where he could cut some printed text and splice it without explanation or transition into what he was writing, With Mel Clay, one of the actors of the Living Theatre, Cohen created a text called *The Majoon Traveler—majoon* a North African hashish confection. Ira then wrote a piece on hash for *Playboy*, and then under the pseudonym Panama Rose *The Hashish Cookbook*.

Returning to the Lower East Side, Ira began taking photographs, making films, and writing poems. He worked in a technique called Mylar, photographing the reflected surface of a golden polyester, a radiant effect that the musician Jimi Hendrix compared to "looking through butterfly wings." In 1968, he filmed the Living Theatre's most controversial play, *Paradise Now*. Then he went to India and Kathmandu, Nepal, where he ran The Spirit-Catcher, a second-hand bookshop. Using a hand press he published manuscripts and poems on exquisite rice paper, sometimes flecked with gold powder.

I saw him in Kathmandu in 1975, an astonishing figure draped in a cape emerging from a rickshaw, and he handed me an invitation to a poetry reading that evening. The French poet Henri Michaux once stated that reading Ira Cohen was "like smoking raw nerves." In a shabby café on what the hippies called Freak Street, Ira's voice was oracular, dissidently bohemian, bituminously vitriolic, a scream in the expatriate night full of a malicious energy. He looked gaunt, dressed all in black, coughing tubercularly until the blood splattered his page, radiating spectacularly (on a pharmacopoeia of drugs, I assumed) like some demoniac resurrection of Edgar Allen Poe. Ira Cohen was the poète maudit of Kathmandu and his language seemed incantatory, raging, madly humorous, and apocalyptic.

By the beginning of the 1980s, Ira was back in New York City, now living in his mother's small apartment on 106th Street and Broadway where I sometimes would visit. Every time I went there I thought of my high school English teacher, Dr. Elizabeth Gordon, who had lived in the same building and had so inspired me. In Ira's apartment, the couch, every chair, even the window sills and all the available floor space was claustrophobically cluttered with stacks of papers, letters, magazines, books, records, an entire archive of hoarded accomplishment. It felt like a storage compartment. It did not relieve my feeling of confinement to hear that Ira's first cousin was Edward Koch, the former mayor of New York. It was a grand claim I could never verify and that I accepted as another of Ira's gripe jokes.

Ira had a bit of the editor's impresario left in him, and he invited me to read what I had written about Henry Miller at the Knitting Factory and the Nuyorican Poets Café, both humming places on the Lower East Side. He asked me to contribute poems I had written decades earlier to little poetry zines, and I complied, though with a dislocating sensation that the person who wrote those poems was no longer me. Whenever he had some event to announce, Ira would also call me to overwhelm my ear with one of his endless rants, quotations from what he had written or what he was reading, complaints about Ginsberg who would not fully accept him. Ira leaves one trace of his feeling of rejection by the Beats in his best book, *Poems from the Cosmic Crypt*, at the end of a poem called "Mirror Poem for Allen Ginsberg" where he proposes to discuss matters of mistaken identity:

> we will meet on the George Washington Bridge
> where we will settle these questions and decide
> why you were chosen to impersonate us all—
> even before we knew who we were
> we will embrace each other in empty movie
> theatres in the Bronx &
> we will play ping pong in the Byzantine madhouses
> where Carl Solomon is the head psychiatrist
> & commits us to infinity where we disappear at last
> with no more curtain calls, save one.

I suspect that like most artists Ira felt neglected and only wanted me to write about him. Instead he led me to Judith Malina and the Living

Theatre and reminded me so often that I had to write that history that I ultimately relented and spent years buried in archives. When my history was published, I dedicated it to him because Ira was a prototypical under the underground artist. His birthday parties were all at other friend's homes or cafés or clubs, fabulous all-night extravaganzas of Moroccan food, flutes, and gyrating bodies in a thick haze of marijuana smoke. Although he ended up on the Upper West Side of Manhattan, his soul belonged downtown, which is where I often saw him.

I would argue that while there are no survivors of the Beats, their spiritual effusion is now part of the air we breathe. But in the fin de siècle on the Lower East Side of Manhattan in the 1980s and 1990s, one might have detected simmering signs of the same energies that made the Beats so prominent. Ginsberg was still alive during almost all of that period and his sustained commitment to the Poetry Project at the St. Mark's Church was centralizing. Newspapers like the *Village Voice* (before it was purchased by real estate interests to sell porn), *Soho News* (for which I covered the twenty-fifth anniversary reading of *Howl* at Columbia University), and the *East Village Eye*; small presses such as Raymond Foye's Hanuman; and journals such as Sylvère Lotringer's *Semiotext(e)* helped keep the word current.

The poet Richard Hell characterized his generation as blank, but many of these artists were as intransigent as the Beats and some were more politically outspoken. When the poet Eileen Myles quixotically advertised herself as a write-in candidate in the 1992 presidential election, her platform was strikingly progressive and radically ahead of its time, proposing to tax assets instead of income, guaranteeing health care for all, and reducing defense spending by 75 percent.

Artists gathered in the dilapidated area of the Lower East Side of Manhattan and fostered a sense of a besieged community. Patti Astor and Bill Stelling's FUN Gallery introduced Jean-Michel Basquiat and Keith Haring and suddenly there were over two hundred small galleries like Franklin Furnace, CB's 313, and PS122 competing for an uptown audience that would end up by gentrifying the neighborhood. Andy Warhol, with his implacable I-can-do-anything attitude, and the circle of artists and performers who surrounded him were a key influence. One of them was Gerard Malanga, a poet who did Warhol's silkscreens, who had danced with the Velvet Underground, and who became the first editor of *Interview Magazine*. I knew Gerard because he interviewed Mellon in *Scopophilia*, a book of interviews and photographs he was editing, and because we had a mutual friend in Ira Cohen.

Theater groups like Richard Foreman's Wooster Group and the Living Theatre, which returned to a new location on Third Street and Avenue C in 1988 after a few decades abroad, contributed to an attitude of experimentation. Open to poetry as well as a punk sound, music venues like the Kitchen, the Knitting Factory, CBGB, and the Mudd Club added to the vitality of the area. One night in 1988 at the Kitchen, Allen Ginsberg, Carl Solomon, Judith Malina, Bob Holman, and a group of other writers read all of Jack Kerouac's *Mexico City Blues*, a book he had written while living on pennies a day on the bowery of Mexico City thirty years earlier. The Mudd Club was on White Street, just off the Bowery, which still had its flophouses, its fifteen-cent beer halls, its anguished procession of deadbeat hobo winos, depleted souls with haunted expressions as if on a final march to extinction. The place was grunge chic, unlike the celebrity culture of the uptown Studio 54. I was often there at 2 a.m., helping my wife photograph a singer named Marilyn who was a Monroe look-alike and other punk musicians.

Editors began blending the visual with what young writers had to say, just as some of the writers began to blur the lines between fiction and memoir. Magazines such as Joel Rose and Catherine Texier's *Between C and D*, Kurt Hollander's overtly political *Portable Lower East Side*, the more visual *Red Tape*, or improvisational attempts such as *Top Stories*, *Just Another Asshole*, *Benzene*, *Bikini Girl*, and *Bomb* continued the agitprop and avant-garde priorities of Black Mountain in the 1950s or Ferlinghetti's *City Lights Journal*, and served to disseminate the work of artists such as David Wojnarowicz, and writers including Dennis Cooper, Kathy Acker, and Lynne Tillman. In the tradition of Beat poet LeRoi Jones's *Yugen* and *Floating Bear*, magazines that were challenging but essentially cooked in kitchens, some of these publications were ad hoc, produced by mimeo or photocopy and distributed by hand, and some like *Public Illuminations*, *Wedge*, and *Unbearable Assembly* were more fugitive.

One reason the vaulting creativity of the Lower East Side underground has slipped into history is, to paraphrase Artaud, that its writers did not produce masterwork on the level of "Howl" or *Naked*

Lunch. Burroughs may have been the godfather of punk, but the scene progressed beyond irreverence to a bitterness born from a sense of its own collapse, the AIDS crisis of the late 1980s, and as a profound reaction to the disillusioned aspirations of the early 1960s. Like fireflies of illumination, however, with a potential for a brighter flame, the scene moved west, first to Williamsburg and Bushwick in Brooklyn, then, like *Semiotext(e)*, all the way to L.A.

Three The metaphysics of writing

CHAPTER 13   **BOMBING WITH WORDS**

*Sticks 'n' stones may break my bones,
But words can never harm me.*

I. Beginning Near Babylon

Both the Old and New Testaments deserve consideration as among the earliest, most enduring, and skillful narratives of the last five millennia. Their impact on what we call the Judeo-Christian ethical tradition has certainly been formative and profound. Among the ancient Hebrews, the issue of narrative must have been central, and in their creation myth, Genesis, their God miraculously *speaks* the earth and all its constituents into being. Rarely can we find occasions in human history when the word seems as potent or efficacious.

Throughout the Old and the New Testaments, the word expresses divine will, so it is no surprise that the Gospel of John strikingly acknowledges that "in the beginning was the Word, and the Word was with God, and the Word was God." If there is any potential sanctity to language, surely it is derived from such sources.

There are myriad other instances of the centrality of words and their consequences in biblical narratives and sacred texts of any postliterate culture. Perhaps the most dramatic, however, is the fable of Nimrod, the Babylonian tyrant from Sumer, who ordered the construction of a giant ziggurat, or tower, to be built with baked bricks and mortar instead of stone, essentially a new technology seven centuries before Christ. Nimrod was a descendent of Noah, the biblical hero of the great flood, caused by the God of the Jews to punish humans for their wanton behavior. The tower was said to have had a sword-bearing idol at its peak, challenging and defying that God who, as the allegory would have it, retaliated against its construction by making its builders unable to understand one another and creating multiple languages instead of one.

Balal, the Hebrew word for "jumble," leads to Babel, which becomes the name of the tower, the city of Babylon near it, and the word "babble" that for us signifies nonsense. All the difficulties associated with the word ever since may derive from this fable.

II. Pugilistics

My familiarity with linguistic misuse and distress is based more on the last century or so than on what may have occurred in prerecorded time. The issue with which I am concerned here is the way words can be misunderstood, or incite either anger or pain.

I don't mean in the burlesque sense in which very early in the twentieth century the Georgian poet Lascelles Abercrombie offered to resolve a quarrel over Wordsworth with Ezra Pound. Abercrombie had published an essay urging a return to Wordsworth in a search for true values. Pound, with his own delusions about the twelfth-century Provencal troubadour as courtier, who deplored the romantics as a modern model, retorted in a letter challenging Abercrombie to a duel: "stupidity carried beyond a certain point becomes a public menace," he declared. The hapless Abercrombie heard that Pound had been a skilled fencer in college. As the challenged party, he had the right to choose weapons, and he proposed that they bombard each other with the unsold copies of their books. The absurdity of the proposition itself ended the threat.

There can be a very competitive, pugilistic edge to some writers, particularly those like Pound who always seem on the pinnacle of controversy. He took boxing lessons from the young Hemingway in Paris after World War I, which is another scene of ridiculous posturing: two men swinging at each other in a small Parisian kitchen. Afterward, at least, did they recover with Pernod and snails?

This was the time when the Dadaists were confounding language by inverting or parodying the meaning of words and tradition; when Pound read Hemingway's early stories, he showed him how to trim the fat, expunge the unnecessary, believe in the defining image. Decades later, when Hemingway saw himself as the heavyweight champion of literature, he would have a boxing ring built outside his home in Key West, challenging much younger men to stay in the ring with him.

We all know that words, when they denigrate or insult, can wound, and sometimes when words are used in what a majority considers a politically incorrect manner, severe punishment can occur. If a professor should argue that "enhanced interrogation techniques" are only an Orwellian euphemism for torture, will the consequence be loss of tenure? If the Second Amendment justifies guns in the hands of a trained militia, how does that right get extended to the deer hunter? (Or is the war against nature?) Even a writer has to wonder whether words have inherent meanings, or whether their application is always relative. To what extent is "meaning" itself subject to the superior power of bureaucratic authority?

Consider, for instance, an episode in the history of the Living Theatre, a small, radical group of actors who in the conformist moment of the 1950s were helping to create a very politicized kind of production influenced by the French playwright Antonin Artaud. The theater, which the actors had helped renovate themselves as a sign of their commitment, was on Fourteenth Street and Sixth Avenue, and it was the beginning of the off-Broadway movement, which then moved more marginally "off-off" and regionally around America.

Judith Malina and Julian Beck, who formed and led the company, did not believe in the Broadway model that theater was merely an entertainment to divert an audience from the cares of the world. Beck and Malina were nonviolent anarchists influenced by the writer and social critic Paul Goodman, who had advised that there were moments when political argument, if genuine, should be powerful and brazenly honest and antinomian enough to risk jail. If there was a metaphorical line in the sand that demarcated the socially acceptable from the unacceptable, the anarchist was bound to cross it when a valued moral principle was at stake.

In 1963, the Living Theatre was performing a play called *The Brig* when the theater was seized by agents of the Internal Revenue Service. A siege ensued with the police barricading the theater while protesters marched. When the actors broke into the padlocked theater and performed again, the power was turned off, but the lights of television crews were sufficient. Then Beck and Malina were arrested and incarcerated for a month.

Our secular version of Moses's Ten Commandments is our Bill of Rights, which insures us the liberties of free speech and inquiry, but somehow it had been decided that this legally chartered nonprofit, which like churches was exempt from taxation, was in violation of law. Actually, the problem was the play itself. Written by Ken Brown, it naturalistically documented what he had seen when serving in the U.S. Marines in Japan. He had received a four-hour recreational pass and, like many of his fellow soldiers, decided to spend it in a bordello rather than a museum. He had such a good time that he returned to his base ten minutes late and was given thirty days in the Marine jail as punishment.

In the play the guards, like the prisoners, are Americans, but the prisoners have no names, only numbers, and they are forced by their screaming, abusive guards to move in the confined space of the Marine brig with robotic precision. If they cannot conform, they are beaten. The play is a demonstration of what Artaud called the "theater of cruelty," and the lights and sound are intensified so that the audience might share the prisoner's pain. The play was powerful enough to get the *New York Times* theater critic, Howard Taubman, to call for an investigation of Marine penal practices.

Like the sword-bearing idol at the peak of Babel, the play was seen as a provocation. Terrified, after Beck and Malina's release from prison, the entire company, with their children and spouses, fled to Europe where they would perform the most innovative theater on the continent for the next five years. The legal process dragged on for a decade at the end of which the Living Theatre was fined a token dollar. The object of the prosecution, however, had been quite successful—intimidation, harassment, and, ultimately, censure.

III. Ithkuil

We will all understand that words can often be seen as instruments of sophistic seduction, as in the world of advertising or public relations, when the "truth" seems subservient to the promise of potential sales, whether the product is a politician or a pharmaceutical product. Even as language exists as our primary means of reading the mind and its mannerisms, the insufficiencies of language, its ambiguity and vagueness, the polysemy of words with their denotative and connotative possibilities, all contribute to the hazardous stumbling blocks of interpretation. "The limits of my language," as the philosopher Ludwig Wittgenstein once put it, "mean the limits of my world."

Joshua Foer has written on Ithkuil, a newly invented language that attempts to be more precise, logical, and efficient than any of the approximately six thousand languages still extant. He begins his *New Yorker* piece by considering the various ways we can express looking, as basic a human act as listening: "We can glimpse, glance, visualize, view, look, spy or ogle. Stare, gawk, or gape. Peek, watch or scrutinize." Each choice, he points out, suggests a subtle difference: "looking implies volition; spying suggests furtiveness, gawking carries an element of social judgment and a sense of surprise." Each choice, Foer also alleges, involves some sort of linguistic compromise, part of the disorderly evolution of languages over time.

While I agree with Foer that most language is quirky, riddled by irregularities, I hesitate to accept his verdict of "compromise." To succeed, written language, much more than speech which rushes past too quickly, depends on selection, and the right choice does not depend on compromise. When the bullet hits the bull's-eye, we applaud the act as marksmanship. The eccentricities of any language—and particularly the version of English used by Americans, which draws on a huge reservoir of assimilated energies, the result of a global influx—present an advantage for the writer. It is a language with enormous range and variability. Consider the simple three-letter word "set," which has over fifty uses as a noun and more than a hundred as a verb. The *Oxford Unabridged Dictionary* needs sixty thousand words to describe it.

Selection is key. Though it cannot always prevent either misunderstanding or confusion, language is our most subjective medium, and linguistic attempts at objectification like Ithkuil or Esperanto before it have as much of a chance of popular adoption for discourse as mathematical formulae. The grammatical rules governing language are themselves only a recent innovation—a few hundred years old. These rules evolve in a fluid field in the way Foer, in the lines I quoted above, and in as elegant a magazine as the *New Yorker*, is permitted to use sentence fragments promiscuously. The ungovernable subjectivity of language is a source of nourishment, vitality, and abuse.

IV. The Bombast

Sometimes, the most violative use of language is the most personal and painful. Let me tell you the story of the friend I call Professor X. Almost fifty years ago, I met him in graduate school at New York University where we were both on the grinding path to the Ph.D. Professor X was, perhaps, a little slower than I was in his academic pursuits, but in the end no less successful. I had introduced him to my sister's best friend, the woman who became his second wife, at one of the overcrowded BYOB parties I used to throw when I lived on the Lower East Side in the early 1960s. I may have been insufficiently discreet about whom I invited, but I was young and in a celebratory mood.

It was a particularly hot night and the future Professor X went up to the roof to court my sister's friend (with whom he would later raise two accomplished children). Drunkenly, he tossed a half empty can of beer at a police car down below. Justifiably enraged, two policemen stormed up to my fourth floor walkup and served me with a summons.

I have to explain I was particularly apprehensive about the law and usually circumspect and cautious when it came to police authority. All I knew about the unfathomable mysteries and absurdities of law had been formed by reading Charles Dickens's *Bleak House* and Franz Kafka's *The Trial*. Dickens's huge novel was a warning that any legal process could become interminable enough to overwhelm a life; Kafka's baffled and beaten central character Joseph K seemed to inhabit a universe with few rational options, thwarted by an arcane language where justice usually was fickle or arbitrary and often brutal in its consequences.

When I went to court to answer my summons, I was quite terrified. Correctly berated by a judge, I paid a stiff fine, but I forgave my friend. He invited me to attend a weekly writing workshop that included poets such as Richard Howard and Charles Simic on occasion, which I enjoyed more for its social interactions than for aesthetic instruction. The workshop lapsed with his first marriage, but for the next four decades, Professor X and I would meet once a week or so for a few drinks and dinner, usually in an Indian resto near his apartment uptown or a more elegant Spanish one near me.

Over the years, I had learned not to ask Professor X for advice because it was invariably, and comically sometimes, cockeyed, or at least nearsighted. When I was writing my first book, *Naked Angels*, I told him I planned a historical and biographical approach, which he insisted was inadvisable. What I should do, he urged, was scrutinize the texts exclusively as if they existed in a vacuum. I knew that that was the New Criticism approach favored when we were graduate students, but I wanted to write an account that would go beyond a merely academic or purist audience. Somehow, my approach offended him and when I was done he accused me of having created a tapestry of generalities.

Subsequently, when I was writing about Pound and modernism, Professor X, a poet himself, decided he could improve my literary style, and would parse my sentences with his suggestions. If anything, they served to flatten my expression and deaden it in a formalistic manner. I knew he needed his wife to correct his grammar, and I was unconvinced that he had much that was useful for me. Although I enjoyed his poetry and attended his public readings, I didn't think he was on the level of an Ezra Pound, who had tutored William Butler Yeats in the principles of imagism. At some point, when he saw that whatever I wrote was published and translated without the benefit of his suggestions, he relented and no longer marked up my manuscripts, and maybe no longer read what I wrote.

It did not matter though. When I was researching Judith Malina's archive in the early 1990s, I would go to his house more often than he visited mine since he lived less than half a mile away from Judith. Although I felt that because his wife was often away in the evenings, he was scheduling me more as an entertainment than anything else, that didn't matter either since I would be entertained as well. We enjoyed single malt scotch together, enjoyed our Indian curries, and found enough to say to each other about family matters or the educational bureaucracies in which we worked. Inevitably, though, we would also discuss past literature. I knew that with Professor X this could be a contentious arena, especially if I was writing about it, and I had to maintain a sense of humor.

The Spanish place in my neighborhood is called Sevilla, and it has occupied the corner of West Fourth and Charles Street for as long as we have been friends. I never found the food particularly good and a Spanish friend of mine declared it was a terrible fraud for tourists. They served a house salad with what they called a secret recipe, iceberg lettuce with a dressing concocted of sugar and ketchup, and a garlic shrimp with a ton of saffron rice. You could smell the garlic on Charles Street, just down from where Sarah Jessica Parker used to live. I would go there with Professor X because he insisted it was his favorite downtown restaurant, the first one he had ever gone to without his parents.

We were going there on the night of his final visit, preceded by the single malts. My friend seemed high when he arrived at my place and immediately began complaining that I had been speaking too loudly at our last meeting. I was slightly taken back by this remark because we had eaten in a very small French bistro whose din was so overwhelming that I could barely hear myself, but I let his chastisement pass because my general impression was that Professor X had never listened to anything that I said.

Professor X had retired from his academic duties and was now devoting all his efforts to his verse. Over the years, he had created five slim volumes, the last few published by a dubious firm in Detroit, and another by a publisher I had never heard of in upstate New York. Now he had arranged for a volume of *Selected Poems*, a few hundred copies whose publication he may have partially subsidized. It is a difficult time for writers and I could understand and sympathize: at least, he was persisting, and he was regularly welcomed by a following in a narrow cellar under a bar in my neighborhood where poets would gather and read. As a poet, Professor X delighted in the sounds he could produce, in the jazz accompaniment he insisted on, and would read whenever or practically wherever asked. I don't see this eagerness to be heard as being indiscriminate, but part of the basic drive of many writers. On the one hand, he may have thought that he had finally arrived as a poet, even though his publisher was not Knopf, Harper Ecco, a distinguished house like Norton or New Directions, or one of the better small presses like Hanging Loose or Coffee House. It did not matter to me; I was happy for him.

Usually, we stopped at two drinks, but on this evening Mellon had joined us for a few moments, and we proceeded to a third. At several points in the conversation, grinning sheepishly, he assured me that I was surely "a good person." I wondered whether he intended this ironically, as when the novelist Ford Madox Ford in *The Good Soldier* used the word "good" as a rubric for the hypocritical values that led to the First World War.

Then, Professor X announced to Mellon and then reiterated to me that I was also bombastic! My livelihood depended on public speech and writing so the word "bombastic" seemed so disproportionate, so debilitating and devastating. Why couldn't my friend more generously have declared that in his view I was as expansive as the American economy and as capable of "excessive exuberance"? I admit I was, for once, just too stunned to retort. Perhaps, I was inhibited because my wife was there. I didn't think friends would try to inflict such damage in front of spouses except in an Albee play.

Professor X, who at the beginning of our friendship had flung a beer can from my roof at a police car below—a bombing that did not involve language—was insisting that I was bombastic! That was a word I associated with Hitler and Mussolini, whose speeches I had read and whose histrionic gesticulations I had certainly seen on film in connection with my biography of Pound. If I had one singular talent as a writer, I thought it was finding the right words for the occasion. If a writer was bombastic—flinging words as recklessly as bombs—he was an irresponsible, *bad* writer, a spastic with words, a flagellant of sorts abusing the trust of any reader.

Sadly, the friendship capsized on the hidden shoals of that one word, or my inability to retain my sense of humor. In a subsequent e-mail, Professor X attributed the word to my wife and even denied that he had used it. Professor X was quite social with lots of friends, and certainly did not deserve a bombastic one, a word I perhaps unfairly connected to Babel, to a bloated botulism, to the confused, blaring, braying of a bubble-brain. Maybe, in his eyes, I stand convicted of his accusation with the previous sentence, packed as it is with the plosive "b" sound? There were one or two subsequent e-mails but sometimes, as T. S. Eliot observed, things can end less with a bang than a whimper.

CHAPTER 14   **A WRITER'S RETREAT**

The man of wide international experience, much learning and leisure—luxurious product of our long and sophisticated history—may with good reason wish to live simply, with few tools and minimal clothes, close to nature.
—Gary Snyder, "Why Tribe"

I. Flatlanders' Paradise

I've spent much of my life in the cauldron of lower Manhattan, a place governed by the roars of traffic, over a quarter of a million cars crowding into Manhattan over bridges and through tunnels, the grating racket of garbage trucks, the stampedes of the tenants above, and the street screams full of terror, despair, and anguish that occasionally violate the night.

Such noise would disturb anyone, but the citizens of the city everywhere soon become inured, and as they accept the airport drone of air conditioning in the summer, they find ways to bear the raucous cacophony. Perhaps, my compromised ability to tolerate the sound distractions of metropolitan life is lessened by my work—for me, at least, writing requires solitude and some degree of quiet, though sometimes certain music can provide an insulating barrier.

A composer like John Cage might advocate integrating the actual sounds of the street, no matter how dissonant, into what he was creating, but the Zen of such spontaneous accident would only work for musicians as free as Cage. The rhythmic counterpoint of Johann Sebastian Bach has assisted my concentration and his "Well-Tempered Clavier" has helped me write many pages. Even so comforting a resource might not prove as effective in the warmer months when city sounds seem more penetrating, more frequent, more explosive and reverberating.

I teach writing and American literature at a university, and most of my own writing has to be accomplished during the summer months. I knew early on in my academic career that I would need a place to which I could retreat in order to read and write fruitfully.

In the spring of 1971, driving to work, I stopped off at my landlord's office to drop off my rent check. As I entered his office, a narrow space on Seventh Avenue around the corner from my apartment, two men pointed pistols at my temples and ordered me to be still. Barney Levine, my landlord, was an elderly obese man sucking perpetually on a cigar, and spitting often in his office or outside. He had a prominent safe in the rear; luckily he was not in his office because he was stubborn enough to have shrugged when the bandits demanded access and could very well have replied—"so shoot!"

My little Austin Mini was running outside on the avenue but I was handcuffed to a heat riser with a bawling secretary for twenty minutes until the police arrived. The incident precipitated my desire to find that country retreat, but given the modesty of my assistant professor's salary, my problem was finding the money.

That summer a classmate of Mellon's offered to let us rent her glass chalet on Stratton Mountain in Vermont for a nominal sum. We could never afford it in winter, she explained, because it was heated by electricity and the bill then was over eight hundred dollars a month. But we could use the opportunity to look around and perhaps find something in our budget. I had a small nest egg saved from the royalties from a successful anthology, and I wanted to use that sum as a down payment.

Stratton was being developed as a ski center by real estate interests for people from Boston and New York with lots of money, people who wanted the convenience of skiing right into their garages with all the comforts such a cartoon notion implied. Through friends we made locally, Mellon had met the novelist Norman Mailer, who was living nearby in South Londonderry. Mellon was photographing him boxing under the tutelage of José Torres, a former middleweight champion. In his Hemingway mode, Mailer was quite serious about boxing, running for miles in the morning and then sparring for three rounds later.

One morning, when I was in the glass chalet trying to write, Mellon took a drive with one of Mailer's sparring partners who brought her to an abandoned farmhouse near the top of a hill, three and a half miles above a tiny town. Big wild turkeys impeded their progress up the dirt road, and birds were squatting in the unlocked house, which Mellon said looked like a cross between Tobacco Road and Little Bo Peep. A giant cobweb crowded with Adirondack wicker furniture and lots of debris, the farmhouse had been built by a French architect before the American

Revolution, and the Green Mountain Boys had reputedly shot a Tory on its front steps.

Out back, there was a breathtaking view of the spine of the Green Mountain National Forest. The house had a slate roof, imposing thirty-foot, exposed hand-hewn beams notched into place, and had been unoccupied for thirty years as well. Its previous tenant had been a nurse who before World War Two had worked in Rutland, fifteen miles to the north, and her wild reputation had survived as local legend among some of the old-timers in the town.

The house had no insulation, few plaster walls, and few comforts: a couple of potbellied stoves for heat, one cold-water tap, an old-fashioned icebox in which a big block of ice would melt on a warm summer day, extra-wide sideboards called King's Boards, and the quaint romance of a two-seater outhouse, which was reached through a decaying attached shed. The exact opposite of Stratton Mountain where it seemed everyone drove a Mercedes or at least a red Audi, the old place exuded ancient solidity, a paradise of privacy with no neighbors within a half mile, a cornucopia of wildflowers and drunken yellow finches, inebriates of the air as Emily Dickinson had called them, veering wildly in flight.

We were immediately intoxicated and to some extent, for years, addled or addicted. Suddenly, I had the urgent need to enjoy the changing lights at sunrise and the sunset, to hear the trees whispering in the wind, the yellow jacket buzz, the cooing doves or the barking dirge of the crows, the crickets comforting with their wild ascending vibrato. In concert with the country sounds and smells, I would fill the house with giant bouquets of wildflowers, black-eyed Susans in one room, purple clover or daisies in the next. If I wanted to see the flowers dance in midair, I could study the hummingbird poising for its nectar and then darting off.

Not satiated by our summer sojourns, we started using the house on holiday weekends, despite the five-hour drive from New York City, and during my January recess. I would build roaring fires, boil water for bathing in a big turkey pot in the evening, and at night we would curl up in sleeping bags around the stove, which I would fill with soft coal for extra heat. I was too inexperienced at country life to realize the soft coal burned too rapidly to last and that its high heat would only melt the interior guts of the stove. My immediate remedy was to insert the flywheel of a car in place of the original grate, but that was not the safest route. The folly of youth, alas, is often to disregard safety, but fortunately I didn't burn the house down in my sleep.

In those early days, the tax bill was minimal. In fact, for the first five years, the town failed to bill us at all for our house and ten acres. They finally sent us a bill for one hundred dollars. These were the days before all-wheel drive when the town did not have the tax revenue to properly care for the fifty miles of dirt roads that flowed into it. My vehicle always seemed too puny, dwarfed by the pickup trucks and the protruding fins of the Chevy and Ford boats. The curving dirt road was often rutted after rain, and the winter ice could cause catastrophic slipping and sliding. Once, in snow, our car crawling cautiously at five miles per hour just decided to slide off the road to the side where we waited in a freezing field until three strong Vermont men in a pickup stopped and lifted our car back on the road. In the backcountry, people would help each other when needed.

There were years when my wife or I were able, with a writing project or a grant, to spend four consecutive seasons on our hill, attending to the daily chores required to maintain an old house. In winter storms, the howling wind and the snowdrifts could blanket the windows and turn our house into a sort of igloo. One time, Mellon had to be dug out from the outside, and she has a wonderful photograph of a snow tunnel to the road twenty feet away. There were also years when we rented the house to others in exchange for improvements like replacement windows and insulation.

The inhabitants in the tiny town in the valley below us thought our house was too exposed, too far from any center to be safe. There was only one time when we did feel threatened. While we were preparing a barbecue in front of our house one warm summer evening, a jalopy with two unkempt, surly young men kept slowly cruising back and forth. They kept staring at Mellon, a beautiful young woman in shorts. Back then, we only saw a few cars pass in a day so when they disabled their car on a ledge just a few feet from the house, Mellon went inside and called our only neighbor, Jack Finch.

An elderly, retired man who sang in a barbershop quartet in Rutland, Jack Finch was the town moderator, and lived with his wife in a small cottage at the very peak of the hill with spectacular, panoramic views. The winter winds could get so fierce at their modest place, it was anchored by a steel bridge beam seamed into the foundation. Jack drove down immediately, his Saab arriving in a cloud of dust. Waving a pistol, with another in his belt, he demanded to see a driver's license. Both men bolted down the hill, through our field, and into the woods. The State Police arrived a few minutes later and declared the car had been stolen.

From 1970, when we acquired the house from a "land poor" family that had owned the entire hill for a century, until 1990, we dug a three-hundred-foot well, made necessary repairs to our foundation mostly with our own sweat equity, patched up the leaking shed, replaced the unlined chimney, added electricity, changed the windows, installed insulation and interior walls, and burned a forest of wood in our potbellies. I spent 1993 there writing a book, and Mellon moved up to our house in 2000 when our dog could no longer walk up the stairs of our brownstone residence in the West Village. I joined her in 2001, taking a sabbatical to complete a memoir.

II. Neighbors

We had begun to notice surprising changes on our hill and in Vermont. Initially, we had no neighbors for a half mile in any direction and only a few cars a day would pass our house. We were surrounded by the most palpable silence interrupted only by the creaking of the house, the wind and rain, coyotes howling at night, or crickets in season. When we found our house, the state was staunchly Republican and conservative. Vermonters were known for their stubborn independence and had only been persuaded to join the union in 1796.

Frugal, wry, laconic, skeptical of urban mores and manners, Vermont folk could speak with an indecipherable accent with a high nasal twang—using "ayah" for assent or "eh?" for undecidedness. Like any province with its own particular legacy, the area was rich in expressions that could seem puzzling to the outsider. "Heels over teacups," a sweet elderly woman with a flyswatter exclaimed to Mellon one afternoon to express her surprise that we had bought the old farm just three miles up the hill. Mary owned a small general store located in a hamlet called Four Corners—although I could only detect two. Her remark echoed a time when women were still expected to wear whalebone corsets and hooped skirts, a time when tea was still the ceremonial adventure of the afternoon.

At times some Vermonters could seem mischievous, but like the quickly changing mountain weather, the humor could turn into cantankerousness too. We were tolerated as the outlanders or "flatlanders"—as the locals called those like us—who had decided to salvage the old house on the hill. The stone walls lining the fields had led the poet Robert Frost to conclude that good fences made good neighbors, and our immediate neighbors were a summer herd of fifty heifers who occasionally would get through their fences to lunch on our flowers and plants.

Slowly, we began to acquire closer human neighbors. The family that had owned the hill for so long sold out to a restaurant owner with a steakhouse chain. He would drive by our house in a red Caddy convertible to inspect an abandoned house he owned with its huge barn a tenth of a mile to our north and would cavalierly toss us a loaf of bread each time he saw us. He also kept five huge American bison on his land so people came from all over to admire them snorting in his fields. Suddenly, he decided to sell all his restaurants and parcel out the hill so he could move to Montana for a more reclusive existence.

Our new neighbor to our south purchased 150 acres on what the locals were now calling "rich man's hill." He commissioned a McMansion complete with a guesthouse and a looping paved driveway. The townsfolk hated what they derisively termed "the hotel on the hill" and assessed him for an annual tax bill of seventeen thousand dollars. His house seemed to have more than seventeen poorly designed rooms, and his heating costs were astronomical.

Affable, a good-natured, big young man from Mississippi with a white Mercedes, a wife, and two sons, he had gone to Harvard to play football and major in business. He worked for Ted Ammon, a financier who was murdered by a carpenter who was having an affair with Ammon's wife. It was rumored that Ammon and the executive officers of his firm had been investigated by the Securities and Exchange Commission for trading improprieties, and my southern neighbor had brought his family from Bronxville to Vermont in a change of direction.

If he represented the future, our other new neighbor to our immediate north provided a remarkable contrast while seeming like a strange echo of Vermont's past. Victor Gordon found our hill because someone below us raised Lipizzaner horses, an all-white Austrian breed associated with European aristocracy. The abandoned house that the restaurateur once owned had been sold and moved up the hill. The barn had been partially refurbished for human habitation by a tiny woman named Tina, a sister-in-law of the rock musician Jim Croce. A kitchen had been attached to one side of the barn and an apartment built under the barn in which Tina had lived with a couple of dachshunds and an alcoholic carpenter who also murdered someone in town a few years after Tina moved on to Florida for warmer weather.

A solidly built man with a round, open, ruddy face, Victor Gordon bought a pair of Lipizzaners and moved into the barn in the summer of 1996. He went right to work putting up fence posts, building field shelters for his horses, painting the barn with a fresh coat of red, and loading it with bales of hay. His clothes were quite weather-beaten and old, and he washed them by hand and hung them outside to dry on a line. A man of very few words, when he did speak it was only about the habits of the horses he intended to breed. He was infatuated by them.

The most intriguing aspect of Victor's life was that he owned no vehicle and in fact never learned how to drive one. He would walk three and a half miles down the hill to get his provisions or to reach the bus on the highway when he needed to go to Rutland. I gave him rides when I could but warned him of how vulnerable he was without a car in such a remote location. Victor had joined an evangelical church whose members drove him to their services and he was confident. During his first fall season on the hill, after foliage, the wind blew so hard for three consecutive days and nights that lots of the slate tiles on his roof flew off, his chimney caved, and stress fractures formed in the interior plaster walls of his subterranean space. Undeterred, Victor had his chimney repaired and all the slate removed the next spring and replaced with tin.

Although Victor always complained that he was short of funds, he bought two more Lipizzaners and foals were conceived. Pretty soon he had six horses grazing behind the barn and had secured grazing rights in exchange for gardening on adjacent land. He was devoted to these horses, which he never rode but led like oversized dogs a mile or so down the dirt road to Burr Sprague's vegetable stand. He served his horses faithfully with pails of oats, dragging bales of hay to his various fields, and immaculately maintaining the stalls in the barn and the small ring he designed next to it.

People would bring children to admire the horses and Victor seemed to become a fixture in the town. The general store down below agreed to deliver his food to him once a week, mostly TV dinners and cans because Victor didn't cook much. He seemed to work all day caring for the horses and his dilapidated barn, but as if it wasn't enough, he purchased a pair of blonde Haflingers, a breed related to his Lipizzaners. One of the Haflingers came with the pedigree name McKenzie, and Victor began to ride Ken bareback when he had free time in the late morning, although it would often take some time to catch and bridle the reluctant horse. Although he spoke of it, Victor would never sell any of his horses, and when one of the male Lipizzaners born on the place became unmanageable, he had it transported to a friend's place in New Hampshire where the horse could get care.

Like a character in E. L. Doctorow's *Ragtime*, Victor's curious equestrian romance had begun when as a teenager he had worked as a hostler for Troop C of the New York City Mounted Police, which used to train a large contingent of officers to serve on horseback. Victor was raised in Hell's Kitchen by a father who repaired motion picture projectors—his mother had died when he was an infant—and he worked as a stable hand at the Ninety-Sixth Street Armory when it accommodated five hundred horses, and then in smaller facilities on Washington Street in Greenwich Village.

When the financial decision to diminish the numbers of mounted police occurred, Victor was in Vietnam in a mortar unit. After completing his service, Victor passed the exam to become a motorman in the transit system, and for the next twenty-four years he drove trains through the dark labyrinth of tunnels under the city. As soon as he could retire, he came to Vermont to realize his dream, a complete throwback to the way Vermont had once been. The poet Donald Hall has written a gem of an essay, "A Hundred Thousand Straightened Nails," that captures the frugal concern of New Englanders for every scrap of metal, wire, or string, which could have been written about Victor who also checks out the town dumpster when he is in that vicinity.

Victor is also a concerned citizen who videotapes the select board meetings held once a month just adjacent to the dump. There was a bad smell about the way the town was being managed and Victor believed matters had to be clarified, records maintained. Neighbors, there were many more on the hill now, would bring him to the meetings and home afterward. He did not miss a meeting for a decade.

As a reminder, perhaps, of his lonely work as a transit motorman, locked in a narrow cubicle with nothing but an illuminated view of the track ahead, a sort of coal miner without coal or companions to dig with, Victor has constructed in one section of his barn an elaborate circuit of track for his Lionel trains, which he maneuvers with gleeful intensity. He is also adept at his computer and plays video games skillfully with younger people on the Internet who could be his grandchildren, complaining about their cursing and overt sexual references too.

My wealthier McMansion neighbor bonded with Victor, invited him over for barbecues, and when Victor had a stroke would drive him regularly to a clinic thirty miles away for observation and medication. In the collapse of 2008, however, he went bankrupt, and his wife left him and took their two sons. His guest house and million-dollar mansion still stand vacant, no Jay Gatsby to pay the fuel bills, the entire property now forfeit to a bank that cannot find a buyer in America at a fraction of its value.

Last summer, we had a colossal thunderstorm on our hill as if Zeus himself had come back hurtling bolts of lightning and causing the heavens to collide. One of those heavenly bolts struck Victor's roof, disabling his computer. I drove him to the post office to mail it to his serviceman—a rabbi, he advised—and he devoured three slices of pizza at a gas station on the highway. He is sixty-eight now and survived the stroke without visible impairment. He is still as active and engaged as when I first met him.

The old collapsing shed on one side of our house has been replaced, and the house is heated by oil now. For emergencies, we have a few cords of wood stored in our cellar, which still has retained its dirt floor. The house has not changed much in the forty years I've benefited from it, used it as a sanctuary of sorts to read and write my thoughts while looking for the hummingbirds and drunken yellow finches when I can. Like Victor, I've been privileged, able to pick my own wild apples in the fall and simmer them with some brandy to temper the tartness of winter. For matters like that, I can only express my gratitude.

CHAPTER 15

POETIC FAITH
RELIGION AND THE WRITER

My endeavors should be directed to persons and characters supernatural or at least romantic; yet so as to transfer from our inward nature a human interest and a semblance of truth to procure for these shadows of imagination that willing suspension of disbelief for the moment, which constitutes poetic faith.
—Samuel Taylor Coleridge, Biographia Literaria

1. Worship and Political Change

Voltaire's slogan of *écrasez l'infâme*—crush or eradicate the infamous—was a rallying cry of hatred directed to the Roman Catholic Church in France before the French Revolution weakened its hold on the European imagination. Before Voltaire, the church was powerful enough to organize the burning of members of Protestant sects or heretics, even devout believers like the maiden Joan. Now, in Europe, the churches are reported to be less populated, the faithful less credulous and less adherent.

The dissident English separatists called Puritans who emigrated to Massachusetts in the early seventeenth century effected a repressive, intolerant theocracy—a highly regulated social system governed by a priestly caste with inflexible rules—no singing except hymnal, no dancing or physical displays of Quaker emotion, which would have been seen as diabolically inspired. Instead, they insisted on mandatory appearance at church services to hear intricate three-hour sermons on the most recondite theological matters. These sermons were often a dry punishment for parishioners seated on bare benches in poorly heated churches, unrelieved by what the Puritans denounced as the "dumb show": the marvelous theatricality of the Roman Catholic communion, the candles, incense, organ music, flowing priestly vestments, altars decorated with Titians and Tintorettos.

The Puritans appreciated the value of education and a strict work ethic, but they suspected writing and saw art as an outgrowth of the artificial. In England, their ministers had been quick to denounce

Shakespeare's plays as obscene and immoral invitations for divine wrath and retribution, which would conveniently be provided by the black plague at the end of the sixteenth century that wiped out a quarter of London's population. The literature conceived by the American Puritans was mostly didactic sermons—Cotton Mather's "Sinners in the Hands of an Angry God"—and some doggerel verse in praise of their demanding, intransigent God.

The Puritans were grimly characterized by the humorist H. L. Mencken as afflicted by a sickness based on the "haunting fear that somewhere, someone might be happy." The Puritans gave us no Emily Dickinson—they might have interpreted her indirection as witchcraft. Fiction as a genre was condemned as fabrication, an entertainment based on lying, which is what Melville's mother still believed in 1845 when Melville locked himself in her attic after five years at sea to write *Typee*.

The Puritan theocracy had already lost most of its power by the time, almost a century earlier, that an English corset maker named Thomas Paine arrived. Paine had been persuaded to emigrate to the United States by Ben Franklin, whose older brother James had taught Ben how to set type and established our first newspaper, the *New England Courant*, to attack Cotton Mather and the leading Puritan theocrats and weaken their power. Mather called James Franklin the leader of the Hell-Fire Club and denounced his paper as "A wickedness never paralleled anywhere on the face of the earth!"

Paine had been influenced by Voltaire's anticlerical rage, the Enlightenment view that the church had allied itself with aristocracy to monopolize power and profit and to guarantee order in Europe for a millennium before the Reformation. If monarchs proclaimed their rule by "divine right," a clergy was convenient to ratify such a fabulous assertion, one that derived from the legends of Odin, Zeus, or Krishna. To indulge themselves with the best butter and wine in the land, to wear the finest fabrics, the church tended to collaborate with aristocratic rule and prospered.

Paine was one of the firebrand triggers of our revolution, and he argued with a staggering directness in the famous pamphlet that triggered the American uprising, *Common Sense*, that religion was merely the result of human fabrication. The political figures who chartered the American republic at the end of the eighteenth century are reputed to have been mostly deists—that is, those who chose not to question the existence of deity but its relevance in human governance—and our separation of church and state was intended to further the possibility of religious tolerance. For the revolutionary generation, if there was a divine force in the universe, there was little sign it had shown much interest in human development. The American Revolution itself, of course, can be seen as the culminating reaction to the repression of the Puritan state that had preceded it on these shores.

II. A Young Pilgrim in New York

I offer these historical reflections as a framework for the evolution of my own theological understanding.

I was brought to New York as a refugee child of two by a family of desperate, terrified Belgian Jews fleeing the Holocaust in Europe. Belgium is a little country, but also a natural corridor from Germany to France, so it became a devastated battlefield. My father was so traumatized he would never return, even to visit the few surviving family members. In Europe, his family had been quite secular for at least a century, some of them Zionists after the First World War, but most of them acutely conscious of their compromised status as Jews and their vulnerability in an age when anti-Semitism was normative.

I remember as a child reading early accounts of the Holocaust in the *New York Times*, the horror of which I could barely ascertain. Those early reports—like blows from an unknowable origin—may have pushed me into the deist camp of some of the "founding fathers" of the republic. If the Jews had regarded themselves for centuries as "the Chosen People," why had they been so persecuted for centuries in Europe, exiled from England, burned alive during the Spanish Inquisition, my mother's grandfather wantonly shot in front of his home in Odessa in a pogrom by officers of the czar. Why did a madman and his zealous followers finally designate the Jewish people for universal annihilation?

My father's father, Grandpa Jacques as I called him, was a diamond merchant who located his new office on Forty-Seventh Street in Manhattan, just opposite the Gotham Book Mart, then the most literary bookstore in New York and maybe in the country. My father worked for him, and they tried to teach me, by the age of ten, how to weigh and classify the stones. In Europe, they had learned, you did what daddy did, particularly when most professional opportunities were denied to you because of ethnicity or religion. Though the diamond trade sounds prosperous, the level on which my family participated was marginal; their rewards were perpetual tension, constant bank loans, high risks for small gains. Still, a very portable asset, the small cache of diamonds had saved the family in Europe and bought their way to freedom.

Grandpa Jacques was always attired in the most luxurious shirts and suits, with a vest and silk tie in cool weather. He had diminished most of his assets in the year of flight it took to reach the New World, and spent what he could of the remainder with a hedonistic pleasure. Although he had never been religious, never even a habitué of the temple, he insisted that I, his only grandson, receive a proper education in Hebrew so that I could be initiated at thirteen in the Jewish custom.

The only observation of Jewish ritual I noticed in the family was an annual Passover seder at Grandpa Jacques's where I was chosen to ask the key question: "Why is this night different from all other nights?" It was difficult for a child to comprehend that the night commemorated the end of another period of slavery for the Jews. The long mahogany dining room table could accommodate a dozen adults with a few kids squeezed in. With its mirrored wall, the room seemed very full and was noisy. Everyone at the dinner table seemed intent on discussing the latest clothing fashions or the vagaries of the diamond market—whether one-carat emerald cuts would be more in demand than round stones—and no one was as intrigued as I was with the plagues that had beset the Egyptians when the Jews were enslaved.

Children can sometimes be as serious as they are frivolous, but the contradiction between the solemnity of celebrating freedom from slavery and issues like the most fashionable shoes on the street was too great for me to contain. It usually ended with my sequestration on a green velvet daybed in my grandfather's study after a massive allergy attack.

Sent to Ramaz, a private school with a Hebrew curriculum in the morning and an English one in the afternoons, I hated the Hebrew and became a disciplinary problem in the first grade. I taught myself to vomit on the doorstep on the way to school, to feign illness and miss another day of instruction in a language that sounded so often like the rasping of a dry throat. I suspect it was part of a general disavowment of my own heritage (or was it the shame of not belonging?) and the European inflections of my parents and grandparents that was reflected in every word they said as well as every custom.

After I transferred to a neighborhood public school, my work improved though I was handicapped by problems with my eyes, which required surgery. I was still obligated by my grandfather to continue my studies in Hebrew after school, and I know I resented the lost opportunities to play stickball in the streets of upper Manhattan or roller-skate with my pals.

I admit I was confused about the Jewish part of my identity as a boy. I was on occasion taunted and beaten by groups of classmates after public school and would come bruised and sore to the Hebrew school, located across the street from my parents' apartment in Temple Ansche Chesed on One Hundredth Street and West End Avenue. Though I knew the beatings were unfair, I learned to defend myself. In the sixth grade, when I fought back and beat a bully I was called a "Christ killer" by some of his angry cohorts who had actually placed wagers on the event, a boxing match without rules after school where one's head could be pounded on a car. I had been taught the Romans had crucified thousands of Jews like Jesus, that the terror caused by nailing a man to wood usually served to subjugate any population. One of my Hebrew school teachers explained that the Romans did not use a cross shape for this purpose, but an "X" formation, architecturally more sound if an impaled victim was squirming in his blood. The X, he told us, was too negative a sign on which to base any religion.

I had problems with some of my Hebrew school instructors who were so convinced of the truth of their message that they would not countenance questions. I was twelve when Mrs. Spector, a stout middle-aged woman with enormous black spectacles and a black hair bun fastened tightly behind her head, was discussing the Ten Commandments as one of the foundation stones of Western morality. To me, Mrs. Spector looked like the Wicked Witch of the West, and she even wore pointed black shoes as if to confirm this slander. Referring to the commandment that "thou shall not kill," I asked whether killing was justified if the state ordered me in its service to go abroad and combat an enemy.

My precocious implication may have been too much for Mrs. Spector to bear at that moment, or perhaps it was the irritation of my constant questioning, but she struck me sharply in the face. The stinging humiliation of that sudden blow was probably more scarring than all the abuse I had encountered with elementary school bullies. That smack left my face red and slightly swollen for a half an hour, but it hardly seemed worth remembering in the dim light of my Grandpa Jacques's death in his bed a few weeks later. I was at his bedside with my father when he shuddered for the last time. My father removed his signet ring and fit it smoothly on my finger because we had the same initials.

Perhaps, this ritual transfer helped me to realize that although I could not countenance the Spectors of my world, that the rigidity of their belief system interfered with my ability to see, I still had to fulfill my grandfather's wish and perform the bar mitzvah ritual in a manner he would have admired.

Impressed by my grandfather's death, I wanted to become an observant Jew and even tried to learn how to tie the tefillin around my arms in the early morning to pray in the Orthodox fashion. Alas, I was always hopeless with ropes and could never progress in the Boy Scouts because of my inability to tie the required knots, so I gave up after a few weeks of fumbling, unsure that I had performed the rituals correctly and whether my ineptness would be considered an offense.

The rabbi who taught me to sing my haftorah portion was like an accountant of language, sober and circumspect and dedicated to exactness. Even though the synagogue was not Orthodox, every Hebrew syllable had to be enunciated and accented perfectly, and since I had very little understanding of what the words meant, memorizing was difficult. I had always felt claustrophobic during the Jewish services I had attended during the year when I was studying my haftorah portion. At a certain point, my eyes would itch and my nose would run, or I would start sneezing uncontrollably before my retreat to the vestibule.

I did my best before the assembled congregation on the day of my bar mitzvah, wondering then whether my Grandpa Jacques's spirit was watching with approval. During my performance, which only lasted for a few moments, the rabbi was still correcting me, my voice still the high alto before full puberty, but cracking and surely off pitch. Although I cannot now remember a word of what I sang, I see that my delivery before the congregation was my first attempt to stand before a class or reach an audience with language, that everything I have tried to do has been an extension of what I did for Grandpa Jacques. I did not know then that after my bar mitzvah I would never return, never attend another service.

In high school I was an angry atheist, and by the time I reached university I subscribed to the existentialist conjecture that God was dead or, at least, disinterested in human fate. I became an agnostic, less concerned with my own spiritual capacity than finding myself in the world. I never denied my Judaism, but accepted it as part of a cultural identity. If asked, I would joke that I was a literal descendant of King Solomon, and then quickly add that since he was reputed to have had some eight hundred wives, my legitimacy was dubious at best.

I had one brief brush with a rabbi subsequently, which seems to fit into this little history of apostasy. I was twenty-eight when I was married in my future mother-in-law's backyard in Great Neck, Long Island, by a dangerously good-looking Reform rabbi. The ceremony was simple with the yard full of my mother-in-law's neighbors and friends enjoying a brief respite from their cocktails. Striking, tall, and erect, the rabbi was graying at his temples and could have been a double for the next mayor of New York, John Lindsay. Like a character in a novel by Scott Fitzgerald, he resembled the sort of person who succeeds as a virtue of good looks. He was quite distinguished and his words, though formulaic, were mellifluous and comforting. As soon as the rings were exchanged and I kissed my bride, he collected his fee and said he had to depart. I followed him through the house with some inane anxiety about receiving a certificate of marriage.

The rabbi was in a rush. He had another engagement in Montauk, he claimed, and he swung lithely into the driver's seat of a red convertible Maserati. The sports car was stunningly vibrant, a long projectile of power with a modest compartment for its passengers. There was a small red suitcase protruding from below the rear bucket seat. The passenger seat was occupied by a fidgety, primping blonde, looking at least twenty years younger than the rabbi, whom he introduced perfunctorily as his secretary. Suavely, he assured me, Myrtle would send the certificate. With a deep rumble from the engine, they left me gaping in the exhaust.

III. Reversion/Conversion

Modern American writers have tended to be unsympathetic to religion, particularly to fundamentalist or revivalist expressions since Sinclair Lewis's *Elmer Gantry*. Perhaps, this should be considered as a belated reaction to the cultural consequences of Puritanism, which like British Victorianism had a pervasive, formative, and long-lasting influence. Perhaps, it is because so many charismatic American religious leaders, especially the television preachers, now seem to attract fleets of Mercedes cars.

Ralph Waldo Emerson, early in the nineteenth century, provides us with an early sign of a change in American religious temperament. Emerson's ancestors had been Protestant ministers in France—Waldensians, from which persecuted group he gets his middle name—and his father had been the minister of the First Congregational Church in Boston and the chaplain to the Massachusetts Senate. An honest preacher, he served his parishioners with little thought for his own family's future welfare. When he died suddenly, he left his wife with two young sons. She began renting rooms in her house but had so little money that her two boys were obligated to share a winter overcoat. It is the stuff of fable, I suppose, and a writer like Gogol could have made something of it.

At the age of fifteen, Emerson was a charity student at Harvard, an institution created by the Puritans to train their clergy. After completing his studies in the divinity program, he found a ministerial position in the Unitarian Church, then the most liberal Protestant sect. Early in his ministry, he suffered a series of disasters: in 1831 his young wife died of tuberculosis after seventeen months of marriage and a child. Her death caused Emerson to suffer a nervous breakdown. Then he was discharged by the Unitarian Church when he began to emphasize the humanity of Jesus, seeing him more as a prophetic rabbinical messenger than the actual Son of God.

Emerson lived in Concord, just outside Boston. To earn a living, he went on the lecture circuit. Before the evolution of modern mass media, for edification or entertainment, lecturers toured towns and villages in defined circuits. Emerson's circuit was New England and his method was to speak about his subject again and again. By the time he completed his circuit, he was ready to formulate his observations into an essay.

Some of Emerson's ideas—"society everywhere is in conspiracy against the manhood of every one of its members"—were galvanizing enough in New England to attract followers who began to be called transcendentalists. They tended to agree with Emerson's proposition in his essay "Self-Reliance" that "nothing is at last sacred but the integrity of your own mind." Some of the hardier followers of Emerson would join communal farms; others would gather to hear him speak in Elizabeth Peabody's bookshop in Boston or read him in Margaret Fuller's *The Dial*. Emerson and disciples such as Thoreau and Bronson Alcott were joined by a growing legion that agitated for such causes as abolitionism and women's suffrage. This was the beginning of a tradition of progressive change in America, but it also had a spiritual dimension.

The transcendentalist, Emerson explained, was an idealist inspired by the miraculous in the everyday and the power of individual will. Unlike the materialist who responded to "the force of circumstances and the animal wants of man," Aristotelian logic, or John Locke's reason based on sensory experience, the transcendentalist was motivated more by intuition and an almost pantheistic appreciation of nature. This is evident in Emerson's first essay, "Nature," which simultaneously is his most dense and vague. Essentially animistic and pagan, Emerson locates his notion of deity in nature—the prevalent belief system for half a million years on the planet before monotheism—and compounds his view with a Buddhist awareness of an unimpeded interdiffusion of spiritual energy in all living things, which he calls the "over-soul."

In 1842, Emerson's lecture "Poetry of the Times" was attended by Walt Whitman, then a young reporter assigned to cover the talk. Excited by comments such as "language is fossil poetry," "it is not meters but a meter-making argument that makes a poem," and "the experience of each new age requires a new confession and the world always seems to be waiting for its poet," Whitman began scribbling free verse notations in the margin of his notebook. For Whitman, it was a breakthrough that changed his life.

"I was simmering, simmering, simmering," Whitman wrote to a friend after the lecture, "Emerson brought me to a boil." It was the start of his life as a poet although he would continue to support himself as a reporter and editor for another decade. In 1853, abruptly discontinuing his career as a journalist, he began writing a long epic poem. In that poem, "Song of Myself," we can find the most lyrical and persuasive application of Emersonian pantheism beginning with its central image of the grass, a "uniform hieroglyphic" whose "smallest sprout shows that there really is no death," a mere leaf of which he finds to be no less miraculous "than the journeywork of the stars," the urine of the ant, the egg of the wren, or a grain of sand.

I took a class in graduate school on Emerson and became intoxicated by him despite the sweet decrepitude of my professor and the inconvenience of the hour—a Saturday morning seminar when I had worked all night as a hospital emergency room registrar to pay my keep. Emerson's reverence for nature was a refutation of our Puritan past, which saw the wilderness as the place where Satan cavorted. For me, it became a substitute religion, a way out of my Hebrew heritage, and maybe a way to become an American, and certainly my way to Vermont.

CHAPTER 16

A WRITER'S PASSAGE

What logic is there in things? None really. We're the ones who look for links between one segment of our lives and another. But this attempt to give form to that which has none, to give form to chaos, is something only good writers know how to do successfully.
—Enrique Vila-Matas, *Dublinesque*

Stories are antibodies against illness and pain.
—Anatole Broyard, "Intoxicated by My Illness"

I. The Death of Print

The worst professional possibility for a writer is the news that your work has been rejected again. Second to that, I suppose, is the discovery, sometimes months after the fact, that your previous book has disappeared from a publisher's list, still available, perhaps, used on Amazon for a pittance, or even found with the occasional coffee stain in a public library.

In more gallant times, publishers would remainder such titles and offer their authors an early opportunity to purchase copies at a greatly reduced rate. Henry David Thoreau once boasted that he had a library of over 1,000 books, 998 of which he had written himself. His book *Walden*, it needs no explaining, is one of the classics of our literature.

In my attic in Vermont, I have hoarded a similar supply, each disowned title stacked in boxes to the eaves like so much ballast in a ship's hold. The marauding mice and the more destructive red-tailed squirrels, which eat clothing and most anything else, have not yet resorted to this obscure library. Perhaps, my private stash for posterity doesn't taste as good as the holey argyle of last winter, or maybe it lacks sufficient nourishment, or is my subject matter a literature too refined for country tastes?

Today, short-staffed publishers may not even inform you that they no longer wish to represent your work or even store it in warehouses they cannot afford. If the public library, then, becomes the cemetery for old books, my attic is sort of a private burial ground, the weight of all those words an anchor in the winter winds.

Each book I've been lucky enough to have written and seen published represents a particular journey. Since what I write is nonfiction, literary biography and criticism, the journey involves bibliographic preparation, reading relevant primary and secondary material, travel for research in library special collections, negotiating permissions from literary estates, and interviewing my subject (if still alive and willing) or those who knew my subject. Some of these journeys have lasted for five years, some longer. So prior to the actual work of composition, there has been a lot of patient commitment.

Publication can seem like a validation. Here is this document of fifty thousand or a hundred thousand words, the result of years of research and both contemplative and hopefully imaginative consideration in the attempt to coherently present the life and work of an important, often misunderstood or unappreciated, artist. In one sense, when the publisher decides your book no longer has currency—that is, not selling enough copies to justify warehouse costs—it is the terminus of that journey.

Contemporary writers may have the grim satisfaction of seeing copies of their books in electronic versions blinking into an uncertain future, though such a possibility may seem more spectral and less substantive than seeing a book displayed in a bookstore window. For the writer, the death of a book is akin to what a parent must feel when a child dies first.

I realize that the child's death is inconsolable. In the writer's case, the void may be filled with a new project. The writer may be more prepared, the death of the book more expected so less shocking, but the loss may still be profound. The deceased child's memory remains in the heart while the lost book may resonate more in the mind, but both losses have metaphysical connections to the soul.

I don't mean these words as a professional grouse. Personally, I consider myself fortunate that at least one of my books, *Naked Angels*, has remained in print for forty years. Several others have managed to remain in print or reappear, sometimes in remote incarnations in South Korea or Turkey in languages I cannot decipher. Sometimes a book can be stolen, and I remember my shock when I discovered that the Chinese had pirated *Naked Angels*. The book had appeared in a number of foreign countries: Japan, Germany, even Czechoslovakia. The crushing fact about the Chinese piracy was that they did not even attribute the book to me! When I approached a leading intellectual property rights attorney—this was a decade ago, and hopefully things are changing—he consoled me with the news that I had no recourse. Anyway, he suggested, I should feel flattered because that was what the Chinese had done to Mick Jagger and Paul McCartney.

In some sense, of course, any translation becomes a remaking and on some level an appropriation, as I learned when a French publisher bought my biography of Ezra Pound. Seghers omitted the book's introduction, commissioned originally by *Vanity Fair*. When I complained, the editor wrote to me, with more than a touch of arrogant superiority, that the French were too sophisticated to require such assistance. But at least my name remained on the book.

I admit that there is an organic necessity for the death of a book as for any form of life. Times change, perhaps a better book has been written on the subject, and perhaps the subject itself doesn't seem as significant over time. The journey for that book, its future passage, becomes questionable.

Sometimes, however, the uncertain status of a book may be reversed by an intervention. When *The Solitary Volcano*, my biography of the poet Ezra Pound, was discontinued by its original publisher, Doubleday, I received a call from Joseph Parisi, the editor of *Poetry*, who years earlier had given my book a rave on the front page of the literary section of the *Chicago Tribune*. He insisted the book was too important to die and found another decade of life in print for it with a small publisher in Chicago. My biography was the result of a deliberative process, a human act, and Parisi's enthusiasm was the result of human choice, so I suspect the analogy I want to propose between the life passage of as inanimate an object as a book and the vitality of its author may seem plausible.

II. Another Intervention

The preceding has all been theoretical and then literary. I want to focus here on a particular passage as a matter of life or death. My wife Mellon had created *My Lucky Dog*, a moving book of photographs and text about her devotion for our dog Hunter that HarperCollins published in 2008. In late August, we went to Burlington, Vermont, with our new dog, a rescue we named Frank, for a book signing. The day was warm but dry and sunny; I spent most of it walking Frank by the lake while Mellon attended to signing her books.

Driving back to our old farmhouse, I felt weak and in the evening a severe indigestion that I attributed to some very spicy Tibetan food

I had eaten in the farmer's market earlier that afternoon. During the night, my abdominal cramps got worse and nothing I took seemed to relieve the excruciating pain. Mellon pleaded with me to drive to the emergency room or call an ambulance, which was a step we had never had to take anywhere—we are twenty miles away from the nearest hospital in Rutland.

At dawn, with the pain now unendurable, Mellon insisted that we call the Manchester Rescue Squad. The measure seemed disproportionate, extreme even, but I could no longer rationalize the pain with a theory of digestive disorder. The technician who arrived initially to measure my vital signs told me he remembered cutting my lawn almost forty years earlier. That news somehow seemed reassuring. Mellon followed the ambulance, honking wildly, demanding that I be conveyed to the Southwestern Medical Center in Bennington, forty miles away but with a better reputation than Rutland. When the gurney was wheeled into the emergency room, I was delirious with pain.

Perhaps that is why, when I saw the surgeon on call, I thought she was the actress Christina Applegate when she was playing a fifteen-year-old bimbo beauty, the daughter of a bumbling, bragging shoe salesman on a television soap called *Married with Children*. When I asked her how long she had been practicing, her reply was quite disappointing, only a year, but at least she had done her surgical residency at Georgetown, a highly respected medical facility.

I knew I had no choice at this point, and Dr. Elizabeth Warner did save my life. Before my CAT scan, I was injected with Dilaudid, a drug as powerful as heroin, which I had read about in the fiction of William Burroughs. Reading is a vicarious pleasure and lacks the experiential impact of the actual. The reader's imagination, no matter how active or fluent, is rarely a match for the passion of a drug or the blood coursing through one's veins. The Dilaudid floated me into an enormous brightly lit space with the smell and texture of cotton candy, relaxing my body and assuaging my fears. Somehow, the drug made me see my condition as comic. I was joking with the anesthesiologist, and though it seemed like the best joke I ever told, I cannot remember what it was.

At the same time, I could not help but remember that my father had died instantly of a heart attack when he was sixty-five—my age! He had dropped on the corner of Forty-Seventh Street and Fifth Avenue, a half block from his former office where he had just picked up two new suits. When I identified his corpse in the morgue at Bellevue, the expression on his face was like a crucifixion to behold. My mother died an awful death at the same age. She had battled leukemia for a decade and before she succumbed, her body had swollen to twice its size and her kidneys and spleen had failed to function. She looked like one of the bloated, leering monsters at the Macy's Day Thanksgiving parade to which she used to bring me as a child. It was my sad duty to plead with the physicians at Mt. Sinai Hospital in Manhattan to administer morphine to ease her passage.

I had suffered a strangulated hernia that would have been fatal had it not been for Dr. Warner's skill. Part of my colon had died during my night of pain and needed to be removed, but what are a few inches of intestinal coil in the long run? The colon—where we process our food, derive our nutrition from it, and excrete the rest—is only another sort of messy passage, a sort of corridor between life processes and death. As the journalist Gail Sheehy has proposed, life is a series of passages, and as the rock lyricist Jim Morrison—who died in a bathtub when he was twenty-seven—used to proclaim, "no one gets out of here alive!"

Although in my fear and apprehension, Dr. Warner had resembled a fifteen-year-old television comedienne, she was twice that age and had two children of her own. She also had the skill to repair the collapse of my internal plumbing and bring me back, as it were, into print again. I could not claim to be a new edition of myself; I had a prominent red scar up my middle—the new zipper to my soul, I joked. It did give me entry to a new perspective, the probability that beyond our all-too-human capacity for denial, all my books, even the hundreds preserved in my country attic, would pass back to the dust—as I must one day.

III. Hurricane

During Sandy, the much-too-diminutive name for what was called the hurricane of the century, my neighborhood in lower Manhattan lost power for five nights. I kept a flashlight in my pocket for the dark stairway, filled my tub with water, threw out the spoiled food, walked a few miles uptown for supplies.

My cell phone almost depleted, with the help of a group of neighbors I hooked into a portable generator set up on my corner by the city's emergency services. Our act of communal larceny was interrupted by the police precinct captain who explained that the generator was placed there to prevent looting at night, which was disquieting news.

That night, chilled and clammy, desperate for a bath, I boiled water and cleaned myself for the week. Whatever deprivations I experienced, of course, were minor compared to those who lost their homes on the waterfronts in Queens, Staten Island, and New Jersey.

The hardest part was in the evening as the dimming light disappeared. We had a half-dozen candles, but it got so chilled that I wanted to read in bed by eight, both to stay warm and because there was little else one could do. I used the flickering candlelight but also my flashlight to illuminate the page and focus my beam on words and sentences. While such a procedure would seem disadvantageous, it enabled a pace that was more deliberate, slower than usual. Like eating, perhaps, the more slowly one chews, the more one may savor.

On a shelf I was reserving for summer reading I had a novel called *Dublinesque* by Enrique Vila-Matas whom I had never even heard of previously, much less read, although he was reputed to be one of Spain's leading novelists. Despite his European reputation and his appearance in thirty other countries, Vila-Matas has only recently been brought to an American public, thanks to the agency of a fine small publishing firm, New Directions, which specializes in such corrections of our insularity.

I have a propensity for Dublin and James Joyce. I often use *A Portrait of the Artist as a Young Man* in classes, though my students usually find Stephen Dedalus, its protagonist, too precious for their tastes, and Joyce's language too rich and rambunctious, too self-consciously poetic. I even devoted a semester in a seminar to *Ulysses*, a novel set in Dublin over thirty-six hours, which is still considered the masterpiece novel written in English in the twentieth century.

My predisposition for Dublin was also a matter of heritage. My mother spent her refugee childhood in Dublin and could have been a character in Joyce's book of realistic stories, *Dubliners*. I told her story of bathing in a wooden tub and fetching a wooden bucket of stout for her father every afternoon on the way home from school during the First World War in the *James Joyce Quarterly*.

With the first almost fatuously funny words of *Dublinesque*, Enrique Vila-Matas defines his valiantly quixotic narrator, Samuel Riba, as belonging to "an increasingly rare breed of sophisticated literary publishers." For the thirty years that Riba has been in the book trade he has watched its members—"publishers who still read and who have always been drawn to literature"—"gradually, surreptitiously dying out."

He sees himself as the last genuine publisher. Riba tells us his firm has gone bankrupt because he refused to exploit the cheap Gothicism of vampire stories, but if such failures can ever be regarded as surreptitious, it is because they are considered insignificant from both the business and human perspective, as negligible as a farmer selling his fields to a real estate developer, though much less profitable.

Riba takes great pride in the novels he has published though he has never managed to find the unknown genius he wanted to publish for the world. All he has are a lot of unsold and out-of-print editions he has published and a literary catalog that is the record of his efforts and a lifetime of selection. He has been a compulsive reader, and he even reads his own life as a literary text. He sets an inordinately higher bar for reading and writing than for living: "The same skills needed for writing are needed for reading. Writers fail readers but it also happens the other way around and readers fail writers when all they ask of them is confirmation that the world is how they see it." For Riba, reading is a "way of being in the world: an instrument for interpreting sequence after sequence, his day-to-day life." He sees his own financial catastrophe in the world of literary publishing somewhat romantically, spending "his life feeling that it's the end of an era, the end of the world," doubtless, Vila-Matas reminds us, "influenced by the sudden cessation of his activities."

Fifty-nine, insomniac, he is unhappily married to Celia who has distanced herself with her own conversion to Buddhism. A former alcoholic who has damaged his kidneys with excess, he survived surgery and for two years has struggled to refrain from the alcohol that he believed formerly fueled his friendships. He fills his life with routine gestures: a contentiously irritating phone call on odd-numbered days at noon from Javier, a novelist he once published; regular visits to his parents for dinner each Wednesday, avoiding their often senile concerns while meticulously relating to them the details of his life, which he represents as being much more glamorous than it is. They are unaware that his firm has failed, and Vila-Matas presents these family encounters with a grimly brittle satiric bite.

His wife complains that all his social involvements have collapsed with his publishing house, and that he has retreated from life to the Internet, becoming a boring *hikkokomori*—a Japanese term for a zombie fixated on a screen. Without his firm, he admits he lives in an anxious state of "end-of-everything psychosis." Furthermore, he believes he can communicate with ghosts who drift into his world when he visits his parents and at other times.

Vila-Matas has said that his novel was conceived when he was recovering from major surgery and dreamed that he was in Dublin, a place he had never visited. In the novel, Riba has a weird dream of abjectly relapsing in a pub in Dublin, only to be discovered groveling by his disapproving wife. To save himself from the rut of his own decline, perhaps to save his marriage, he concocts the plan to invite three of the novelists he had once published to join him in Dublin. Their grand purpose will be to hold a funeral for the world of literary publishing, its genuine writers and talented readers. The sanctimony of this ritual announcement of the end of the Gutenberg era will occur on Bloomsday, June 16, the date of the action of *Ulysses*, and a day celebrated internationally in honor of Joyce since the publication of the novel in 1922. Lugubriously, it will occur in the same cemetery where Paddy Dignam is buried in chapter 6 of the novel.

Dublinesque is written with a postmodernist fascination with the flux between fantasy and the actual, and all through it there are echoes and parodies of Joyce and reflections on his work. Key quotations from *Ulysses* run through *Dublinesque* and correspond to the action. Vila-Matas often breaks into dramatic form as in a screenplay just as Joyce did in *Ulysses* (anticipated by Herman Melville in *Moby Dick* nearly a century earlier). The novelists join Riba in a reading of *Ulysses* in a theater, and continue in Finnegan's Pub in Dalkey.

What ensues in Dublin is a minor comic tour de force as the three novelists who accompany Riba (reflections of Joyce's characters attending Dignam's funeral in *Ulysses*) are all so sharply etched, so querulous, so eccentric, so pretentiously inflated, so opinionated on the subject of James Joyce's fiction. As in *A Portrait of the Artist as a Young Man*, aesthetic choices are governing values, but this often leads to the ridiculous and the absurd. Riba is reading a biography about Samuel Beckett, Joyce's first literary acolyte, his friend, and some might argue his successor, and at intervals Riba, who is pathetically drawn but affecting, imagines he sees a mysterious, haunting character who closely resembles Beckett.

I will not prepare you for every hilarious and sad twist in Riba's Dublin misadventure, but he does relapse and realizes he is on the way out. The final fifty pages of the novel are somber but not melodramatic, suffused with a heavy sorrow. Yet the general effect of Vila-Matas's considerable wit is elevating and, if not quite buoyantly, at least with a consistently grinning wryness that engages and pleases the reader.

At the very end of the novel, Riba, still unable to extricate himself from the ghosts of Dublin, is attending another funeral in Glasnevin. In Riba's attempt to live out his dream of discovering a new Joyce or Beckett in Dublin, Vila-Matas has given us a marvelously sophisticated entertainment, full of humor, fancy, and imagination. The implicit teaser that he leaves us with, however, is whether Vila-Matas believes *he* is the discovery that Riba seeks.

Reading *Dublinesque* gave me an equation I could not have imagined. I had had a memoir of my childhood and early years published in 2003, five years prior to my strangulation. The book began when I found an old prewar Dutch poster for the Red Star Line in the trash depicting a ship crossing the Atlantic from "Antwerpen to Amerika." I was born in Antwerp and came here as a child with my parents in such a boat. *Reading New York* was my sixth book, and though it was published by a major house, it went mostly unnoticed in the world, barely reviewed, remaindered, mostly unread. A friend told me he had seen it in the library of a luxurious cruise ocean liner, but I surmised it had been abandoned by one of its more fickle passengers who may have preferred a deep and deserved slumber after a hearty repast and a few glasses of Bordeaux.

Discouraged, my self-worth diminished, I lost any residual ambition and dreaded the enormous effort of writing another book. For several years after Dr. Warner's intervention I did not have the psychic or physical energy anyway. I noticed that even when I attempted to write, certain phrases I had relied on in the past began recurring, almost as if they had become formulaic, easy resolutions for the problems of the intellect. Had the spring been depleted, and was the well now dry? My wife and friends were mystified that for the first time in forty years I was not writing a book, and their disappointment was like a fresh reminder that I had somehow lost my way in a desert.

Though I hope my efforts here are not as quixotic as Samuel Riba's in *Dublinesque*, I realized reading Vila-Matas that I had, unknown to myself, taken a similar turn after surgery and recovered a renewed appetite for reading and writing. The gifted Dr. Warner unscrambled my insides and may have connected an invisible, psychic fuse that caused me to write again. By now you have measured the result and I hope it has afforded some pleasure.

CHAPTER 17   **THE DONKEY AND THE WRITTEN WORD**

The human tongue is like a cracked cauldron on which we beat out tunes to set a bear dancing when we would make the stars weep with our melodies.
—*Gustave Flaubert*

1. A Personal Note

Is it arbitrary, merely odd, or the result of etymological curiosity that the words "write," "rite," and "right" seem somehow related, as do the words "author" and "authority"? Does the writer serve some righteous or ritual function as recorder of the tale of the tribe?

Such questions have their anthropological dimensions in the very evolution of writing, which is not nearly as long as we might imagine. Before exploring that quite recent past, allow me a brief autobiographical explanation of why I chose to write in the first place. Call it "the writer's rite."

I am a European refugee from the Second World War, part of a family whose street in Antwerp—the Rue Quentin Matsys—was being bombed by the Luftwaffe in May 1940 when I was one. A year later, we were lucky survivors who were permitted to embark by boat for New York City. My mother told me, and it may be distasteful to admit it, that my family's frantic year of anxious flight, my second year of life, was my year of constant colic.

Instead of acting like a proper European and accepting the tradition of my father's diamond trade, which is what his father and grandfather had done in Antwerp, my model became my mom, who studied with Pearl Buck at Columbia and tried to write the story of my family's exodus, a story marked by the pathos of sudden departure, the stark terror of newspaper headlines and the indomitable advance of Panzer tanks, the dread of an uncertain future (reflections of which form the music of the posthumously published novel *Suite Francaise* by Irène Némirovsky).

I would return home to the Upper West Side of Manhattan and my interminable D-train voyage to and from the Bronx High School of

Science to read what my mother had patiently written that day. Although she had been born in London and raised in Dublin, her favorite language was French, and she never felt sure about American English, so my job was to help her determine whether her diction and dialogue were sufficient. It was a modest role but it helped form me.

I won prizes for poetry and a short story as a senior at the City College of New York in 1961. I was not an English major though I had taken a course in formal prosody where I learned the intricacies of terza rima, sprung rhythm, and William Carlos Williams's variable foot. This was before creative writing courses began to occupy such a large space in English departments. With the brash and reckless irreverence of the undergraduate, I called my instructor Dr. Dry-as-Dust and learned some of what I needed to deny in my own future fumbling efforts.

Those efforts at self-expression had begun much earlier. I trace them back to the third grade when I received a "D" in penmanship and my mother declared this failure might reveal a character flaw. I suspect she remained perennially suspicious of me. I forgave her that and won the school spelling bee. Later, by trying to write myself I was only doing my best to emulate her. In fact my first two books were written longhand, which seems, in the computer age, so antediluvian.

II. Origins

There is some juice in that word "antediluvian"—that is, before the biblical flood—and it relates to my deeper purpose here, which is to consider our rightful place in the relatively brief tradition of the written word.

I am always surprised at how recently writing has become fashionable. Our species, *Homo erectus*—no gross sexual slur here intended—has been strutting on the planet with a straight spine and a flexible thumb for approximately half a million to two million years, so what astonishes me is that the tradition of the written word that concerns me here only represents less than 1 percent of the entire history of our species. What indeed did we do for at least 495,000 years without writing or monotheism?

Thanks to carbon dating, we know some ancient Chinese records were carved on oracle bones and tortoise shells thirty-seven hundred years ago. Historians of the word tell us that the donkey was crucial for the spread of writing, that it was only because of the domestication of the donkey that trading caravans from the east reached the west approximately seven thousand years ago. Writing fulfilled the need for traders to account for what was ordered and sold. It surely seems humbling to recognize that what we may revere in a Shakespeare or a Montaigne probably began as a series of scratches on small clay tablets, units of commercial measurement that listed the weights and numbers of fabrics or spices loaded on a trudging donkey's back.

Someone should have told that great American poet, William Carlos Williams, whose poem "The Red Wheelbarrow"—composed in the previously mentioned "variable foot"—is the most anthologized and studied in twentieth-century American literature, that so much depends on the donkey, not the wheelbarrow. Incidentally, I was introduced to Dr. Williams in the flesh by one of my professors in my senior year at CCNY, a brief handshake that boosted my sagging spirits immeasurably at a time when I must admit I felt like an anonymous, barely visible cipher.

But I need to return to the donkey. Despite its cartoon political association for Americans, the donkey is such a fundamentally unglamorous beast, sturdier than the camel in its endurance of elemental privations and human abuse, perhaps, stolidly plodding—is it fair or too cute to say dogmatic in its stubborn almost fanatical persistence? Somewhat like the successful writer, I sometimes wonder.

Our first real evidence of organized writing is the Sumerian code, which we date roughly to 2500 BC, and the Mayan codices of 2300 BC. Early writing was often executed—it sounds so fierce, I know—so priests and rulers like Hammurabi could command others to obey.

I use the word "execute" because I see Moses as our first known writer who used the Babylonian cuneiform method of carving into clay tablets with a wedge-shaped rock—an arduous process that makes revision daunting. Was this the awareness behind Jack Kerouac's "first thought, best thought" spontaneity?

I accept Moses as the manufacturer of monotheism, announcing to the worshippers of the golden calf, with his new rules formulated in tablets of clay, the end of the animist era: that long period prior to the written word when nature was worshipped as the source of the godhead, when the divine force could be felt in a tree, when its retribution could be felt in the volcano's wrath, its bounty in the sun's radiance. Moses used writing as an ordering principle, like Hammurabi thirteen hundred years earlier, or the followers of Jesus thirteen hundred years after, all exemplifying a basic quest of the writer—to name things so as to identify, classify, evaluate, hopefully comprehend, and ultimately control. The more utilitarian purpose of writing was to list administrative regulations, accounts of crop harvests, flocks tended, goods manufactured, the exact means of preparing religious feasts and processionals, and to record the glories of battle.

III. The Future of the Written Word

The present generation has been accused of taking writing far less seriously than mine did—and I am a member of what was called the Silent Generation. Some of my students seem to want to write novels on cell phones in class (or are they just gossiping with friends?) as I'm trying to explore William Burroughs's postmodernist pyrotechnics. While the Twitter novel of tomorrow might seem facile, too Zen, or perhaps even blasphemous to a Moses on his mountain, it should be written in stone—like the engraved passages on the Kerouac memorial in Lowell, Massachusetts—yes, it should be written in stone that the technology of writing changes more rapidly than what needs to be written.

Near the end of the sixteenth century, John Donne and Andrew Marvell passed poems still written by hand to the ladies of the British royal court, and Shakespeare only realized a few decades later the necessity of even collating the folios and publishing his plays. If not for a German goldsmith named Johannes Gensfleisch von Gutenberg who innovated a printing system on a wine press using movable metal type in a small dark room in the medieval town of Mainz in 1455, we might not have had the European Renaissance, the modern university, or the novel as an art form at all.

We now explore most of culture through the visual image and the written word. History, except for its oral variants, is usually recorded by writing its story. Since Gutenberg, we have tended to depend on writing as a cohesive tool, a means of organizing systems and nations. However, it is dangerous to overvalue the written word, as entire civilizations and empires seem to have thrived without writing—think of the Incas, who controlled much of South America from the thirteenth through the fifteenth centuries, for example, or of the tribal groups in much of central Africa.

The written word may be less fragile than it was during the classical era—only a fraction of Sophocles's 120 plays have survived, and the same is true of the plays by Euripides and Aeschylus. Now Google wants all my books to flicker however dimly on its vast eternal screen, and in the age of e-mail some of us may titter about what linguistic morphing we must anticipate—Yeats's rough beast slouching toward Bethlehem or New York City?

Before that transformative future, however dismaying to some or grim to others, I want to return to the issue of the future of the written word. We inhabit a culture where writing is said to be taken for granted and endangered, where the young are no longer much concerned with its possibilities, where we are told they cannot concentrate long enough to persuade their teachers with sentences more elegant or complex than advertising slogans, where the coherent paragraph seems like an Everest of undergraduate accomplishment, where everyone on the streets of the American metropolis seems engaged in an endlessly animated conversation with a small portable instrument while newspapers and booksellers are disappearing.

In the spring of 2010, I attended the Fales lecture at New York University where an eminent panel mourned the imminent demise of the literary novel. I admit having heard such baleful apprehensions thirty years ago, and they do sound like perennial complaints of the aged. One of the panelists, Jonathan Galassi, the editor in chief of Farrar, Straus and Giroux, pointed out, however, that he had recently published the posthumous novel 2666 by a Chilean novelist, Robert Bolaño, which had sold over one hundred thousand copies.

I had spent much of the previous winter reading 2666, transfixed by the author's deliberate presentation of the utmost horrors—a series of unsolved brutal assassinations of women, mostly workers in the factories producing cheaply made goods for American consumption in the region of Juárez in Mexico, just south of the Rio Grande. It became clear to me as I read 2666 that it was the most important Latin American novel since Gabriel García Márquez's *One Hundred Years of Solitude*. Bolaño is as enchantingly digressive as Márquez, both writers irresistible fabulists as anecdotes foliate into stories.

At the spiritual center of 2666 is the mystery of an almost invisible, or at least rarely sighted, literary Nobelist, an unusually tall, reclusively misanthropic Prussian novelist who uses the improbable pseudonym of Benno von Archimboldi. Near the end of his 893-page novel, Bolaño tells us the story of Archimboldi's early life, of how as a young German soldier named Hans Reiter (that is, "writer") he is badly wounded on the Russian front during the First World War when a bullet pierced his throat so that he lost the ability to speak. After an operation, while recuperating in an abandoned farmhouse, Reiter finds a cache containing hidden papers by a Jew whom he names Abraham Ansky, whose family had lived in the farmhouse, and by a Russian novelist named Efrain Ivanov. As Reiter heals from his war wounds, his fascination with these papers makes Reiter write.

Like Archimboldi, Efrain Ivanov is one of Bolaño's innumerable inventions like all the writers whose histories Bolaño fabricates for a much smaller, though equally imaginative, earlier novel entitled *Nazi Literature in the Americas*. Ivanov eventually writes a novel called *Twilight*. There is a detail in this surreal science fiction story that seems so central to the origin and persistence of the written word.

Twilight is about a fourteen-year-old boy who joins the Russian revolutionary forces and is badly wounded on a battlefield. Just before vultures are about to descend, a spaceship appears and takes the boy along with other mortally wounded soldiers to the stratosphere. The wounded are healed and then perplexed by a series of metaphysical questions about god, creation, and the universe posed by an extraterrestrial who looked "more like a strand of seaweed than a human being." The seaweed image might suggest one of Bolaño's typically absurd reversals between power (the extraterrestrial has saved the boy) and the appearance of helplessness.

After a series of adventures, the boy becomes a reporter for a Moscow newspaper who accepts an assignment to interview a communist leader in a Peking cellar. This occurs during the early 1930s when militant Chinese communists formed an underground insurrection against Chaing Kai-shek's nationalists.

Both men, the reporter and the Chinese leader, contract a mortal fever in the cellar and decide to escape Peking on horseback. Freezing, shaking with fever, their horses submerged and sinking in snow, the Chinese revolutionary begins to ask the reporter the same perplexingly existential questions as had been posed by the extraterrestrial on his spaceship: "How were the stars created? Who are we in the middle of the boundless universe? . . . What trace of us will remain?"

That final question—what trace of us will remain—is both haunting and anguished. At the same time it seems to tingle with egotistical assertion in the face of annihilation. Would it have been as present a concern in the animist era, that period before the written word of approximately 495,000-years or longer? Would it even have been asserted as a valid perspective in that time when writers were mostly anonymous, as Homer might have been and as are the author of Everyman and the medieval monk scribes copying and illuminating biblical texts?

I suspect Bolaño, facing the prospects of his own death at the early age of fifty, was reflecting on what might seem to be an unconsciously axiomatic premise for writers, the deeply centered yet submerged desire to leave some trace behind. In the great scheme of things, even colossal achievements, such as *War and Peace* or *2666*, are only traces of our mutual destiny, dancing dust motes on our human path. But the inclination to leave such traces, and not necessarily in Tolstoy's or Bolaño's epic proportions, but often as grand as Flaubert's intention to "make the stars weep with our melodies," seems to be a universal imperative, one that promises that the continuation of the written word is as viable as it is vital.

www.ingramcontent.com/pod-product-compliance
Lightning Source LLC
Chambersburg PA
CBHW030110010526
44116CB00005B/180